EAST LOTHIAN FOURTH STATISTICAL ACCOUNT
1945 – 2000

VOLUME FOUR: THE PARISHES OF
Aberlady, Athelstaneford, Dirleton (with Gullane),
North Berwick, Whitekirk & Tyninghame

Edited by Sonia Baker

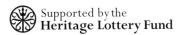
Supported by the
Heritage Lottery Fund

East Lothian Council Library Service
for
The East Lothian Fourth Statistical Account Society
2006

Published by
East Lothian Council Library Service for
the East Lothian Fourth Statistical Account Society, 2006
*Publication of this volume was made possible by funding made available by
East Lothian Antiquarian and Field Naturalists' Society*

Designed by
East Lothian Council

Printed by
Howie & Seath Ltd

ISBN 1 897857 32 2
2006

Project Manager
Veronica Wallace

Illustrations
© East Lothian Council Library Service
except where otherwise stated

Web page design: Peter Gray

Web pages: www.el4.org.uk

The Fourth Statistical Account of East Lothian 1945–2000
Volume One: The County
Volume Two-Six: The Parishes
Volume Seven: Growing up in East Lothian

VOLUME FOUR: THE PARISHES *of*
Aberlady, Athelstaneford, Dirleton, North Berwick, Whitekirk & Tyninghame

Contents

Additional Information

OVERVIEW

During the 50 years that have passed since the publication of the East Lothian volume of the third statistical account, great changes have occurred both in the situation in East Lothian and in the study of local history in Scotland. In this field there has been a great expansion with increasing recognition of its importance in university departments, in local authority library and museum services, and in the setting up of local history societies. There has also been increasing recognition of the importance of the three existing great statistical accounts, which gave reports of Scotland, parish by parish. They were produced at three critical stages in our history. The first was written when the work of the agricultural improvers was virtually complete, and proto-industrial changes were under way (1789-93); the second was written just at the beginning of a period of vast industrial change (1845), and the third when the country was coming to terms with the aftermath of large scale war (1953). All gave important analyses, both of stability and change.

As the new millennium approached, it became clear that the last, the third, account of East Lothian had become, like its predecessors, a historical document and that since its publication, the county had been subject to enormous social and economic change.

By 1997, there was a feeling that it was time to do the exercise again. The council of the East Lothian Antiquarian and Field Naturalists' Society, under their president, Professor Mitchison, decided to explore the feasibility of such a project. Professor Mitchison fully endorsed the proposal for a Fourth Statistical Account of East Lothian.

The account is presented in seven volumes: the county (Volume One), the parishes (Volumes Two to Six), and reminiscences of growing up in the county (Volume Seven). The countywide essays are complemented by the detailed parish contributions, which themselves vary in style and approach; some contain more oral material than others. Additional information and some longer versions of both are presented on the CD-ROM version of the work.

These volumes contribute to our understanding of the economic and social history of the county, 1945 to 2000; they should in no way be seen as the complete story of the period, as each topic could, in itself, be the subject of far more research and study. There are omissions too. Some topics have not been addressed, as there simply was no existing research available, at the required level. There is always more to discover; we have made a start. East Lothian is in many ways, Scotland in miniature; it has a wide range of landscapes, occupations and experiences. Inevitably, the county's experiences mirrored the Scottish and even the British picture; the difference lies in the detail.

This mammoth task has been a labour of love, but has been more testing than any love affair. East Lothian is worth such effort. We hope this Millennium landmark will be read, be useful, but above all be enjoyed, for a good part of the third millennium.

Stephen Bunyan   Sonia Baker
Chairman   Editor
East Lothian Fourth Statistical Account Society

EAST LOTHIAN PARISHES
INCLUDED IN VOLUME FOUR

ABERLADY
ATHELSTANEFORD
DIRLETON
NORTH BERWICK
WHITEKIRK & TYNINGHAME

ACKNOWLEDGEMENTS

On behalf of the society, I would like to acknowledge the support and help that we have received from a vast number of people.

First of all, we must thank the Heritage Lottery Fund without whose financial support we could not have begun. We are grateful for the extensive support of East Lothian Council, and for contributions from the following community councils: Cockenzie & Port Seton; Dunbar; Gullane area; North Berwick; Pencaitland; Prestonpans; Tranent & Elphinstone; West Barns; and from other organisations and individuals. We appreciated the support of East Lothian Council Library and Museums Service. *East Lothian Courier* and *Musselburgh News* back numbers proved to be a mine of information. We are grateful to the *East Lothian Courier* for permission to reproduce the quote from its pages which appears on page 23 of this volume.

We were encouraged by the interest and support of 14 local history and amenity societies who provided representatives on the committee and who, by and large, took on the responsibility for the parish volumes. The Haddington Remembered group volunteered much useful information.

Where there was no such society in a parish, we managed to find volunteers in almost all cases. Their input was invaluable. It soon became clear that the changes in most parishes were greater than we had realised and we are grateful to the parish representatives and the many local volunteers who have produced such a range of material, and to those who have responded to a wide range of queries on a myriad of subjects.

Particular thanks must go to those who took on the role of parish representatives for this volume – namely Peter & Hermine de Iongh (Whitekirk & Tyninghame), Malcolm Duncan (Athelstaneford), Norman Hall (North Berwick), Iain Macaskill (Aberlady), and Anne McCarthy (Dirleton). Each parish record contains a wealth of information, some of which might have been lost forever.

Many of the photographs used to illustrate the work came from East Lothian Council Library Service, supplemented by private photographs.

We are grateful to East Lothian Antiquarian and Field Naturalists' Society for their support in funding the publication of this volume.

I must also pay tribute to our editor, Sonia Baker who has been indefatigable and whose perseverance has kept the show on the road. We are also grateful for the support and assistance of staff in the Local History Centre who solved many knotty puzzles and showed great patience, and also for secretarial help from Doris Williamson and Jackie Stevenson.

Stephen Bunyan
Chairman
East Lothian Fourth Statistical Account Society

INTRODUCTION

This volume covers the parishes that encircle historic North Berwick burgh, with only Athelstaneford being landlocked, the rest abutting the Firth of Forth. Aberlady, Athelstaneford and North Berwick parishes are of a similar size, although much of the latter is now part of the town itself. Rural Athelstaneford is home to farms, to Drem railway station and, until 1997, East Fortune Hospital.

While Dirleton and Whitekirk & Tyninghame parishes are similar in size, otherwise they are very different. Whitekirk & Tyninghame remains largely agricultural, with a scatter of farms and its two small delightful villages. Meanwhile, the rolling dunelands of Dirleton have been much exploited by the golfing fraternity, and Gullane is now far bigger than the village that named the parish. The golfing industry is evident in all the parishes excepting Athelstaneford; nevertheless, this group of parishes is situated on rich farmland, and the land is used mostly for arable crops, in spite of the exposure to the sea.

The parish representatives who produced the material in this volume are:
Peter & Hermine de Iongh (Whitekirk & Tyninghame)
Malcolm Duncan (Athelstaneford)
Norman Hall (North Berwick)
Iain Macaskill (Aberlady)
Anne McCarthy (Dirleton) on behalf of the Gullane and Dirleton History Society.

Malcolm produced his material largely single-handedly. Peter and Hermine divided their workload: Peter worked on the factual material while Hermine collected and wrote up the oral recollections. Norman initiated and collected the North Berwick essays from a large number of contributors – including many oral recollections on education - and Sonia Baker collated and edited it all. Iain took on the additional work of collecting and then editing down the material collected from many individuals, in addition to taking on the main writing role for Aberlady. The Dirleton contribution was an impressive joint effort by the Gullane and Dirleton History Society; it was edited for the society by Anne McCarthy.

The series editor, Sonia Baker, Stephen Bunyan, David Moody and the Local History Centre team carried out additional research.

Considerable effort has been made to check the information given in the account, but many facts proved elusive, hence the use of approximate dates. There is still more to discover about the history of these parishes 1945-2000; this account makes a start.

The parameters of this work are the years 1945 – 2000. We realise that a number of important changes have occurred in East Lothian since that date but we have kept to the original timespan and these changes have not been recorded.

The East Lothian Fourth Statistical Account Society

ABERLADY

PARISH REPRESENTATIVE & PARISH EDITOR: *Iain Macaskill MBE*

Introduction

Situated between the wooded estates of Gosford and Luffness at the head of the great tidal bay, Aberlady remains one of the most attractive of East Lothian villages. The parish boundary runs from Gosford Bay eastward along the shoreline to the Peffer Burn, thence to Luffness Mill, south towards Mungoswells, west to Ballencrieff, Lochhill and Spittal, and northwest along the line of the Redhouse Burn. Aberlady parish covers some 2029 ha (5014 acres).

The restoration of normality to village life in the aftermath of the second world war came about gradually. In 1945 the canteen in the drill hall, which was run by the Women's Voluntary Service (WVS), was closed. The villagers celebrated Victory in Europe (VE) day in May and Victory over Japan (VJ) day in September 1945, and the names of the four local men who had lost their lives were duly added to the War Memorial. In 1947 children at the primary school enjoyed their first summer trip since 1939. German PoWs from the military camp at Gosford removed concrete anti-tank blocks from Kilspindie, and the camp was still occupied by the army when the Haddington fire brigade attended a serious fire there in 1951. It was to be the mid-1960s, however, before the ten postwar prefabricated houses, the 'prefabs', at Kirk Road were dismantled and the air-raid shelters removed from the school.

For about 20 years after the war the physical appearance of Aberlady did not change much, with the attractive Main Street displaying a variety of architectural styles and building materials, and many single and two-storey houses dating from the 18th and 19th centuries. Distinctive dwellings include Red Row, a series of early 19th century cottages with Gothic windows and doors, and Gable Cottage dated 1684. A notable feature - and a reminder of Aberlady's former importance as the port of Haddington and burgh of barony - is the 18th century stepped Mercat Cross.

Mercat Cross, Aberlady. The red-pantiled ∘ss Cottage (right) was author Nigel Tranter's first home in the village,1938-50, apart from war service.
(Jean Curnow)

Introduction (cont)

Aberlady was fortunate in that its existing charm protected it from unchecked (indiscriminate) development; what was built from the 1960s was carefully monitored, and efforts were made to keep the village style intact. From about the 1990s, this monitoring appeared to be less in evidence.

Environment

Land use is primarily for arable farming. The policies of the two estates - Gosford and Luffness – add scenic beauty, but it is for its coast that Aberlady is renowned.

Aberlady Bay was designated a Local Nature Reserve in 1952, the first in the UK; it is also a Site of Special Scientific Interest (SSSI). The reserve area comprises about 1440 acres of tidal mudflats, saltmarsh, sand dunes, scrub and grassland extending east towards Gullane links, as well as some woodland and the small freshwater Marl Loch.

For some years Archie Mathieson, the then county ranger, had oversight of the reserve until the appointment of the first full-time warden, Russell Nisbet, in 1974. Peter Gordon took over in 1980 and Ian Thomson, the present warden, in 1992. The Aberlady Bay Local Nature Reserve Advisory Group, representing local and wider interests, meets regularly.

The birds which nest, breed, rest or winter there - about 250 species recorded, including rare migrants - are the prime attraction, but there is interest too in the great variety of plants, marine life - and dragonflies! Nigel Tranter was intrigued by a solitary green woodpecker, which inexplicably returned 'season after season' to the treeless habitat of Gullane Point (Tranter, N. 1992, p22).

From October to March, the huge V-formations of honking pink-footed geese make an impressive sight and sound over Aberlady as they wing their way inland to feed, or return to roost at night on the long, wide sand-bar of the Bay. A record tally of 25,960 of these annual visitors from Greenland and Iceland was recorded in 1993.

Townscapes, Buildings & Landscapes of Distinction

The Civic Amenities Act (1967) required local authorities to designate areas of special architectural or historic interest as 'conservation areas', and in 1970 the historic core of Aberlady, with its coastal and rural surroundings to the north and east, was so designated. In 2000 it was proposed that this be extended westwards to include the playing fields, primary school, and pre-war council housing of Kirk Road, Elcho Terrace and the Pleasance.
Within the parish are three large houses of note:

Ballencrieff Tower was originally a 5-storey fortified house of the 16th century, and was incorporated in a Georgian-style mansion in 1730. Long ruinous as a result of a fire in 1868, the building was saved from imminent demolition and restored over a period of eight years (1992-2000) by Peter Gillies, a civil engineer, with advice and a grant from Historic Scotland. Local author Nigel Tranter encouraged Peter Gillies to undertake the restoration and took a personal interest in the project.

The A listed Gosford House has been home of the 12th Earl and Countess of Wemyss since 1951; it was designed by Robert Adam. Gosford was requisitioned in 1939. In 1940 a fire damaged much of the roof; years of temporary roofs permitted leaks, and dry rot followed. A new roof was constructed in 1995-6 over the central block, the work being overseen by local architect Fred Giffen, and assisted by Historic Scotland. Restoration of the sandstone is ongoing, with chimneys and balusters replaced and repaired in 2000. A programme of internal restoration is ongoing. The landscape dates from at least 1799, with later additions, though now masked by two centuries of growth.

The present A listed Luffness House building incorporates a 16th century tower house and later extensions. Until 1946, Luffness House was used to accommodate Mayfield House Girls' School, which was evacuated there. After they left in 1946 it was used for a time as a convalescent home for Polish personnel who had served with the armed forces during the war. This ceased in the early 1950s although some of them stayed on. Some actually did not survive and are buried in Aberlady churchyard. A baronial wing of the house (1841) was demolished in 1959. The house is now available for functions. The landscape is of significant value, and the double walled *jardin clos* (walled garden) is reputed to be the only one in Britain (Land Use Consultants, 1987, p152).

Population
By parish, from the General Registrar's office

1931	1094	524M	570F			
1951	1519	867M	652F	*By locality – census –*		
1961	1089	511M	578F	*ie Aberlady village itself*		
1971	1071	509M	562F	746	351M	395F
1981	1114	515M	599F	885	408M	477F
				By Small Area Statistics - census		
1991	1027	484M	543F	815	377M	438F
2001	1210	571M	639F	--	--	--
By parish, from ELDC				*By settlement, from ELDC*		
1991	1081			815		
1997(est.)	1226(sic)	578M	650F	895		
2001	NO DATA			873 (ELC)		

Population figures are difficult to compare, as no two sources extract data in the same way.

Belief
Aberlady Parish Church continued to loom large both in village life and in public awareness though, in line with national trends, communicant membership fell from 500 in 1953 to 349 in 1999. A notable feature of the past century had been the remarkably long and devoted service rendered to Aberlady Kirk by some of its servants. The ministry of the Rev Dr Thomas Caldwell, who was exceptionally supportive of village activities, lasted from 1918-58. Cornelius Smith was session clerk and kirk treasurer from 1912-54, and for almost 70 years two men served successively as beadle, Andrew Thomson (1918-53), then John Fortune (1953-86).

Dr Caldwell's ability and vigour did not pass unnoticed. He was appointed depute-clerk to the General Assembly of the Church of Scotland in 1946, and principal clerk from 1949 to 1953. Dr Caldwell died in 1966, and the following year a Celtic cross dedicated to his memory was hung in the church.

Belief (cont)

Aberlady Parish Church, 1940s.

His successor, the Rev David MacFarlane (1959-70), prepared a guide to Aberlady church. It was during his tenure that a pipe organ was installed, the vestry relocated in the 15th century church tower, and the manse stables converted into a hall. The former UP church, which had served as the church hall, was sold for housing in 1969.

The Rev Robert Lennie was inducted in 1970, and remained at Aberlady until 1986. In 1980 the first ordination and admission of women elders to Aberlady Kirk Session took place - a proposal rejected in 1945 by both the Kirk Session and the congregation. In the 1980s Aberlady church became the venue for concerts and other fund-raising events, including the Garleton Singers, (of which Mr Lennie was a member), the Kevock Choir, two weekend flower festivals, and an annual plant sale. This tradition continued in the following decade with another flower festival and concerts by brass bands and Welsh male voice choirs.

As early as 1972 there had been a Presbytery 'Readjustment Plan' for reorganising the parishes, in which a union or linking of Aberlady with Longniddry was suggested. Though this proposal found no support in either Kirk Session and was abandoned, it was clear that a union might be necessary in the future. The impending retirals in 1985 of both Mr Lennie and Dr David Whiteford of Gullane parish church revived the issue. After lengthy discussions and negotiations, in which the Rev Kenneth Hughes, minister of Prestonkirk, representing the presbytery of Lothian, played a pivotal role, the final arrangements for linking Aberlady and Gullane parishes were approved by both congregations, and the Aberlady manse of 1864 was put up for sale.

The Rev Norman Faulds was inducted as the first minister of the linked charge in 1986, and several notable events preceded his retiral in 2000. 1987 marked the centenary of Aberlady parish church. Two former ministers, the Rev D. MacFarlane and the Rev R. Lennie, participated in the communion service in May, and the Moderator of the General Assembly, the Rt Rev Dr Duncan Shaw, preached at the centenary service in June. A centenary stained glass window, *The Crucifixion of Christ*, was commissioned from artist Christopher Sachs and unveiled by Lord Wemyss.

In March 1989, an event of exceptional significance in the history of Aberlady church took place when a Requiem Mass was celebrated at the funeral service of Mrs Elizabeth Hope of Luffness, with permission granted by the principal clerk to the General Assembly. The participating clergy included Cardinal Gordon Gray, six Roman Catholic priests, and four Church of Scotland ministers, including Mr Faulds. (Until the mid-1980s some villagers attended Sunday Mass at a chapel in Luffness House).

The manse stables were demolished and replaced in 1990 with a purpose-built hall officially opened by the Earl of Wemyss. Renamed Aberlady Kirk Stables, the hall was to prove a major asset both to the church and the wider community.

Ways of marking the Millennium, under consideration since 1995, included a memorial rose garden, and presentation of a bible to each child in the Sunday school, and a new stained glass window depicting Jesus as a boy in the Temple, commissioned from artist Garion Jack and unveiled at a special service in January 2000.

Homes

For 20 years, from the late 1940s, council houses were built along School Road and, in the 1960s, in Rig Street, Rig Place, Kilspindie Court and Luffness Court - a total of 162. Many of these houses were roofed with modern pantiles to blend with the vernacular style of the village. Pantiles were also a feature of several of the subsequent private developments, notably the 13 houses built in 1977 at 'The Gardens', ground at the east end of the village that was previously a market garden, and the enclaves of Sinclair Court and Golf Court off the south and north sides of Main Street.

The Maltings, the old malt warehouse in the Wynd, long derelict and an unsightly roosting-place for pigeons, was restored and converted into six flats and a house in the mid-1990s.

Other developments included the 21 Miller houses at Luffness Gardens, 'infill' in Back Lane, and the 23 'executive-style' houses at Craigielaw Park completed in 1999. All this additional housing arrested the decline in population, which rose to 1226 (ELCC parish estimate) in 1997. Wemyss Estates still maintained and rented out 35 houses within the parish.

The Draft East Lothian Local Plan (1994) designated a large area for new housing south of School Road, extending from Haddington Road westwards to Kirk Road. In Main Street, 'The Poplars', opened in 1933 as a holiday home for poor adults and children from Edinburgh's Grassmarket, and later a home for the elderly, closed in 2000 and was sold for redevelopment as private housing. There were also plans for housing developments at the Wagon Inn and Aberlady Garage.

Utilities

The public toilets, located at The Wynd, were demolished in 1991 after the Maltings had been sold for conversion into flats.

*Old and new Aberlady.
The house on the right
is reputed to be the
oldest in the village.
Quill House on the left
was once a bakery.
In the background,
with modern pantiles
to match, is the 1990s
development of
Golf Court.
(Jean Curnow)*

*The Maltings in
The Wynd, Aberlady,
before conversion.*

*High Street, Aberlady,
c1940s. The trees on
the left are those of
'Glebe House', and the
railings of 'The Lodge'
can be seen on the right,
in the middle distance.*

The Aberlady & Gullane Gas Light Company's gasometer was situated adjacent to Aberlady station, supplying gas to Aberlady and to Gullane. It was closed down in 1958, having been nationalised in 1949 (Hajducki, A., 1992, pp79, 128).

A Miss Fortune operated the telephone exchange at Haddington Place, with helpers during the war years; it ceased in the 1950s, when the system became automated.

Dealing with rubbish: the vast increase in all kinds of packaging, the use of drinks cans and plastic bottles instead of the old-style returnable glass bottles, and the modern habit of both children and adults of casual eating and drinking out of doors or in cars, has produced a perennial problem of unsightly litter, particularly on the verges of the roads leading to and from the village. By 1980 Ally Punton, the last street sweeper - the old Scottish word 'scaffie' (scavenger) seems to be unknown to many younger people - had been replaced with his broom and barrow by a squad of men descending on the village periodically, but obstructed in their efforts by parked cars. The convenience of the modern 'wheelie bins' was perhaps discouraging some villagers from recycling their cans and bottles.

Shops & Services

Up to the 1960s, Aberlady was fairly self-sufficient, with a wide range of shops, including a bakery and grocery in what later became the Quill Gallery, where the ovens could still be seen, a butcher shop, now part of the Wagon Inn, a confectioner in the Wynd, and a haberdashery in a front room of 'The Neuk' at the eastern corner of the Wynd. In 2000 there remained only a privately run general store (run by East Lothian Co-operative Society until 1995), the 'chip shop', and the village post office.

The village had many services on offer as well, with a chimney-sweep, a coal merchant, a boot repairer, an undertaker, and a golf club maker, Willie Waggott, who specialised in wooden-shafted clubs at his shop in the Wynd - W. Waggott of the Wynd. Aberlady even had its own registrar, Alec Yorkston, until the parish records were centralised in 1968.

A mobile library service was introduced in Aberlady by East Lothian County Council in 1968, before which the village library - with books donated by the Traill Bequest - was kept in the primary school. By 2000, the van visited the village every Friday, with additional services for schoolchildren and the Mothers & Toddlers Group.

Robertson's sweet-shop, The Wynd, Aberlady, was once occupied by a golf club maker, then a cycle shop, then was a sweet shop from 1950s - 1970s. Bay Cottage now stands on the site.

Healthcare

There was no medical or dental practice in Aberlady. For medical advice most villagers attended the long-established surgery in Gullane, with prescriptions dispensed at the Gullane pharmacy. For dental treatment local people might go to Longniddry or North Berwick, but a dental practice was established in Gullane in 1991. Prior to the mid-1980s, before general nursing was separated from midwifery, the district nurse worked from home and sometimes had to travel well beyond the boundaries of Aberlady parish. Subsequently, two district (or community) nurses were based at Gullane surgery.

Education

The present Aberlady Primary School was opened in 1931 with a roll of 126 pupils under the headmastership of Alex Ross, who remained in office until 1960. In 1945 there were two assistant teachers and 119 pupils, including 39 evacuees from Mayfield House Girls' School, who lived at Luffness House until their return to Edinburgh the following year. Ten candidates sat the Qualifying Exam or 'Quali' (soon renamed the Promotion Exam) in 1945, and a record 22 in 1959. In 1947 there was a summer outing to the Three Lochs, the first school trip since 1939, with a reassuring ratio of 29 adults to 44 pupils! A visiting schoolmaster from Grenada in 1946 recorded his impressions in the logbook - 'a happy and orderly little school.'

It could not, of course, be all 'sweetness and light'. Attendance was quite badly affected throughout the 1940s and 1950s by outbreaks of infectious diseases, including whooping cough, scarlet fever, chicken pox, mumps and measles. Immunisation against diphtheria continued at least until 1952, to be followed by anti-polio vaccinations in the later 1950s. As late as 1967, a quarter of the pupils were off school with measles. Monthly 'cleanliness inspections' by the school nurse were a regular feature during these and subsequent years.

Weather too could affect the smooth running of the school. When the roads were blocked by snow in the severe winter of 1947 and 32 pupils were absent, it is recorded that Miss Jane Havery, with commendable devotion to duty, walked to school twice from Gullane. When she retired in 1954, Miss Havery had served Aberlady Primary School for 36 years, and was a living link with the earlier school that once occupied part of the Kilspindie Hotel site in Main Street.

In 1950-1, when the school roll rose to 108, an additional (third) assistant teacher was appointed, who used the dining-hall as a classroom. Visiting specialist teachers were still comparatively rare, with none at all in 1959-60. Gradually the situation improved, but there does not seem to have been a full range of specialists until the late 1970s. Under headmaster William Doig (1960-72), summer school outings were resumed in 1962 with a forenoon of cruising on the Forth, a welcome break from school routine even for the four pupils who were seasick! The following year there is the first mention of a cycling proficiency test, conducted by 'Lothian & Peebles Constabulary'.

Aberlady pupils had long supported National Savings, and in 1968 the school was awarded the John Archer Memorial Trophy by the National Savings Committee for Scotland, of which John Archer had been chairman. With 80 regular savers out of a roll of 94, Aberlady Primary had come top out of 804 entries. Mrs Archer later planted a young oak tree in the school grounds.

The educational experience for Aberlady children continued to broaden under Mr Doig's successors David Bruce (1972-8) and John Roy (1978-86), though a more ominous sign of

Education (cont)

Aberlady Primary School.

changing times was the showing in 1972 of the film *Never Go with Strangers*. There were more frequent school outings, science lessons in P6/7, mention of social education and environmental studies. In 1977 some pupils appeared in a TV programme about Aberlady Bay, and P7 pupils spent a day at North Berwick High School for 'familiarisation', an innovation that was to become an annual two-day event. On Saturday, 23rd May 1981, the Golden Jubilee of the present school was celebrated with a party!

The designation 'headmaster' finally disappeared from use when Elizabeth Way became the headteacher in 1987, followed by Dorothy Hermiston in 1989 and Jacqui MacKinnon in 2000. A falling roll - 57 in 1989 - caused concern, but by 2000 it had risen to 90. The school continued to 'punch above its weight' with many successes recorded, such as winning the under-11s Scottish Lacrosse Championship in 1999.

The duties of a teaching headteacher became increasingly onerous in the 1990s, with many new directives and initiatives. These included Devolved School Management (with budgetary control), the 5-14 Curriculum, multicultural and anti-bullying policies, national testing, tighter security, and increasing emphasis on Special Needs Education. A nursery class was set up within the school in 1993, with room for ten pre-school children. After initial problems over accommodation and staffing, the nursery unit was finally established in a new purpose-built classroom in 2000, with a full complement of 20 children attending five morning or afternoon sessions.

Following The School Boards (Scotland) Act of 1988, Aberlady school board was established in November 1989. Members took a special interest in the welfare of staff and pupils, being actively engaged with such issues as road safety, school meals, accommodation and staffing. The school was equally fortunate in having a long established PTA, which organised fund-raising activities, notably the annual Autumn Fayre. The links between the school and the village community have always been strong. In recent years, for example, OAPs had been invited to a preview of the annual Christmas concert in the community hall.

Transport

It is difficult to imagine that Aberlady residents once had the option of travelling by train from their own railway station, on a branch line from Longniddry to Gullane that was opened in 1846. The station was situated outside the village on the Haddington road. The branch was closed for passenger traffic in 1932, unable in the end to compete with the convenience and comparative cheapness of the new SMT (Scottish Motor Traction) bus services dating from the 1920s. The line continued to be used for freight traffic until the Beeching 'axe' fell in 1964.

In the 1950s the station building at Aberlady was let as summer holiday 'camping apartments', the accommodation for six people comprising two bedrooms, living room, kitchen and bathroom, with gas for cooking and lighting. An advert of 1958 mentions 'bracing climate, good sands, safe bathing, golf and bowls' (Hajducki, A. 1992, p163). Eventually, Eastern Scottish, then Lowland succeeded the familiar green SMT buses plying between Edinburgh and North Berwick. Since 1997 First Bus, whose evening and weekend services are subsidised by East Lothian Council, has maintained the route. A limited bus service has connected Aberlady with Haddington since about 1987, and is currently provided by Eve Coaches. This subsidised service also connects Aberlady with Port Seton and Newcraighall. In recent times the cost of petrol and city parking has prompted more local people to travel to Edinburgh by train from Longniddry. Public disapproval of 'drink-drivers' and increasingly severe penalties for offenders have encouraged greater use of taxis, including the service provided in recent years in Aberlady.

Police

The last village policeman, PC Tommy Campbell, was withdrawn in 1971 and the police house subsequently sold. Ten years later the first local community policeman, PC Des Bathgate, was appointed, a post held currently by PC Willie Innes. He reports to Gullane area Community Council and liaises with local people and organisations. Crime was not a significant problem in Aberlady, apart from occasional burglary, minor vandalism, and theft from cars parked at the nature reserve - all usually perpetrated by outsiders. The Neighbourhood Watch scheme was set up in the village in 1991.

Leisure

Facilities

The original drill hall (built 1883-4) was reconstructed as the community hall and gifted to the village by the Earl of Wemyss, with the official opening by the then Countess of Wemyss in 1953. The original Deed of Trust stipulated at least three trustees - the schoolmaster, the minister and the postmaster - and latterly there were four. The general management of the hall was to be entrusted to a council appointed by the Aberlady Community Association, which had been formed in 1949. In the following years the hall was used by many local organisations, as diverse as the WRI, the Kirk Session and the amateur dramatic society, with a bingo session every Saturday!

However, use of the community hall gradually declined as the facilities did not keep pace with modern requirements, while conversion of the manse stables to a church hall in 1963 (and its replacement by the new kirk stables in 1990), had created an alternative venue for many activities. In 1994 renewal of the public entertainment licence for the community hall was refused because the kitchen did not comply with food and hygiene regulations. This unhappy situation, compounded by lack of funds, was to change dramatically from 1995 onwards, due to an active and enthusiastic committee, fund-raising, several grants, and skilled tradesmen. The aim of a fully modernised village hall generating a self-sufficient rental income, even a profit, was achieved, with regular bookings from local clubs and individuals, table sales, and donations. The huge open coal fire, originally installed in the 1940s for the comfort of servicemen, is an attractive feature.

The British Legion hut, Haddington Road, was used for some village events (eg whist drives) until 1952 when the land it stood upon was sold for housing – two houses were built.

Organisations & Clubs

The Third Statistical Account (Snodgrass, C.P. 1953, pp330-9) recorded that about 27 organisations were meeting regularly in Aberlady. In addition to boy scouts, girl guides and cadets, there was a young people's club associated with the church, with about 30 boys and girls over age 14, and village committees for the British Legion and the Vert Hospital. The advent of television and the increase in car ownership, which made city attractions more accessible, were two factors which gradually led to the demise of many village-based activities, including the rifle club, the pipe band, the amateur dramatic society, which flourished until 1971, uniformed organisations and, in 1997, even the Woman's Guild. The Saturday club, established in 1971 by two kirk elders, Laurence Goudie and Ross Allan, as an 'outreach' group to promote Christian fellowship, was non-denominational and open to those aged 11-17 within the parish and beyond. This club, with its varied programme of games days, guest speakers, visits to places of interest, community service and venture holidays, made a significant impact until a change in the attitude of local youth and consequent decline in interest forced its closure in 1997.

Branches of the SWRI and OAP Association still existed by the end of the period, while bookings for the community hall included badminton club, volleyball club, dog training club and the newly formed Aberlady Craft Group, which produced an impressive Millennium wall-hanging for display there. Young children were still well served by brownies, swimming club, Sunday school and Monday club.

Bowling and golf (see *Economy*) share an enduring popularity in Aberlady. The Aberlady Bowling Club celebrated its centenary in 1988, and the green was opened by the Earl of Wemyss, who was presented with a commemorative quaich. The annual rent for the lease of ground from Wemyss Estates was originally one shilling (5p) until 1971, then £1, latterly £50. The original clubhouse was replaced in 1977 and extended (with a bar licence) in 1985 and again in 1998. Members - currently about 80 - compete for various club and county trophies and participate in national championships. The oldest local trophy is the Halkett Cup (1895), which is contested annually by Aberlady, Athelstaneford, Dirleton and Gullane. The five shillings paid by veteran member Alex Birse when he joined the club in 1956, contrasts with the subscription of £40 in the year 2000.

The club was fortunate in having many skilled and enthusiastic players of long standing, including Jock Brodie and Jack Greenwood, who were the Scottish Pairs champions at Queen's

Leisure (cont)

Park, Glasgow, in 1986, and who repeated their success the following year at the British Isles championships at Llanelli, Wales. Jock Brodie was team manager for East Lothian for four years (1996-2000). Another stalwart of the club was Jock Cunningham, who gained a Scottish cap against Wales in 1983. In 2000, Jim Florence, Billy Dunleavey and Charlie Greenwood, were Scottish Triples champions. The ladies' section, which dates from 1956, had enjoyed success too. Cathie Walkingshaw and Linda Black won the East of Scotland Pairs championship in 1987, and Aberlady came top of the East Lothian Ladies' League in 1992.

Aberlady Curling Club is a very old club, dating from 1860. It was accepted into the Royal Caledonian Curling Club in 1926. The curling stones were originally held in the curling house on Gosford estate and when the ponds were bearing during the winter (the ice there had to be 4″ (10cm) thick) they held bonspiels (matches) there. There was only one occasion - during the 1980s - in recent times that this was possible. Indoor rinks at Haymarket (1912-1978) and Murrayfield (c1980) provided the facilities. Up to about 20 years ago, inter-club competitions were held in the county. But by 2000, Aberlady no longer participated in inter-club competitions, although the other clubs – Athelstaneford, East Linton, Dirleton, Haddington and Yester - still existed. John Niven was president in 2000. Membership numbers varied, being highest in the 1930s. By the end of the period there were about 25 members, enjoying both the sport and the social side of curling. Curling tends to be a family sport - once one member begins, others follow; club members are drawn from all over the county and beyond. Nowadays, coaching is given before curlers begin – in the past they just started, often working out their own ways of curling.

The modern Aberlady gala was established in 1949, and seems, in its early years, to have been restricted to a single day of activities on the Sea Green, with the village pipe band contributing to the festive atmosphere, and refreshments to follow in the community hall. In more recent years the opening events, including competitive sports, parade of floats, various stalls and entertainments, and the crowning of the gala queen, with Primary 1 and 7 children forming the 'royal court', have been held on the playing-fields near the school. The music is supplied now by bands from outwith Aberlady, such as the Haddington Pipe Band (1989) and Dalkeith & Monktonhall Colliery Brass Band (1996). Typical evening events during gala week include inter-schools seven-a-side football, a social evening for senior citizens, a children's fancy dress party, and a gala dance. The kirkin' of the queen in the village church usually takes place now on the Sunday at the end of that week. The first gala queen, in 1949, was Jean Watson (Mrs Denholm), and the Millennium gala queen Amy Nash. Great commitment is shown by the gala committee, which organises fund-raising events during the preceding months and is determined that Aberlady will not lose this annual summer event.

Aberlady participated in Scotland's Gardens Scheme one Saturday in June 1999, the local organiser being Elaine Carnie. Enthusiasts from as far away as Ayrshire and the Borders viewed over 20 gardens in the village, from The Pleasance to Cockle Square; teas were provided in the community hall. 40% of the income was donated to Children in Need and the community hall fund. The intention was to take part in the gardens scheme again in 2001.

Economy - Tourism

The Aberlady Nature Reserve attracts walkers and bird-watchers all the year round, with an estimated 30,797 visitors in 2000, and the car park is often filled to capacity. Golfers were soon to have the opportunity to play two 18-hole courses, Kilspindie and Craigielaw, the latter to be opened in 2001. Another attraction near Aberlady is the Myreton Motor Museum, established in 1966. On display is a large collection of vintage cars, vans, military vehicles and motorcycles, as well as period posters and enamel signs.

Provision of 'bed and breakfast' accommodation for visitors was no longer so readily available in the village, but the three hotels - Kilspindie, Old Aberlady Inn (formerly the Golf Hotel) and Green Craigs - were fulfilling this need, while the Aberlady caravan park, with storage, servicing, and holiday chalets, had been in existence for about ten years at the station site. An earlier park for caravans at Gosford, leased to the Caravan Club for 25 years in 1974, closed in 1999.

Economy - Agriculture

The period saw truly dramatic agricultural changes (see *Farming* by Fiona Dobson & George Barton, county volume), which, on a parish level, resulted in a reduction of the work force, from perhaps 100 full-time farm-labourers to about a dozen in farming, with about another 40 regular and casual employees involved in work associated with agriculture. This greatly contributed to migration from tied houses to the villages.

Huge changes in environmental and conservation practices had been brought about, largely because of pressure from the urban population. There had been a very noticeable reduction in the number of songbirds, attributed to loss of habitat, changes in farming practice, and the increased number of raptors resulting from legal protection and lack of gamekeepers.

Regarding the original post-first world war development of smallholdings on the 600-700 acres of Ballencrieff - there were 30 in 1945 - the pendulum had swung significantly towards these lands being amalgamated or incorporated in neighbouring farms. They had continued as small units, often worked by the owner or tenant single-handed, until by the 1970s, when only 14 remained, they had become quite uneconomic. Increasingly, the occupier had taken on an outside job to supplement his income, or developed some separate business. In 1979 the government introduced legislation whereby smallholdings could be bought from the state at attractive prices. This resulted in some owners selling the ground and outbuildings, but retaining the dwelling and taking up some alternative career.

One of the original Ballencrieff smallholdings became the Myreton Motor Museum, while immediately adjacent was a modern processing-plant, preparing leeks from neighbouring farms to meet the high standards required by supermarket buyers. Other vegetables are occasionally produced for supermarkets by specialist growers with short-term renting of fields. Another new enterprise was the provision of horse-riding facilities and stabling.

In spite of so much rapid and technological change, there remains a strong thread of continuity, with, for example, the third generation on the smallholding at Ballencrieff where tomatoes and chrysanthemums were once specialities, but which now produces high quality pork and bacon products for specialist demand. The third generation too was now farming Ballencrieff Mains, and likewise Luffness Mains, although a professional manager was taken on there in 1973.

Economy - Agriculture (cont)

Aberlady Mains and, with reduced acreage, Lochhill continued as working farms, but Gosford estate no longer had its home farm, Craigielaw, due to poor agricultural returns from the early 1990s onwards. Over the last 50 years or so the agricultural income of the estate had declined from 75% to perhaps 25%. There were no longer any estate workers employed outdoors, where 9 or 10 were full-time up to the 1980s, including foresters, gamekeepers, groundsmen and maintenance staff. Sub-contractors were being used for such work as vermin-control and mowing of amenity areas. The predominantly arable land previously farmed by the estate had been distributed among existing tenant farmers under various 'share-farming' agreements, generating useful income from previously tied estate houses.

Economy - Golf

The Kilspindie Golf Club (originally the Luffness Golf Club established in 1867) was formed in 1898. It remained a private club, with members drawn from professional people living mainly in the Edinburgh area and East Lothian. After 1945, there was a decline in membership to around 200, but after a recruiting drive in 1957, membership rose from 330 to 400, and remained around that level to the end of the century. For most of that period there were about 130-150 lady members.

After the war a lot of work had to be carried out to restore the course to pre-war standards. To help finance the cost involved in restoration work and buying new equipment, the entrance fee was doubled in 1946 to £7.7s. (£7.35p), with the annual subscription set at £3.3s. (£3.15p). However, to attract new members, the entrance fee was reduced in 1957. By the 1970s the entrance fee was £70 and the annual subscription £35. In 2000 the respective charges were £720 and £360.

Joe Dickson, who had started as a greenkeeper in 1925, became head greenkeeper in 1950, and doubled as the first professional from 1961 until his retirement in 1975. In addition to restoring the course, he had to deal with the damage done by sheep and rabbits. Flooding by the sea occurred on occasion, as well as damage caused by coastal erosion. In 1982 it was estimated that some parts of the course had lost 10 feet in ten years. Sadly, it is recorded that a member was killed by lightning in 1953.

Jim Orsborn became the next head greenkeeper, retiring in 1991. Since then the head greenkeeper has been Alan Aitken. All three men have overseen many changes, such as alterations to the fairways, bunkers and tees. The first full-time professional, appointed in 1988, was Graham Sked. As the financial situation became much better, improvements and extensions to the clubhouse were carried out from time to time.

In 1967, the centenary of the original Luffness Golf Club was celebrated with a number of events, culminating in a ball at Gosford House. In 1992, the club celebrated its own 125th anniversary with a number of well-attended events. In 1998 discussions were held with the proposed Craigielaw Golf Club to consider a merger, but it was subsequently agreed that the two clubs would remain independent.

The Aberlady Golf Club, sometimes known locally as the Artisan Club, dates from 1912, when the Kilspindie Golf Club committee granted permission for the Aberlady Working Men's Club to play the course at reduced fees. Members, who are limited to 30 and must be resident in the village, hold competitions every month and play matches against similar local clubs.

Construction of the new Craigielaw Golf Club, the first new links course in East Lothian for 80 years, was completed in 1999 and due to open in 2001. A six-green junior course was under construction, and it was planned to convert the former Craigielaw farm steading into a clubhouse.

Local Government

For local elections after 1975 Aberlady was linked with Gullane and Dirleton and, until 1999, Drem and Athelstaneford. From 1975 to date, the ward always returned a Conservative councillor, currently Gilbert Meikle, to East Lothian Council.

Gullane Area Community Council, established in 1976, incorporated Aberlady, Dirleton, Drem and Gullane, with four councillors representing Aberlady ward. Local issues included the condition of the roads, planning applications, and housing developments, while allocations from the Local Priorities Fund are made to village groups and projects.

Miscellany

Events

On VE Day, 8th May 1945, Aberlady was 'profusely decorated with flags and coloured streamers, almost every house contributing its quota and the main thoroughfare presenting a gay aspect.' *(Haddingtonshire Courier)*. The parish church, the chancel decorated in the national colours, was filled in the evening for a short thanksgiving service, conducted by the minister, the Rev. Thomas Caldwell, followed later by a dance in the drill hall. The schoolchildren had been granted two days' holiday to mark 'the cessation of hostilities in Europe'. All the uniformed organisations, including ARP wardens, air training cadets, women's voluntary service, local observer corps, boy scouts and cubs, girl rangers, girl guides and brownies, attended another thanksgiving service on the following Sunday morning.

Later the same year, on 15th August, the people of Aberlady celebrated VJ Day, with a bonfire on the Sea Green built by the local troop of boy scouts. Children and adults took part in community singing, and danced until after midnight. An evening thanksgiving service was held, and Sunday was observed as Thanksgiving Day.

As part of the celebrations for the Coronation of Queen Elizabeth in June 1953, Aberlady school was closed for three days, and commemorative mugs from the county council were distributed to the pupils along with gifts from the village Coronation committee. A tree gifted by the local boy scouts was planted in front of the school, and it is recorded that the remaining chestnut tree of the two planted at the previous coronation in 1937 was in flower for the first time. Cornelius Smith, for long village postmaster and office-bearer in the parish church, was awarded the Coronation Medal for services to the community.

The Aberlady Millennium Committee, with grants and fund-raising, ensured that this significant date was celebrated in style, with a torchlight procession, a bonfire and fireworks in Butcher's Field, a Hogmanay party in the community hall, a Millennium calendar featuring early views of Aberlady, and 'celebration packages' of whisky and shortbread for senior citizens. A more permanent feature, set up on the Sea Green, was a telescope with two illustrated explanatory panels.

Miscellany (cont)

*Celebrating
the Millennium:
preparing the village
bonfire in Butcher's
Field, Aberlady.*

*Left to right:
Brian Ford, Alan
Wood, Ian Main,
Andrew Shaw.
(K. Macaskill)*

People

The 12th Earl of Wemyss KT (and 8th of March), who succeeded his grandfather in 1937, has long been a notable figure in Aberlady and on the wider Scottish scene. He was appointed Lord High Commissioner to the General Assembly of the Church of Scotland in 1959, 1960 and 1977, the then minister of Aberlady church acting as his chaplain on each occasion and staying at Holyrood House. He has for many years held office as honorary president of the Old Edinburgh Club, vice-president of East Lothian Antiquarian & Field Naturalists' Society, and, from 1967-91, president of the National Trust for Scotland. The Earl was Lord Lieutenant of East Lothian, 1967-86. He remains a long-established elder of Aberlady Parish Church, where there are several memorials to members of the Wemyss (Charteris) family in the north aisle.

Nigel Tranter, OBE (1909-2000), prolific author of well over 100 books and champion of many causes, including the campaign for the Forth road bridge, settled in Aberlady in 1938 at Cross Cottage. He later moved to Quarry House, a short distance from the wooden bridge over the Peffer Burn - his 'footbridge to enchantment' - that leads to the nature reserve, where almost daily for nearly 50 years he could be seen walking and making notes for his next book. A cairn was erected in his memory 'by East Lothian Council and public subscription' at the Aberlady Nature Reserve car park in October 2000 - a deserved tribute to one who was so intimately associated with the neighbourhood, and who gave scholarly and entertaining talks to so many local societies over the years.

Another Aberlady resident, Patrick McVeigh, a dealer in antiques who had originally traded from a shop in Edinburgh's West Bow, set up in business on the west side of the Sea Wynd in premises which had earlier been a confectioner's shop and would later be converted into a single-storey house. His authoritative book, *Scottish East Coast Potteries, 1750-1840*, was published in 1979. His memories of a Longniddry childhood, no. 8 in the 'Flashback' series - *Look After the Bairns* - were published in 1999.

People (cont)

Other local authors include the late Marie Muir, who wrote historical novels and children's stories under the pen-name Monica Blake, and Elizabeth Stuart Warfel, who co-edited *Bright Ring of Words,* a compilation of extracts from the writings of Robert Louis Stevenson, in 1992.

In 1993 the late Dr David Hutchison, who was interested in local and ecclesiastical history, produced *A Brief History of Aberlady Village and Church,* a useful source of information about the village. Dr Hutchison's house at the eastern end of Main Street incorporates the old smiddy, a building at least 300 years old.

Another well-known Aberlady personality, Archie Baird, retired veterinarian and golf enthusiast, wrote a history of Gullane golf club, *Golf on Gullane Hill,* to mark its centenary in 1982.

From 1986, soon after she made her home in Aberlady, Jean Curnow began to produce a wide range of photographs and postcards of the village and its neighbourhood, as much a hobby as a business.

This account of Aberlady Parish was written and edited by Iain Macaskill. Additional information, research and essays were provided by the following:

Alison Andrews	Environment - Boundaries; Homes
Martin Andrews	General - Gosford estate
Archie Baird	Economy - Golf, Aberlady course
Michael Cox	Economy - Golf, Kilspindie course
Bill Doig	Education
Laurence Goudie	Belief - Aberlady Parish Church
Jack Greenwood	Leisure - Aberlady Bowling Club
Hilda Nicoll	Leisure - Aberlady Curling Club
John Stevenson	Economy - Agriculture

The following provided a useful summary of Clubs, Shops and Services (past & present):

Mr Bill Cockburn
Miss Margaret Guy
Miss May Guy
Miss Margaret Hamilton
Mrs Isabel Heenan
Mrs Edna Parker

FURTHER READING & REFERENCES
Hajducki, A. (1992) *The North Berwick and Gullane Branch Lines* Oakwood Press
Land Use Consultants for the Countryside Commission for Scotland, CCS (later Scottish Natural Heritage, SNH) and Historic Buildings and Monuments Directorate, Scottish Development Department (first published c1987, 1997 reprint) *The Inventory of Gardens & Designed Landscapes in Scotland: Volume 5: Lothian & Borders*
Snodgrass, C. P. (1953) *The Third Statistical Account: The County of East Lothian*
Tranter, N. (1992) *Footbridge to Enchantment,* Lochar Publishing

ATHELSTANEFORD
PARISH REPRESENTATIVE: *Malcolm Duncan*

Introduction

The land-locked, mostly agricultural parish of Athelstaneford is hemmed in by the parishes of Haddington, Prestonkirk, Dirleton and Aberlady. It covers some 2045 ha (5053 acres). There are two small settlements - Athelstaneford itself - and Drem, which clusters around the railway station. Athelstaneford at the beginning of the twenty first century was recognisably the place described by the Reverend A. Downie Thomson in the Third Statistical Account 50 years ago. Housing was still an issue but rather than the 'shortage' he identified, the 'new' problem was affordability and the pressure from outside for evermore expansion. And the locals may then have had 'general contentment' as he says: maybe they still had this, but not because of his then given reason that 'their work is here and not far distant'.

Changes and development there had been, in housing, transport, communication, employment - the common social and economic development of the second half of the twentieth century which at least lapped at the built environment of Athelstaneford even if it had not, yet, inundated the parish with the full flood of the urbanisation of central Scotland. At night, without travelling far, one could see the ever-spreading light pollution from roads and communities. From Aberlady and the coastal communities to the north and the Fife villages across the Forth to bright lights on A1 roundabouts away to Dunbar in the east; to the glow in the sky to the south where the street lights of Haddington reflected on the clouds. And yet more menacingly to the not so very distant glare in the west from the lights not just of Edinburgh but also of its environs in Musselburgh, Prestonpans and Tranent and every piece of road and dual carriageway and public and private development in between. It seemed that flaring orange sodium lighting was required all night long for a society that appeared no longer able to live or travel in the dark. A far cry from 1953 when Downie Thomson could note, with no apparent real sense of anything unusual, that very few houses in Athelstaneford now lacked sanitary arrangements 'though some still lack electric light'. Today one might enquire who 'lacks' computer access?

Main Street, Athelstaneford, 1964

Introduction (cont)

Yet Athelstaneford in 2000 still straddled its ridge, a conservation area (designated 1969, extended 1979 and to be so again in 2001); the church abided, the school was open and the village hall opposite, where the Sunday school and the SWRI and the guild and youth club and village events took place. The bowling green, tennis court, public park and play area were down the street. The post office and village shop were long gone as was the village blacksmith, the smiddy closing when Alex Ainslie died in 1982. But the post box was still there, in front of the hall. There were future doubts over the once perennial certainties of daily rural post deliveries and collections in the modern age of privatisation and profit but the school across the road from the post box remained a healthy indicator.

Townscapes, Buildings & Landscapes of Distinction
Of the two principal mansion houses, Kilduff House had changed hands once or twice since it was one of the Kinloch properties (and an RAF officers' mess in the war). Gilmerton House itself and parts of the original estate continued remarkably in the Kinloch family, the 'lairds' of the parish, although it was 80 years since the estate village of Athelstaneford and some of the farms were sold off in some 70 or so lots after the first world war.

The East Fortune airfield was an entire listed ancient monument because of the completeness of its second world war remains and ambience (and some first world war corrugated iron huts also survived among the former hospital buildings).

That didn't stop the regular Sunday market (which began c1976, though latterly was a lesser attraction), and microlight flying and the occasional bout of motorcycle racing on parts of the old runways. The Museum of Flight (opened 1971), part of the Museums of Scotland, occupied most of the hangars and site and afforded of course a visitor attraction while performing a very serious museum role.

Stall at East Fortune Sunday market, 1990s (Linda Sneddon)

Population

With a population of some 650 people, this figure is very similar to the 1931 and 1951 levels of population if the hospital numbers are taken out. Athelstaneford lies squeezed between the A1 and the railway only 22 miles from Edinburgh.

By parish, from the General Registrar's office

1931	945	431M	514F				
1951	1205	648M	557F				
1961	982	515M	467F				
1971	866	457M	409F				
1981	791	399M	392F				
				By Small Area Statistics - census			
1991	631	299M	332F	257	123M	134F	
2001	659	326M	333F	--	--	--	
By parish, from ELDC				*By settlement, from ELDC*			
1991		535		--			
1997 (est.) 644 (sic)	329M		316F	260		87 Drem	
2001	NO DATA			NO DATA			

Population figures are difficult to compare, as no two sources extract data in the same way.

Belief

The Church of Scotland minister still lived and worked locally. The Rev A. Downie Thomson retired in 1974. The parish was linked with Tyninghame and Whitekirk on 4 June 1974 and the joint charge was briefly held by the Rev John Blair. The Reverend Dr Kenneth Walker succeeded in 1976 and had completed 24 years' service. The old manse was sold off and the Walker family moved into a new bungalow manse at the east end of the village in 1977.

Ministers

1944-74   A. Downie Thomson
1974 Linked with Whitekirk & Tyninghame
1974-75   J. L. Blair
1976-date   K. Walker

Until about 1960, there was a church hall in Drem where evening services were conducted and the Woman's Guild met. Situated past the last house before the road at the northeast end of the village green, it passed into use as a joiner's shed and was demolished in the 1970s, the site then being used for the garage of that house.

The first interment in the 'new' Athelstaneford burial ground, located near the airfield, took place in 1964 although holders of old lairs were occasionally still buried in the churchyard.

Homes

Almost all the remaining 18th and 19th century cottages and houses had been substantially refurbished and upgraded since the mid-1970s, some before. New 'Goxhill' pantiles from East Yorkshire lay along the roofs maintaining the look of tradition, smart but with an evenness and regularity that indicated that they were not the originals. Some of the work was necessary modernisation but there was a steady move upmarket, which more than hinted at a gentrification, the placing of former modest workers' cottages in a high price bracket.

The economic effect of the national housing market had more than rippled into Athelstaneford. The renovated older properties, whether small cottages or larger houses like the former manse, attracted prices which no doubt reflected the East Lothian and Scottish demand but which were unimaginable 20 or 30 years before. The housing developed by the county council in Glebe Crescent and Saltire Gardens brought modern homes in the years after the war, some for local people who had been occupying and waiting in former RAF huts at Needless and Athelstaneford Mains after the hundreds of air force personnel departed in 1945-6. Further to the dozen or so cottages built in the thirties along the Main Street that Downie Thomson mentions, Glebe Crescent, mainly built under the 1946 Housing Act, had eight houses by 1951 and all 40 houses by 1954. A further ten houses, also by the county council, were completed in Saltire Gardens by 1971.

Cottages at Needless, Athelstaneford.

But the economics had changed. The 'right to buy' was introduced for house tenants in 1980, and around half the former council housing stock was bought by former tenants. This allowed many long-term residents to stay on with security. Yet when these houses themselves began to fall vacant, they were sold on the open market and purchasers moved in from anywhere, often at substantial prices, unless a local connection allowed a local deal to be struck. 15 houses were opened by the East Lothian Housing Association at Mansefield in 1996, an

Homes (cont)

attempt by public landlords both to avoid the tenants' right to buy legislation and to provide affordable housing for rent, but local people may not finally benefit and tenants can be allocated to these houses from elsewhere in East Lothian and beyond.

In Drem, the Drem farm steading was converted into homes with new houses tacked on behind. A highly visible development of some 20 new dwellings was begun in 2000.

Athelstaneford still retained a sense of place: however, with the pressure on housing prices moving upmarket and the lack of local affordable housing, the sense of a balanced community may be in future danger.

Standards of living – some recollections of homes in the parish

As a teenager, and on into early adulthood, Mrs Moncrieff lived with her parents (then in their 60s) in Athelstaneford.

'Between c1945-55 we had a holiday cottage in Athelstaneford. During the war my mother and I stayed while my father came at weekends. After 1945 we continued to do this until 1951, then came to live there. The cottage was modernised c1959-61.

There were two/three rooms and a cellar: a living room, a scullery (WC off it), bedroom (off the living room, which was portioned off latterly to make two rooms). There was one window in the living room, one in the bedroom (door with glass top half after division into two areas), one in the WC, and none in the scullery which opened straight off the front (only) door. We used paraffin lamps (Aladdin).

The walls were plaster over original 'bullet' stone walls, and they bulged in places. Gloss paint (often green or cream) was used on the top half, a dado (paper frieze), and wallpaper (often a leafy pattern) on the bottom half. The low plaster ceiling was gloss painted (white or cream).

The scullery/kitchen was long and narrow, immediately opening from the front door. There was no door except for the WC at the end. It had a wooden worktop, draining board, and a stone sink with cupboards below (curtained); there was a large larder with shelves, an air vent, and curtained at front end. Linoleum flooring. [We cooked on] A paraffin cooker, with an oven and two burners, each heating a hob. The WC had a small window, opening on ratchet, and a door from the scullery. The toilet had linoleum flooring, and a small rug'.

The living room

'This had one window, with a net curtain part way, and a wooden rail holding two cotton (summer) or velvet (winter) curtains. There was a drop leaf mahogany table – covered with chenille or oilcloth. Furnishings were four dining chairs, a horsehair (one ended) sofa, two armchairs (with wooden arms), a mahogany sideboard with long upper drawer, chest of drawers (mahogany), stool, radio and a bookcase (oak). Flooring was linoleum on a concrete floor, Axminster rugs, and a half-moon wool type fireside rug. A Sofono fire had a tiled fireplace and surround, with brass coal box and tongs. The full-length (built-in) cupboard held books, papers. The few ornaments included a crystal bowl with fruit; two large china dogs; a Chinese vase, and a large green vase with a red flower'.

Bedroom(s)

'These had originally been one, opening off the living room. A partition of wood divided it into two smaller rooms, and the rear one had a door (partly glass) opening onto a yard. The rear part had a double bed, chair, small table, a large built-in cupboard, and a chest of drawers. There was linoleum on the wooden floor, and a rug. The front part had a window to the front, a single bed, rug, a chest of drawers *(small), and a small harmonium. There was a large framed sepia print of a Victorian family scene in the bedroom. We used feather mattresses, eiderdowns (satin), and candlewick bedspreads.*

The outhouse (known as the cellar) was one of the three cottages purchased in the 1920s but which was not made habitable. It had a floor of beaten earth, with flagstones; the walls were of original large stones, whitewashed. There were shelves fitted to hold boxes of tools of all kinds (nails, electrical wire, switches, shoe last and shoe repairing tools, joiner's tools, gardening tools etc).

Water was collected from a tap at the wall. There was a wooden 'stall' for supplies of coal, wood, and storage for 5 gallon drums of pink or blue paraffin which was delivered alternate weeks by Robertson, Dunbar. The large boiler at an open fireplace provided hot water for washing (clothes and baths); we had two large zinc bathtubs, and a freestanding mangle (wringer) with wooden rollers and large handle. Fuel used was a mix of wood blocks (off cuts of oak wood from an Edinburgh Cooperage), and coal – delivered by the ton (by Dobson).

The post-war (date not known) change to electricity meant an electric (one bar) fire then stood in the fireplace, and lights came on at flick of a switch!'

Personal hygiene
'Twice daily washes were provided by heating water in the kettle, and used in a basin. For the weekly bath, the water was heated in the boiler, and the zinc baths were used. Soap used was either scented (Lux) or carbolic (Lifebuoy)'.
Pat Moncrieff

Compton Lodge, 1954
'This was a tied house, and my husband was a lorry driver for Baillie of Haddington.

There was a big garden at the back and a drive down to the big house at the front

You went in the front door, turned to the left into a small bathroom; straight in from the front door was the big bedroom, you then turned right into the living room. There was a little bedroom off the living room. And then out of the living room into the back kitchen – a teeny wee back kitchen, but there was also a big larder, a big walk-in larder. No back door. There was no electric – we used a Tilley lamp.

In the living room were a dining room table, four chairs, a settee and two armchairs, and a sideboard. On top of the sideboard was a radio – battery. In the sideboard, some food kept in the sideboard. There was a big range fire – a black range with a tank to the side – for cooking. In the bedroom were a double bed, single wardrobe and a double wardrobe.

I think the house was all white, with lino on the floor.'
Jenny Gray

Gilmerton Lodge, 1954-57
By this point Mrs Gray had a new baby
'This house was quite nice; it had 2 bedrooms, a bathroom, living room, a little front porch, front and back doors and a wee tiny kitchen; I cooked on a wee electric cooker, which was on a meter, fed with shillings.'
Jenny Gray

Utilities

Because of the proximity of the airfield, Athelstaneford benefited early on from 'modern' sewage and electricity supplies. By the end of the period the sewage works were at capacity, limiting, perhaps temporarily, more development.

Utilities (cont)

A gas pumping station is located near the old airfield. A national gas pipeline came through the parish in 1981, taking North Sea gas at immense pressure from Peterhead down to England. Too strong though, for the village, which still has no gas supply.

Shops & Services

While the supermarkets of North Berwick and Haddington and Edinburgh dominated the shopping patterns, a few local services continued. Tait's butcher van from Haddington and the Co-op grocery van stopped in the 1980s but vans with fresh fish and with vegetables still 'tooted' their way round the village and the council mobile library stopped weekly. Drem post office remained open, with Mrs May Fairbairn in charge. The signal box and resident railway workers there were long gone.

Education

Downie Thomson reported four teachers and a roll of 104 pupils, who went on to North Berwick at secondary stage as they mostly still did by 2000. The headmaster Dick Ross lived next door in the schoolhouse; he still lived there in venerable retirement although by then it was a private house. By the end of the 1990s the school had a recently completed extension by East Lothian Council and all the teachers travelled in to work, the head teacher Ronnie Grieve from Dunbar and others from Haddington and elsewhere. There were three teachers plus a variety of visiting assistants and specialists with a school roll of 45 and a nursery class of 14.

There were seldom fewer than six or eight cars parked outside the school and those were only the staff vehicles. The parental 'school run' cars dropped off and picked up at the start and end of the day. There was still a school bus service provided by East Lothian council but the mobile car society had affected Athelstaneford like everywhere else.

Transport

The village is only two miles from Drem station and arguably rural isolation was cut 155 years ago when the railway came through and opened the world to anyone who could walk to the station with a train fare, like John Muir's family from Dunbar station in 1849. From the late 1990s, public policy was to encourage and enhance public transport and to reduce inward car commuting to Edinburgh but increasingly, Athelstaneford looked routinely to Edinburgh and beyond not just for work but for shopping and leisure. The attractions of the national road network accessed only four miles away on the A1 dual carriageway coupled with an intended further improved train service from Drem and the possibility of more housing developments continued to press on the identity of Athelstaneford.

In 1951 the valuation roll disclosed six 'railway servants' at Drem. By 2000, the signal box was demolished, the station open (i.e. unmanned) and the line electrified. East Fortune station had also closed in 1963.

There was a bus service still between Haddington and North Berwick. It was not as busy as when East Fortune hospital was going strong, and dependant on council subsidy, it ran some ten times a day, which compared remarkably with the eight journeys each way reported by Downie Thomson in 1953.

Post Office, Athelstaneford, 1950s, when it was situated in part of the blacksmith's forge, partitioned off from the rest of the building. It was run from 1951-1978 by Mrs Dora Ainslie, wife of Alex Ainslie, the blacksmith, who also sold groceries, confectionary and newspapers. (Dorothie Reilly)

Children of Athelstaneford Primary School, 1950s, with teacher Mrs Ross

Economy - Tourism

By the end of the period, the parish was able to make a small contribution to the tourist industry:

The Flag Heritage Centre is located behind the church, in the Hepburn doo'cot (dated 1583) that was restored in 1996 by the Scottish Flag Trust. This is a memorial to the legend of the Saltire being seen in the skies of Athelstaneford in a 9th century skirmish, and thereafter becoming adopted as the national flag of Scotland. The late novelist and writer Nigel Tranter of Aberlady was one of the moving forces in the creation of this small but unique public attraction, part of both tradition and the modern cult of leisure and tourism.

The Saltire Memorial was built in 1965 in the southeast corner of the churchyard; this carved battle scene was restored in 1993.

Economy - Agriculture

With the number of people employed in agriculture shrunk to penny numbers, part-timers or contractors, in addition to the job implications, former farm worker cottages lie empty at farms like Kilduff or Athelstaneford Mains or may have non-agricultural lets. The tenanted government agricultural smallholdings at Drem Newmains changed radically. The Conservative government also extending the right to buy to them in the 1980s brought a virtual end to the statutory small tenant working a few acres and created in many cases merely owner-occupied houses.

Economy - Miscellaneous employment

There was a riding school in the Drem Newmains former holdings and a garden centre, that indicator of lifestyle, at Merryhatton.

East Fortune hospital had provided local employment from its re-opening after the war in April 1949 to its closure in 1997 although in its latter years declining, and providing only geriatric care which finally moved to Haddington. In 1963, from matron to pupil nurses, there were 42 nursing staff plus nine part-time, with 27 auxiliaries plus 43 part-time auxiliaries. The following year there were some 300 beds, of which TB numbered only 25 compared with the 338 at the end of 1949, but with other chest cases, convalescents and a small general medical section. The principal occupancy was geriatric and chronic sick and what were then described as 'mental defectives', 45 children and 80 male adults.

Post-1997, the site lay derelict, waiting its planning fate possibly as housing or even the 'East Fortune new town' if the constraints of the sewage system could be removed.

(See *Overview of Health Services* by Helen Zealley, county volume, for extracts from the personal reflections by Professor Jimmy Williamson (TB sanatorium days) and Dr J.S. Milne (geriatric service days). These last are given in full on the CD-ROM.)

'Although East Fortune was the great haven for tubercular patients, with its row upon row of beds under verandas, thus mimicking the cure of Swiss patients, it was so much more. Less well known was the great diversity of roles, interests and talents used by patients, staff and friends of East Fortune who helped to create a community to be proud of. Such was the diversity of this great little community that it was able to have its own magazine; 'Fortune' contributions were encouraged from everyone.

The post office sign was a green painted wooden slat, which I saw a few years ago lying on the ground, I wish now that I had picked up this piece of history.

Economy – Miscellaneous Employment (cont)

The radio network broadcast each day, news, requests for patients and staff. Dr Murray, the Consultant, was a frequent contributor to the network, offering words of encouragement to everyone.

The regular bus service from all over the county ensured that patients were able to enjoy the support of their relatives. The children were involved in brownies, guiding and scout groups. Both staff and patients were adept at producing their own drama groups – including pantomimes, skits, karaoke and comedies.

With the advent of new drug therapy and improved health structures, many vacant beds arose. These were quickly filled with elderly patients from the acute areas – thus many blocked beds were available for emergency use. Parallel to this was the need to house children with learning difficulties (due to the proposed closure of Gogarburn and similar establishments). It is to the credit of all staff that these two groups of patients were successfully absorbed into East Fortune. Indeed many children arrived very young and grew up in East Fortune.

I worked in East Fortune during the last 5 years before its final closure, and heard many confidential experiences of how wonderful this community was. Sadly nature has caused an immeasurable overgrowth. The once lively gardens are now home to foxes, rabbits and pheasants.

It needs to become a community again. What a gem for a hospital site. Who knows!'

Nita Fraser, nurse 1992-97

With the hospital gone and agriculture mechanised there was little other immediate employment. People did travel to employment in the North Berwick and Haddington areas and there was some local self-employment in small business and in gardening and house services but Edinburgh was a main employment centre.

People

SWRI Outing, 1950s. Those pictured include: Mrs Borthwick; Mrs Shaw; Mrs MacArthur; Mrs Chisholm; Mrs Nettie Blackshaw; Mrs Susan Smith; Mrs Pow; Ella Bolton; Mrs Wood; Mrs Lambie. (Dorothie Reilly)

People (cont)

The people of Athelstaneford gather at the school to see Sir Alexander Kinloch present a gift to village milkman Willie Tofts on his retirement in 1980. *(Ronnie Grieve)*

This account of Athelstaneford Parish was written by Malcolm Duncan. Additional information was provided by the following:

Ronnie Grieve
Irene Pow
Dorothie Reilly
Watson Thomson
The Rev Dr Kenneth Walker

Thanks are due to the following for sharing their recollections
Nita Fraser
Jenny Gray
Pat Moncrieff

FURTHER READING & REFERENCES

Bunyan, I.T., Storer, J. D. and Thompson, C.L. (1983) *East Fortune: Museum of Flight and History of the Airfield*, Royal Scottish Museum Information Series

Downie Thomson, A. (1953) *'The parish of Athelstaneford'* Snodgrass, C. P. *The Third Statistical Account: The County of East Lothian* pp323-330

Murray, W. A. (1982) *A Life Worth Living* Croal, Haddington

DIRLETON [1]
PARISH REPRESENTATIVE & PARISH EDITOR: *Anne McCarthy*

Introduction

The parish of Dirleton stretches from the Peffer Burn in the west to the outskirts of North Berwick in the east. To the north it is bounded by the Firth of Forth while to the south are the lands of the hinterland farms. The parish covers some 3978 ha (9830 acres). The area is generally flat with Kingston Hill and Gullane Hill the only outstanding points. The Peffer Burn and a tributary, the Mill Burn, run into Aberlady Bay. Over a period of many years, a sand and silt bar has formed at the river mouth and the water quality became poor due to silting, slow flow and pollution. Monitoring and improvements have been ongoing.

Environment

The area enjoys a moderate almost 'micro' climate and often seems to be on the edge of passing weather patterns. Snow seldom lies here for more than a day or so. Wind is a noticeable element with the prevailing winds being mostly west-southwest with speeds of 70mph not uncommon, with, frequently, cold east or north-easterlies in the spring and early summer. Haar (sea mist) can persist for two or three days, drifting in and out of the Forth during the day.

There are designated Sites of Special Scientific Interest (SSSIs) and much of the Aberlady Bay Nature Reserve falls within the parish. Following a scientific study and reports in the 1960s, the county council started work on a major, and on-going, project of dune conservation and restoration at Gullane Bents. This involved the planting of sea buckthorn, sea-lyme grass

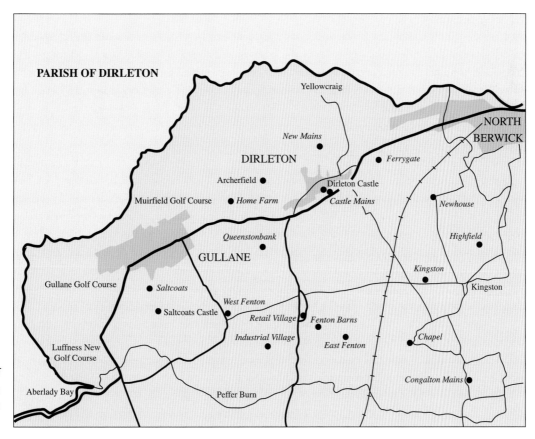

Map of Dirleton Parish

Environment (cont)

Sand dunes at Gullane Bents (John Dewar)

and marram grass. Wooden posts and brushwood fences have also been added and specific pathways designated to allow growth of the grasses and to stabilise the dunes. Although the buckthorn secures the sand, it does squeeze out other species. Another side effect has been to provide more cover for the deer that not uncommonly ventured into the gardens and even on to the streets of Gullane in the 1990s. Yellowcraig Country Park, formerly part of the Archerfield estate, was established by the county council in the early 1970s when a nature trail was also set.

The coastal area is important both for its flora and fauna and for the recreational opportunities it provides. The latter include not only the obvious sea and beach facilities but also the terrain, which shapes the local links golf courses. Natural erosion caused by wind, storms and high tides, together with human use and conservation measures, has ensured a constantly changing scene since the war. Sand winning at the Muirfield end of Gullane Bents has also had an effect. Permission for this was first given to Dobson & Sons in 1951 and although no extraction has been carried out for a number of years, it has been left as an option for the future. In 1990 very high tides and north-westerly gales badly affected much of the work of conservation and the beach was cut back by eight to ten feet, leaving a low 'cliff' of sand.

Seawater quality is now tested regularly. Since 1996, Gullane has achieved a green rating on the European Community scale, indicating excellent water quality and in 1999 Yellowcraig was rated very good. Gullane has also received a Seaside Award for reaching a high standard of land and sea cleanliness and providing good facilities.

Seabirds provide much of ornithological interest along the coast. Winter visitors include divers, seaduck such as common scoter, eider and goldeneye, and waders from the north such as turnstone, knot and dunlin. Fidra is home to a number of nesting seabirds including puffin, guillemot, razorbill, kittiwake and eider. The coastal grasslands have skylarks and meadow pipits and the sea buckthorn thickets provide shelter and nest sites for many birds. In winter the buckthorn berries are eaten by large flocks of fieldfares and other thrushes as well as the resident species such as greenfinches.

Away from the coast many of the breeding bird species have shown a marked decline over the past two or three decades though some such as goldfinches, siskins, long-tailed tits and blue tits which benefit from bird-tables have shown an apparent increase. Also more prominent around the villages in recent years are carrion crows and magpies. Dirleton Castle grounds are excellent for songbirds, particularly when the yew berries are ripe. Modern farming methods have not been good for wildlife although, as part of the set-aside policy, some land has been planted to create wildlife habitats and encourage the reintroduction of lost species. Grey geese and whooper swans are daily visitors in winter to a number of the local fields. The distinctive sight and sound of the comings and goings of skeins of geese is a feature of the parish.

Grey squirrels are very numerous on Archerfield but there also appears to be a very small population of red squirrels and there are roe deer too in the area. With the decline in game keeping, red foxes are now common and have even been known to rear their cubs in garden shrubberies. Weasels and stoats are seen now and then but hedgehogs have become very uncommon. Plenty of rabbits and hares are still to be found on Gullane Hill although less than formerly. Golf course management has had an effect on these and on the proliferation of buckthorn.

Townscapes, Buildings & Landscapes of Distinction

The parish has two main settlements, Gullane and Dirleton, with the smaller hamlet of Kingston on the southeast boundary. Over the years a number of areas of land, gardens and buildings have been listed or classified to note their significance and to ensure their management and conservation for the future. As a result selected parts of Gullane and the whole of the village of Dirleton have conservation area status.

Two factors had a significant impact in Gullane in the 19th century, the coming of the railway and the development of golf. These, along with an easily accessible beach, brought many more visitors to the area and around the turn of the century there was a considerable amount of new building involving such well-known architects as Robert Lorimer, James B. Dunn, Sydney Mitchell and J.M. Dick Peddie. Greywalls, now a hotel, was designed by Edwin Lutyens with a garden by Gertrude Jekyll. Also notable, in Hopetoun Terrace, are the semi-detached houses of Rattlebags stone designed in 1920 for the county council by the firm of Dick Peddie and Walker Todd.

The ruin of the former parish church is to be found at the western end of Gullane. The present Gullane parish church was completed in 1888 and St Adrian's Scottish Episcopal church in 1927. The former United Free Church, which became a church hall before being sold in 1990 and converted to a private house and gallery, is notable for its painted ceiling.

In Dirleton examples of houses and cottages dating from the 17th to 19th centuries, in a vernacular style, survive on the ridge from Chapelhill to the Castle and around the Green. Most of these are built from stone from the local Rattlebags quarry on East Fenton farm, with

Townscapes, Buildings and Landscapes of Distinction (cont)

Houses in Dirleton village viewed from the castle. In the foreground are Castlemains farm cottages. Next to these is the old bakehouse which was a Co-op grocery store till the mid 1960s. (A&J Gordon)

sandstone quoins and lintels. Dirleton kirk with the original manse, on the west side of the Green, dates from the 17th century. Oatfield House and a later manse to the east of the church both date from the Georgian period.

Archerfield estate lies between the two villages. The house, now a ruined shell, originally dates from the 17th and 18th centuries. During the war it was occupied by a series of regiments, latterly Polish soldiers, and was left by them in a poor state. In 1946, the estate was bought by a farmer, Ian Mitchell, who farmed the land and used part of the house as a grain store. He removed the front entrance and installed a grain drier. In 1960, the Hamilton and Kinneil Estates bought the estate and the home farm became the residence of the Duke of Hamilton. The house continued to deteriorate and in the late 1980s it and the eastern half of the estate was sold for development. From then until 2000 three proposals for golf course, hotel and housing developments were made and failed due to planning or financial difficulties. The requirement by the East Lothian Council to restore the house contributed to these difficulties.

There are also the remains of two castles in the parish: the fragmentary ruin of the late 16th century Saltcoats Castle south of Gullane and the much more significant Dirleton Castle within Dirleton village. The Dirleton Castle ruins date from the early 13th century with additions through to the 16th century.

Population
By parish, from the General Registrar's office

Year	Total	Male	Female		Locality			
				By locality – census – ie Dirleton				
1931	2824	1224M	1600F	*and Gullane villages*				
1951	2817	1317M	1500F					
1961	2768	1316M	1452F					
1971	3041	1469M	1572F		*476*	*231M*	*245F*	*Dirleton*
1971					*2046*	*941M*	*1105F*	*Gullane*
1981	3205	1481M	1724F		*458*	*217M*	*241F*	*Dirleton*
1981					*2232*	*1005M*	*1227F*	*Gullane*
				By Small Area Statistics - census				
1991	3278	1575M	1703F		*456*	*213M*	*243F*	*Dirleton*
1991					*2049*	*963M*	*1086F*	*Gullane*
2001	3188	1475M	1713F		--	--	--	

By parish, from ELDC					*By settlement, from ELDC*		
					Dirleton	*Gullane*	
1991	3111				477	2229	
1997 (est.)	3411 (sic)	1666M	1747F		486	2283	
2001	--	--	--		*No data for Dirleton village*	2172	*(ELC)*

Population figures are difficult to compare, as no two sources extract data in the same way.

According to census returns, in 1951 the population of Dirleton parish was 2817. In 1991 the parish figure was 3278, with 2229 of these living in Gullane and 477 in Dirleton. Significantly 30% of the residents at that time were at or over retirement age. The population of Dirleton village is very much the same as it was at the end of the war but living in double the number of houses. East Lothian Council projected figures for 1997 were 2283 for Gullane and 486 for Dirleton.

In the Third Statistical Account of 1953 farming is mentioned as the only industry, providing employment to over 300 people. Gardening and quarrying are also listed along with a dozen girls employed in the laundry at Dirleton and a good number working at golf clubs in Gullane. At that time too there were five joiners in Gullane and two in Dirleton. In 1977, Gullane boasted five joiners/builders, two plumbers and two painter/decorators. At the end of the century there are six joiners/builders, five plumbers/heating engineers and five painters/decorators but agriculture has seen the biggest change with a 40% fall in employment since 1990.

Golf remains a major employer, along with local hotels and the building trade in the widest sense, though the largest single workforce in 2000 was the mushroom-growing operation at Fenton Barns. Many people work outside the parish and, as has been the case for the last 50 years, there are a considerable number of retired residents. A quick rundown of Dirleton's 416 adult residents indicates around half are in employment and about half of these work within East Lothian.

Belief

Throughout the period there have been three churches in the parish: the Church of Scotland parish churches of Gullane and Dirleton and St Adrian's Scottish Episcopal church in Gullane. The major change is that all three are now linked to other congregations. The first of these moves came in 1975, when St Adrian's became a linked charge with St Baldred's, North Berwick, retaining the rectory there and the Gullane rectory being sold. In 1985 Gullane parish church became linked with Aberlady with the manse in Gullane retained. The same year Dirleton kirk was linked with the Abbey church in North Berwick.

In the last 50 years Dirleton kirk and Gullane parish church have each seen four ministers while six rectors have served St Adrian's. A new manse (the third) was built in Dirleton in 1968. In terms of membership Gullane's now stands at around 500 compared to 921 in 1977 and 570 mid-century. In Dirleton the membership was 390 at the time of the Third Statistical Account and is 280 today. By comparison today 143 persons are 'attached' to St Adrian's (93 as communicants) with a quoted membership of 150 in 1977 and 100 in the early 1950s. These figures obviously are more significant when considered in conjunction with population numbers. At Dirleton as well as the Sunday morning service there is a service on Wednesday morning and an Armistice Day service is held at the War Memorial. At the time of the linkage, Gullane morning services were cut back from two to one and Communion services have been reduced from three to two per Sunday and are held three times a year. The use of communion cards ended in 1998. On Easter Sunday an early morning service is held on Gullane Hill or at Aberlady Bay on alternate years. St Adrian's has a sung Eucharist every Sunday morning and an early Holy Communion (1662 Prayer Book) on the 1st and 3rd Sundays. There is also an occasional Evensong. The Sunday school in Gullane parish church had a roll of 120 in 1950 reaching a high of nearly 200 in the seventies. Thereafter, numbers declined but with a change in format - a rota of participating parents and much more emphasis on discussion for the older children. In 2000, there is a lively Sunday school with around 35 children on any one Sunday and a Sunday evening Sun Club attracting an average of 24 in the 11-13 age bracket. Noticeable too is the much greater involvement of Sunday school children in church services.

During recent years some significant changes have taken place. Women elders were first called to Gullane parish church in June 1979. At the end of the century there are 39 elders of whom 14 are women. St Adrian's welcomed its first lady curate, Rev Lorna Mortis, in 1999 following the Scottish Episcopal church's decision to ordain women priests. A number of other church-based organisations have come and gone in Gullane over the last half century: church dramatic group (1947-c57), boy's brigade (1951-85), men's club (1965-95) and young wives and mothers (1951-76). The parish church guild, however, continues to thrive. Towards the end of the 1990s 'Woman's' was dropped from the name and the guild became open to both sexes and men are starting to attend. Equally, membership is no longer restricted to the Church of Scotland, with some coming from the congregation at St Adrian's.

Church halls too have seen changes. In 1990 the Gullane church hall was sold and replaced by the church centre, adjoining the church itself. It has become a well-used facility including being used for the serving of coffee on Tuesday morning and after morning service on Sunday. In the 1990s in Dirleton the church hall became increasingly used for a variety of activities, as the village hall became less usable.

Belief (cont)

The Roman Catholic community in the parish is served by the Church of Our Lady Star of the Sea in North Berwick. A Mass centre at Luffness House, Aberlady, closed in 1992.

Homes

In both the main settlements, housing expansion has continued.

In Dirleton, local authority housing added in the 1920s and 1930s though built of harled brick, retains a vernacular style. Even the housing association development of the 1990s is of a sympathetic scale and style.

Between the wars about 30 houses were built, extending the village to the east and also, to the south at the western end. During the second half of the 20th century the number of houses has grown steadily but not dramatically. After the war five prefabricated houses were built to help meet a post-war demand when conventional building materials were in short supply. They were demolished in 1982 when Maxwell Road was developed. Groups of new houses were built at Gylers Road in the 1940s and 1950s and by the East Lothian Housing Association at Castlemains Place in the 1990s. The latter has two associated workshops to encourage the establishment of small businesses in the village. Cottages in Chapelhill were demolished to make way for houses for the elderly. Major developments were latterly curtailed by the limited capacity of the sewer although this was rectified at the end of the century. This paved the way for a development of five houses at the paddock beside the Open Arms Hotel. Some council houses have been sold to the tenants leaving 73 council houses today compared to 94 in 1985.

Harpenside Crescent, Dirleton, with stooks of wheat in field beyond, belonging to Castlemains farm.
(A&J Gordon)

Homes (cont)

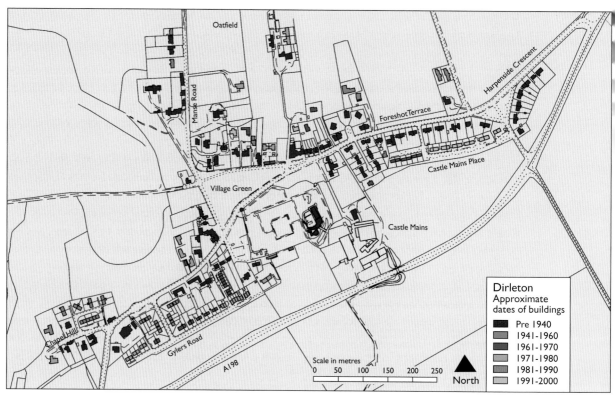

Housing expansion in Dirleton

The first local authority housing in Gullane was built between the wars, with some 80 houses in Hopetoun Terrace, Middleshot Road, Hamilton Crescent and Hamilton Road. The Third Statistical Account, published in 1953, gives the total number of houses as 450 with very little building taking place in the immediate post-war years. However the 1950s saw the beginning of an increase in housing with a large council house development of 135 houses, chiefly in Muirfield Crescent, Muirfield Drive and Muirfield Terrace.

The housing expansion continued in the early 1960s and early 1970s with private developments at Broadgait Green, Erskine Road and Muirfield Park and the nearby 'linked' housing area. At the same time the council estate also grew with houses being added to Muirfield Drive and Muirfield Terrace and the building of Garleton Court. Some of the early large houses have now been subdivided and a significant amount of infill building has taken place, much of it in the gardens of larger properties. Other newer developments include those at the former Muirfield House, at the Paddock (behind Stamford Hall) and, most recently, on the former Gullane station site. The borders of the village have been extended too with developments to the south and east at Muirfield Steading, Fentoun Gait and West Fenton Gait and to the north of Erskine Road. Local authority housing has decreased in the last 15 years with the sale of council houses. In 1999 the number stood at 145 compared to 236 in 1985. Although much of the latter half of the century has seen a drift away of local young people, it would seem that in the late 1990s a noticeable number are choosing to return to Gullane to set up home.

Utilities

Gullane water is distributed from a tank on Gullane Hill, initially pumped from Whiteadder reservoir to Castle Moffat treatment works, near Nunraw Abbey, Garvald, flowing from there via a holding tank in the Garleton Hills. In 2000, work along the A198 was part of East of Scotland Water's new main. Dirleton water comes from a holding tank at Kingston, parts of the main supply having been renewed in 1999.

In 2000, work was completed to link to the main system the sewerage system in a narrow northern strip of Gullane, its sewage until then being discharged untreated into the Firth of Forth. The main system already took waste to the Gullane treatment works on the lower slopes of Gullane Hill and thence into Aberlady Bay. Houses to the south of the Scottish Fire Service Training School, Gullane have a system of collecting 'surface water' separately and channelling it into a burn near West Fenton. In the 1990s a new pipe was connected to the existing system at the Eel Burn bridge to take Dirleton sewage to the North Berwick treatment works instead of its being discharged untreated into the sea near Fidra. The old system, being at capacity, restricted housing development in Dirleton, with septic tanks being used for some new properties.

In the 1990s cleansing, administered by the local authority, ensured that domestic and trade wheelie-bins were emptied weekly, with a special uplift by arrangement for large items. Street cleaning was done weekly, twice a week along the main street in Gullane with a weekly truck handling litter picking and bin emptying, with Gullane Bents and Yellowcraig caravan site included. Mechanical beach cleaning was the responsibility of the Leisure & Tourism department.

There were permanent collection points for recycling bottles and cans in Gullane, a paper bank was available once a month, while used oil and other rubbish could be taken to North Berwick's Civic Amenity Site.

Earlier telephone systems were superseded in 1974 by a partial electronic system when a new telephone exchange was opened at Muirfield Drive, Gullane. A fully electronic system was installed in January 1992. Lines began to go underground in the 1970s. At the end of the century there remain two public telephones in Gullane and one in Dirleton, which is still the traditional red design.

Shops & Services

Shopping patterns have changed generally in recent years, greatly influenced by increased car use. From the 1980s many people have made use of supermarkets in North Berwick, Haddington and the outskirts of Edinburgh where once they would have shopped locally.

Despite this, Gullane has done better than many villages in retaining its local shops.

Nevertheless changes have taken place. The 1953 Third Statistical Account gives around 30 shops in Gullane, reduced to 21 in 1977. In 2000 there were still 21. These include three grocery stores plus butchers, bakery, greengrocers, newsagent with confectionery, men's outfitters and ladies' dress shop. However there is now no ironmonger, fish shop, general draper nor dairy. Other types of businesses, such as a travel agency, antiques, interior design and curtain shops and a health and beauty salon, have moved in. There are, besides, two hairdressers, a solicitor/estate agent, chemist, charity shop, post office and bank. The original four Co-operative shops (bakery, grocery, drapery and butcher) were gradually reduced until, at the

Shops & Services (cont)

Main Street, Gullane, 1940s. The Wishing Well Café on the left has been replaced by 'La Potiniere'. The ivy-covered building on the right is the Golf Inn Hotel. (A&J Gordon)

end of the century, only a grocery store remains. Changes occurred in opening hours in the 1990s with a number of shops remaining open during the lunch hour and on Wednesday afternoons, once a universal half day. The monthly Monday holiday in the winter is now a thing of the past. Both the Co-operative store and Gullane mini-market have late opening until 8pm and 7pm respectively with the latter also opening on Sunday. At the other end of the day, the paper shop and mini-market are both open at 6am and the baker at 7.30am so all in all there has been a noticeable extension of hours.

In the Third Statistical Account of 1953 Gullane is credited with eight hotels along with three restaurants or cafés, with three hotels in Dirleton and a teashop attached to a shop. In 1977 the hotels in Gullane numbered six and restaurants/cafés four. At the end of the century Gullane has five hotels, four restaurants/cafés and one bar providing food. Of the eating establishments, La Potinière has a national reputation. Dirleton's two hotels are the Castle Inn, a 19th century coaching inn, and The Open Arms. The latter was converted from a guesthouse to a tearoom in 1947 and shortly afterwards became a hotel. During the summer a marquee erected in the garden is used for wedding receptions (15 in 1999) and other functions. Throughout the parish a small number of homes offer bed and breakfast facilities.

In 1950, Dirleton had two shops and a post office. During the century the latter has occupied no less than nine different premises. From pre-1950s, it was run from premises on Main Street. By the 1960s it had become the village store as well as a Post Office. The property eventually became an antique shop and the village was without a Post Office until a portacabin was sited in the front garden of Castlemains Farm cottages. The original sign was used and is still stored

*(left) Dirleton village
Post Office,
Main Street, 1950s.
(Gullane & Dirleton
History Society)*

*(below left) Post Office
housed in portacabin at
Castlemains cottages,
1983. (James Simpson)*

*(below)
Post Office,
Maxwell Road, 1990s,
now a private house.*

in the portacabin at Castlemains Farm. When houses were built in Maxwell Road, a tiny building was attached to one of them to be used as a Post Office. At the Millennium there remains only a general village store, which also houses the village post office. The only other retail business is The Gallery, housed in the former laundry buildings. A variety of other small, mostly one-person, businesses operate in and from the village.

Throughout the period vans and delivery services have supplemented the shopping provision in both villages. In this way fresh fish is available every day. Others provide fruit and vegetables, ice cream, lemonade, tea, coal, cleaning products, logs and gourmet foods. Milk deliveries continue by way of the institution that is George Bell who has been delivering to our doorsteps for 28 years, albeit from a variety of suppliers.

Shops & Services (cont)

East Lothian District Library van leaving Ruthven Road, Dirleton. The cottage beyond is Woodend.

Despite there being far fewer cars around, after the war Gullane had four garages (one kept by a blacksmith/motor mechanic) and Dirleton one, compared with today's total of two in Gullane and one outside Dirleton on the road to North Berwick.

Animal health has been served since 1963 by the veterinary practice of Mrs Pat Morris who also has a surgery in North Berwick.

The mobile library from East Lothian Council Library HQ in Haddington visits Dirleton once a week, making two stops in the village.

Away from the two villages, several shops have appeared during the 1990s under the umbrella of Fenton Barns Retail and Leisure Village. The original farm shop dates from the 1950s and sells farm produce and other goods with much of its stock being locally grown or prepared. The later additions include outlets for antiques and collectables, local crafts, designer furnishing fabrics at discount prices, prints, signs, pine furniture and clothing.

In Gullane the incoming mail was still sorted in the back room of the present post office until February 1990. Since then it has been sorted in North Berwick for their own Gullane deliveries by three full-time and two part-time postmen (and women). On weekdays in Gullane there are two deliveries per day and bicycles are still in general use. A team of postmen and women using vans makes deliveries in Dirleton, and the rural part of the parish. After the war there were four letterboxes in Gullane, increasing to seven in the 1970s. Dirleton has two.

Healthcare

General medical practitioners in the parish have been notable for their long service to the local community. Dr H.B. Kirk first came to Gullane in 1916 and remained in practice until his retirement in 1964 at the age of 75. He was joined for a time by his son and later by his son-in-law Dr W.L. Blackett who served in the practice from 1949 to 1984. In 1964, Dr St. C.G. Barr came as an assistant, became a partner, and remained until his retirement in 1996.

Before 1957, surgeries were held in the doctor's private house, the dining room acting as waiting room. That year saw the building of purpose-built premises in Broadgait, which were modified in 1994. Up until 1984 Saturday evening surgeries were held in particular to cater for patients having to come in from surrounding farms. In conjunction the chemist remained open till 7pm.

At the end of the century the Gullane Medical Practice provides most of the general medical services for the parish. There are three doctors, one of whom is part-time and a practice nurse, also part-time. Three part-time receptionists and a full-time practice manager complete the team. In addition there are two community nurses (what would formerly have been district nurses) attached to the practice and a health visitor based in North Berwick runs a twice-weekly child health clinic at the Gullane surgery. The practice serves around 4100 patients, mainly from Gullane and the immediate surrounding district. No appointment is needed to see a doctor. In the 1990s for evening and weekend emergencies the partnership became part of the East Lothian Medical Emergency Clinic and Service, based in Tranent and run by a rota of doctors from participating practices. The retiral of Dr Barr provided the occasion for a real village event when the community expressed its appreciation in a packed village hall, the evening ending with the guest of honour playing Auld Lang Syne on his accordion.

A dental surgery was opened in May 1991, catering for both National Health Service and private patients. The staff consists of one full-time and two part-time dentists, along with two dental nurses and a trainee. Previously residents had to travel outwith the parish for dental treatment. A podiatry clinic is provided by the NHS Trust. For several years it was held in the annexe at Waverley House but later moved to Gullane Day Centre where it operates one day a week.

The present pharmacy follows in the footsteps of the first chemist shop of J.P. Sinclair who opened for business in 1899. At the end of the century there is one full-time and one part-time pharmacist plus two dispensers. Whereas the retail side of the business has not changed greatly, the dispensary has become increasingly busy and, needless to say, computerisation has been introduced and now plays a large role.

Several premises in Gullane have been used as residential and holiday homes. Muirfield House was bequeathed to the Royal Hospital for Sick Children in Edinburgh by Miss Mary Jane Meikleham and used for the treatment of long-term patients. From 1967 it was used as a holiday home by patients of the Royal Scottish National Hospital at Larbert, and lastly by Lothian Health Board as a geriatric holiday home. In the period 1985-87 the site was developed with the building of retirement cottages in the grounds.

After the war, Waverley House was a holiday home for the wives of retired miners. In the early 1970s it was taken over by the Midlothian, East Lothian and Peebles social work group as a retirement home, being transferred to the Lothian Regional Council's social work department in 1975. Despite protests it was closed in 1999 and residents moved to other locations.

Healthcare (cont)

The Miners' Convalescent Home at Whatton Lodge, with accommodation for 20 people, was opened in September 1949 by Lord Balfour, having been purchased for £23,000. The actual ceremony was performed by Joe Neilson who had been a miner for 68 years. An extension was opened in October 1981 by Mr and Mrs James Cowan. It still operates at the end of the century, albeit on a more limited basis.

Coldstones was left to the W.R.V.S. in 1950 by Hon. Percy Thesiger to be used as an establishment for the elderly. It was subsequently passed to the Bield Housing Association, which has since sold it on.

Muirfield Nursing Home, formerly the major part of Bisset's Hotel, opened in 1988 and houses 41 residents.

Linksview Gullane Day Centre was started in 1991 to serve local elderly people who were frail, disabled and/or were suffering from dementia. The former Primary 1 classroom in the playground of the old school in East Links Road was refurbished and adapted for the purpose. It is open five days a week with lunch served on three of them, and provides a wide range of social, therapeutic, recreational and basic health activities. In 1997 a banner representing life in the village was hand sewn by some 18 ladies meeting once a week for two hours. Two more banners, one looking to the future and one to the past were presented to the village in 2000 as a thank you for its continuing support of the day centre. They hang in the village hall. A qualified co-ordinator is assisted by a rota of volunteers and by a management committee of ten members. It has its own minibus with volunteer drivers. Funding is currently provided by East Lothian Council social work department supplemented by fund-raising events to cover extra costs.

Some other voluntary services have disappeared. A local Red Cross members' group ceased and the last local involvement of the W.R.V.S. stopped with the end of the Meals on Wheels service in January 1999.

Education

Each village has a primary school, feeding naturally into secondary education at North Berwick High School, although there is parental choice. The primary school at Kingston closed at Christmas 1974 with both pupils and teacher transferring to the newly opened Law Primary School, North Berwick. A small number of children attend private schools in Edinburgh.

In both schools numbers have fluctuated over the period covered. Throughout the 1940s and 1950s Dirleton Primary School was attended by 80-90 children but this gradually fell away, reaching a low of 33 in 1983. In 1984 a move to close the school was abandoned in the face of strong local opposition. Pressure on North Berwick Primary School has given rise to an increase in the Dirleton roll, which reached 61 in 1999. The number of teachers has varied from two to three during this period.

In the mid-seventies Gullane Primary School was full to overflowing with an additional infant classroom, two temporary classrooms and a dining hut built in the playground. On 27 June 1977, the 225 pupils and 10 staff moved to a new open-plan school at Muirfield Terrace. The local MP John P. Mackintosh officially opened it on 10 April 1978. In 1950 there were four teachers at Gullane and in 1999 there were seven and 155 pupils. In addition both schools have auxiliaries, learning support provision and visiting teachers for physical education and music. Both schools have strong parent teacher associations, which help with fundraising and extra-curricular activities. In 2000 a school dress code is compulsory in East Lothian but Gullane introduced this ten years earlier, with blue sweatshirts bearing a logo of flying geese, designed by a P7 pupil. A nursery section was added to Gullane school in April 1993. The children are mainly from Gullane but with some also from Aberlady, Dirleton and North Berwick.

Since the opening of the new school, dinners have been prepared on the premises at Gullane. Although built as a community school, including squash courts, out of school hours use is mainly by pupil groups. Regular adult use has diminished, curtailed at least in part by the costs of janitorial cover for out-of-hours opening. In 1999 only classes in martial arts and weight training remained. For many years series of lectures were provided via the University of Edinburgh Extra-Mural Department and were very well attended but fell victim to the economic cutbacks in the 1980s.

A change in educational climate saw the end to the awarding of the Dux medal in Gullane in the mid 1980s. However two donated golf trophies are still contested annually. The earlier of these, the Honour Bright, has been in existence since 1922. In the early 1960s George Zaharias gave a sum of money to the school to purchase a trophy in the name of his wife 'Babe' Zaharias who had won the British Open Ladies' Championship at Gullane in 1947.

Gullane playgroup for the under-5s began in the village hall in 1967. In the late 1970s, it moved to the rear portion of the old school and operates four mornings a week, catering for a total of 35 children. A grant is received from East Lothian Council, but not guaranteed. Management is by a committee of nine, plus a further fund-raising committee. Dirleton playgroup has been going for 29 years and was also originally housed in the village hall. Latterly it has used the church hall and takes children aged two and a half to five on three days of the week for a variety of play and creative activities. It has a leader and assistant and operates with parental help.

The former Gullane school building has had a variety of tenants besides the playgroup. The separate buildings of the former infant classroom and the dining hall were used as a base for the Outdoor Education Unit until February 1992. The former was then converted to become the Linksview Day Centre. The front of the main building was for a time used for Youth Opportunities activities and the head teacher's office for child health clinics. In 1981 this space was taken over by East Lothian Council's Library Service, which replaced the voluntary library, which had been housed in the small hall of the village hall, a provision which the village had long outgrown. It is open, and busy, 14 hours a week.

The last head teacher to occupy the schoolhouse was Mr William Bennett who retired in 1979. After lying vacant for some years it was finally sold as a private house.

One other educational establishment has its home in the parish. The Scottish Fire Service Training School (S.F.S.T.S.) moved to Gullane in October 1953, taking over what had been the Marine Hotel. The building was used as an army billet during the second world war but an attempt afterwards to re-establish it as a hotel had not been a success. Since arriving in Gullane the school has gone from strength to strength and has seen substantial expansion.

The original building, known as Henderson House, contains the administrative offices, conference and seminar rooms, a closed circuit television studio, lecture theatre and classrooms, refectory and en-suite bedroom accommodation. An additional residential block containing 120 single study bedrooms was built in 1980 and a gymnasium was opened in 1990

Education (cont)

and extended in 1996. In February 1999 Henry McLeish, Minister for Home Affairs, officially opened the Real Fire training facility and a separate Flashover facility. Unfortunately the latter has rarely been used following residents' complaints concerning smoke emissions. In March 1999, a Confined Space training facility complete with grain silo became operational.

The S.F.S.T.S. provides comprehensive residential training for the Scottish and Northumberland fire brigades involving both basic and specialised courses. A total of 1079 men and women attended 23 different courses in the year to 31 March 1999. In addition 328 people attended courses, seminars or special meetings. Of the 125 whole-time recruits on the three sixteen week basic courses held during that year, nine were female. All fire service staff other than the Commandant and his Deputy live outwith the village but local people are employed in the catering and domestic services provision.

Transport

The main mode of transport in the parish is undoubtedly the private car, ownership of which has been very much on the increase since the 1950s. As an example of its popularity, at the 1991 census Gullane residents owned over one thousand cars with 44 households having three or more. Despite the obvious increased volume of traffic, the road network remained unchanged until the creation of the Dirleton bypass in 1975. By this time it was becoming difficult to cross the road in Dirleton especially on a sunny weekend when many people visited Yellowcraig. A few years later the road at Fenton Barns was straightened and in 1997 a pedestrian crossing was installed at Gullane.

Throughout most of the period the parish has had a half-hourly bus service on the Edinburgh to North Berwick route. In the 1940s and 1950s this was heavily used but as car ownership increased it became less busy. At the end of the century it runs every 30 or 60 minutes, depending on the time of day and follows the coastal route. It is supplemented by a limited stop service running once a day in each direction on weekdays, so serving commuters, and a school-term-time service via Ballencrieff and Drem, by-passing the coastal villages.

Since 1999, on Wednesday and Friday a free, sponsored bus has conveyed passengers to the Gyle shopping complex, west of Edinburgh. The same year saw the introduction of Gaberlunzie, a rural East Lothian service operating on Wednesdays and Fridays between Gullane and Haddington. Intending passengers wishing to join at intermediate points telephone the day before to arrange for the bus to call at or near to a pre-arranged place. Two taxi services operate from both Dirleton and Gullane, one of the latter also having a driving school. In the late 1990s a coach hire service was established in Gullane.

The railway no longer serves the two villages directly. Passenger services, already withdrawn from Gullane, finished at Dirleton in 1952 with a reduced goods facility remaining at both stations. After the war Gullane station buildings along with a camping coach were let as self-catering holiday accommodation. Closure finally came to both stations with the Beeching cuts of 1964. With the closure of the village stations Drem became the nearest railhead, with parking for about 70 cars. With the electrification of the North Berwick to Edinburgh line, in 1991, the frequency of services increased. In 2000, trains to Edinburgh run on a roughly hourly basis Monday to Saturday, with four trains on Sunday. The journey from Drem to Waverley takes 27 minutes.

Police

After local government reorganisation in 1975, the two Gullane policemen were transferred to the North Berwick police station. The Gullane office was then used as a 'policebox' until it was sold at the end of the century. Further changes to policing came to the area in the 1980s with the introduction of the community policeman. The incumbent attends community council meetings, visits the school, advises on security, polices the Gullane Games Week parade and generally tries to create ties between the police and the community, including doing foot patrols. Policing is generally via North Berwick with telephone calls switched to Dalkeith after office hours. Crime in the villages is principally theft from cars, with golf clubs a particular target. In the late 1990s in Gullane there has been vandalism by children with under-age drinking more of a problem than drugs. Dirleton is noteworthy for a particularly low crime rate. Neighbourhood Watch schemes have been set up in both villages though that at Gullane is presently not noted for its high profile.

Leisure

Gullane's original village hall was built in 1902 and by 1945, still under military command, it was looking the worse for wear. A replacement was proposed, a 'memorial hall' to those who had died in the second world war. However, in 1945, permission for new building was strictly regulated and refurbishment of the old hall was agreed on. A village council steered the project and the East Lothian Courier reported on a 'building transformed' on its re-opening in June 1948 after much local fund-raising. The 'memorial' idea was transferred to playing fields and a pavilion, opened in 1952, next to the site of a proposed new primary school and close to planned district council housing.

By 1953, the village council had become Gullane Community Association with responsibility for drawing to the attention of the district council any local matter which it was felt needed to be addressed. It made plain to a well-attended public meeting that it could fund only minor repairs to the hall and recommended that a new hall be built. Thanks to Ian Bowhill of Stamford Hall, who offered to match the village fund-raising pound for pound, the new hall was opened in 1958, at a cost of £10,000 on a site behind the old hall. With the demolition of the latter, it acquired a convenient parking area, which remained for many years rough and muddy. However, it underwent a transformation one Saturday morning in 1995 when public-spirited local tradesmen guided enthusiastic villagers in the laying of a brick paver surface over the whole area. A side wall had to be replaced in 1973 and fund-raising in 1988 provided roof repairs and conversion of the heating system from oil to gas. An access ramp and toilet for the disabled were installed in 1993. A new kitchen, double-glazing and a new roof followed in 1998. Constant fund-raising is needed to keep the hall viable but it would still not have been possible without grants from the Scottish Office, local authorities and the Lottery Fund.

Dirleton village hall was built soon after the war due to the joint efforts of the British Legion and the village association using voluntary labour. It was much used for village activities but the limitations of its construction, due to lack of finance and shortage of materials, began to tell and it became less used. It was taken over by the district council in 1974 and the higher rents they charged further reduced its use. By 1999, it was in need of extensive refurbishment and was little used.

Leisure (cont)

Dirleton itself is centred round Dirleton Green. Formerly common ground, cattle grazed here until 1948. Under council ownership it is enjoyed by both local people and visitors and it is here that the Dirleton Games are held each year. These annual games lapsed during the war but were restarted in 1960 and continued until the 1970s when they again lapsed. They restarted in 1990 and remained an annual event at the end of the century. The format latterly included children's competitions, stalls and sideshows. In the early 1990s a scramble competition for vintage motorbikes took place in Archerfield estate and a dance was held in the evening. A swing park and public toilets are at the top of the Green by the castle.

Gullane Games, with Games Day firmly fixed on the first Saturday in August, has a long history. The original games were professional but since the end of the first world war Gullane Games Day has been mainly a children's day. The arrival of the shows (fair) on Goose Green is also part of the tradition. In the 1970s with a new and younger committee Gullane Games became a Games Week with three or four additional events and the re-introduction of the selecting of a local girl as Miss Gullane. By the 1990s, Games Week covered eight days with a variety of competitions and entertainments for all ages, with many locals and visitors planning their holidays around it. Games Day itself enjoys a very traditional form with races and events for toddlers, children and adults, and a variety of displays and attractions. The Dalkeith and Monktonhall Brass Band provide music throughout the afternoon. The very last event is the fancy dress parade up the main street and back. In recent years, the Games committee has run a Christmas Eve event for the children in the village hall. Gullane Games' success is testament to a great deal of hard work by its all-male committee some of whom have been involved for many years, joined by younger volunteers coming forward.

It is encouraging to be able to report a good number of active local clubs and groups but inevitably some have come and some gone (and some done both) over the last 50 years mirroring the social changes that have taken place. One loss was the Gullane branch of the British Legion, active post-war, which stopped functioning in 1972.

Youth groups

The under-fives still do quite well. Half way through the period there was music and movement along with mothers and toddlers. These have been replaced by mums and tots and tantrum busters, certainly a change in terminology. Their parents also have contact via the National Childbirth Trust. For older children, the boys' and girls' clubs have both disappeared over the past two decades and various youth clubs have come and gone although the situation at the end of the century is encouraging. Interest in scouts was reported to be on the wane after the war but by the mid-seventies there was again a healthy scout and cub membership, which along with beavers now numbers between 40 and 50.

Guides have had an even more roller-coaster time. The number of guides, brownies and rangers totalled about 70 in the post-war period, a number well-maintained 25 years later. By 1995 guide membership was insufficient to sustain an independent company, those remaining joining North Berwick. Brownies, however, have remained buoyant and with a waiting list. Their only restriction is the shortage of adult help and should this be forthcoming, there is even the possibility of Gullane guides returning.

Leisure (cont)

Dirleton Games Day, 1950. Left to right: Mrs Elizabeth Thorburn; Mrs Young (nee Neilson); Jim Inglis; Mrs Alison Nairn; Betty Sherrat (later Timson); unknown; Mrs Victor Pride; others unknown till Mrs Scorgie (far right). Ronald Thorburn is front left ('Tinker') and Andrew Thorburn ('Sleepless Night') next to him
(Gullane & Dirleton History Society)

Float at Gullane Games, c1953. (left)
(Gullane & Dirleton History Society)

Gullane Games Day, c1953.
(Gullane & Dirleton History Society)

Leisure (cont)

On the sporting front the bowling clubs, catering for both men and women, in both villages are in a healthy state, no longer quite the preserve of the less young. The Dirleton club is notable for its use of the historic bowling green in the castle grounds. For a long time the badminton club in Gullane maintained some 20 to 30 members and although numbers are now under 20, it is still enjoyed. The tennis club was re-formed in 1976 by an enthusiastic group and at the end of the century continues all year round, weather permitting. But the football club and the senior squash club no longer function, and participation in men's darts has been reduced from four teams to two and the ladies' team which had been active from 1979, folded in 1999 with the end of the local darts league.

On a more positive side the swimming club was formed in 1972, and since then parents have ferried children weekly to pools at Portobello, Haddington and North Berwick. In 1977, the club had a membership of 180 and still had 90 members in 1999, despite the much-increased swimming instruction through schools. Newer ventures are the cricket club begun in 1997 and a walking group formed in 1985 and drawing members from the parish and beyond. Dance classes, of which there were two in 1977, no longer appear to be the 'in' thing in the 1990s, but Gullane has an aerobics class and regular yoga classes have been run since 1979.

In Dirleton, an outdoor group with a varied programme of outdoor activities first ran from 1971 until 1982 and was then restarted in 1996. It does try to encourage young people to participate but has found this to be difficult in recent years. Castlefield Archers, about 15 in number, use the indoor facilities at Fenton Barns and a field archery course on Chapelhill. In 1950, waning interest in the Women's Rural Institute in Gullane was reported and also the recent formation of The Co-operative Women's Guild. The latter no longer survives, but the SWRI did, with a membership of 107, around the time of its fiftieth anniversary 25 years later. At the end of the century that number is down to 20. The Dirleton branch was founded only in 1947, and in 1999 also has a membership of around 20.

Throughout the 1950s amateur dramatic clubs flourished with regular productions of both plays and pantomimes but it is quite some time since there have been any local drama or musical productions.

Other groups which came and went include a chess club, ladies' social club and a Scottish country dancing group as well as the National Housewives' Register (by then the National Women's Register) which folded in 1994, having celebrated its 20th birthday only the year before. A survivor is the over-60s club, albeit with a much reduced membership and many participants in their 70s and 80s. Bridge has grown in popularity, from one club in the 1970s to three in 2000. Quiz nights are a recent innovation and these are held from time to time as fund-raisers.

The Gullane & Dirleton History Society genuinely involves both communities. It was inaugurated on 1 March 1995, following the amalgamation of the Gullane Local History Society, formed in 1985, and the Dirleton Local History Group, launched in 1982. A programme of illustrated talks alternates between the two villages. There has been an annual membership of well over 100 people throughout the 1990s. Members have been encouraged to undertake research projects, which add to knowledge of the history of the parish. Members of the societies have contributed to ten books published by the societies, two books published jointly with the former East Lothian District Council, and a number published by others. Its programme goes some way to plugging the gap left by the demise of the extra-mural lectures.

Leisure (cont)

Gullane Parish Young People's Association drama section performing 'The House with the Twisty Shutters', 1950. Left to right: Jean Brown, Jean McGraill, John Wood, Eric Rule, David Dewar, Marion Black, George Morin. (Gullane & Dirleton History Society)

Economy - Tourism

Golf is the main attraction for visitors to Gullane, as well as being the dominant leisure activity for residents and an important source of employment (see below).

The most obvious tourist attraction in Dirleton is the castle. Over the years the annual visitor numbers have remained fairly constant, exceeding 20,000. In 1982 the guardianship and responsibility for maintenance of the property passed to Historic Scotland, although ownership was retained by the National Trust for Scotland. The fine beehive doocot was restored in 1983-84. A new shop and revised entrance was erected in 1990, followed in 1991 by the creation in the west garden of an 1850s-style garden design. In 1996 the existing herbaceous borders were joined to form the world's longest continuous herbaceous border, 709 feet long and with around 300 varieties of plants, a fact formally recognised in the 1998 *Guinness Book of Records.*

Still on the garden theme, both villages participate in Scotland's Garden Scheme. In Dirleton every second year about 15 gardens, large and small, are opened to the public one weekend in June and attract around 800 visitors with teas provided by the church. In 1998 the event raised about £2000 for local and national charities. In Gullane several groups of gardens have been open over the years under this scheme. In 1999 Whim Road gardens' opening contributed to both the parish church and St Adrian's. Gardens at West Fenton raised money for Riding for the Disabled.

Gullane and Yellowcraig are popular beaches for day visitors but do not now see the great influx once common on fine summer Sundays through to the 1980s when crowds streamed in

Economy – Tourism (cont)

Holiday-makers enjoying the sunshine at Gullane beach. Note the beach huts behind.
(Valentine & Sons, Ltd)

by bus and car. Yellowcraig Country Park, an area of beach, woodland and bents, was established in the early 1970s, by the East Lothian County Council. The Ranger Service provides guided walks describing the flora and fauna of the area. During 1999 the official number of people recorded visiting Yellowcraig came to 274,000. The area is also well used by local people to exercise both their dogs and themselves and the barbecue area is popular on summer evenings. Edinburgh taxi drivers run an annual children's outing to Yellowcraig in June, a convoy noted for its streamers, balloons and honking horns.

The Caravan Club site at Yellowcraig was opened in July 1973 by the Queen and Duke of Edinburgh. It operates from April to October providing 116 pitches to members and non-members, is well used and brings many visitors to the area.

Gullane Bay in recent years has attracted a regular flow of windsurfers, mostly apparently from outside the immediate area. The last few years of the century have also seen the annual staging by the Edinburgh Triathlon Club of an event from the Gullane beach area, with 1999 seeing an international triathlon event at the same venue. Horse-riders too use the beach and a designated track is provided. The car park at Gullane Bents is managed by the council and has a pitch leased to an ice-cream van in summer. In 1956 the area was extended and tarmac roads put down. In 1957 parking fees were raised from one to two shillings (10p). By 1961, 450 cars were expected daily in the spring and summer period and in 1999 a total of 284,000 visitors were recorded. Improvements in recent years include access to the beach for disabled visitors, better toilet facilities, picnic tables and, in 1999, new information boards.

Economy – Industry

Within the villages small businesses have been the norm. In the 1990s the building trade in its various aspects accounted for 16 of these and gardening for three. One-offs involve health and beauty treatment, picture framing and computer consultancy. More unusual is a small Gullane firm, which specialises in the stringing of all types of sports rackets. It is the only full-time specialist service of its type in Scotland and has a number of well-known clients. The long-established Dirleton laundry closed in 1973 as the result of a huge increase in oil prices the year before. Furniture making took place on a small scale at Dirleton and Kingston and continues at Gullane and Fenton Barns. In 1977, three industrial units were created in the former Kingston school. Two of these were used by joiners and one by a golf club maker. A bakery firm took over one unit in 1995, and subsequently a second. At the end of the century ten people were employed in the bakery and 18 in three retail outlets. One joiner remains. A further joinery business in the area ceased in the mid 1950s and an agricultural engineering firm moved away in 1962.

In the hinterland area, a significant number of small businesses have become concentrated in the region of Fenton Barns, making use of former airfield buildings no longer needed for farming. For two years around 1960, one of the hangars was used to clean and surface coat the roadway sections of the Forth Road Bridge. Other businesses have been more long lasting. A haulage business, founded 40 years ago in Drem, moved to the hangar site in 1984. It employs 20 people, owns 21 haulage vehicles and has contracts UK wide. The turkey-processing and mushroom-growing enterprises begun by the Chalmers-Watson family are covered in the section on farming. A much newer venture is Edinburgh Preserves, the brainchild of two young local men, which began trading in March 1995. Beginning with a single product, they now produce over 50 chutneys, pickles, jams, curds and sauces.

Several businesses appear under the umbrella of the Fenton Barns Retail and Leisure Village, developed in the 1990s. Some of these are retail outlets but others include the Scottish Archery Centre, a fireplace manufacturer, Jane Connachan Golf Centre with driving range and 9-hole pitch and putt course with tuition provided, a ceramics and glass workshop, furniture manufacture, upholstery service, picture framing, sign design, tiling and a cattery. Some other businesses are car-related. The Game Conservancy Scottish Fair is organised from an office at Fenton Barns.

Rattlebags quarry provided a hard, trachyte stone, which has long been used for building in the parish and beyond. After the war, it was worked by Baxters of Tranent and supplied stone for Haddington Sheriff Court. The monks of Nunraw have owned it since the 1960s and used its stone to build their new abbey. Much of the quarry has been filled in but a small working face remains open but unused.

Craigs quarry was worked by Dobsons of Gullane until the late 1950s producing roadstone. It was filled with refuse in the 1970s.

Economy – Agriculture

In 2000, there were 14 farms in the parish, varying in size from 220 acres (90 ha) to 690 acres (280 ha). They were Archerfield Home farm, Castlemains, Chapel, Congalton Mains, East Fenton, Fenton Barns, Ferrygate, Highfield, Kingston, Newhouse, New Mains, Queenstonbank,

Economy – Agriculture (cont)

*Castlemains farm
with Dirleton Ca
behind.*

*Pitting turnips
at Castlemains
(Willie Cowie on le
The tower in the
background was
used by Drem
aerodrome to
monitor position
of planes.
(James Simpson)*

*Castlemains
farm workers on
Yellowcraig beac
lifting seaweed.
Four farms in the
parish had the ri
to gather seaweed
off the shore to us
as a fertiliser.
The men standin
are (left to right):
Kurt Gherke, Ha
Lauder, Willie H
Johnny Mercer.
(James Simpson)*

Economy – Agriculture (cont)

Saltcoats and West Fenton. Apart from Archerfield Home Farm and Saltcoats, during the last 50 years each of these farms has been run by three generations of the same family. In 1945, there were two additional farms, Muirfield and Williamstone. Part of Muirfield farm was sold in 1978 to John Stevenson & Son, potato growers of Luffness Mains, Aberlady. In 1987, most of the remainder was bought by the Royal and Ancient Golf Club, St Andrews, to reserve ground for car parking during future Open golf championships. When Miss Stella Moffat of Williamstone retired in 1983, the farm was sold to the neighbouring farms of Ferrygate and Newhouse, with a portion sold to the Gilsland Caravan Park. All but one of the farms is owner occupied - the exception being Saltcoats, which is part of the Luffness estate.

The growing of cereal crops and potatoes has been the mainstay on most of the farms in the parish during the last 50 years. A diary, kept by William James Simpson of Castlemains from 1913-51, provides a picture, at the end of world war two, of a farm typical of this parish while his son James and grandson Robert have detailed changes up to the end of the century.

Crops (ha)	1950	1999	*Workforce*	1950	1965	1999
Wheat	35	56	Men	12	10	2
Barley	30	90	Youths	1	-	-
Oats	28	-	Casual women	8	6	-
Potatoes	26	10	Working partners	-	-	2
Roots	20	-				
Protein Peas	-	10	*Livestock*	1950	2000	
Oilseed rape	-	11	Horses	8	- (14 during world war two)	
Rotation grass	58	3	Beef cattle	24	98 (¹/2 wintered for a third party)	
Permanent grass	4	4	Sheep (hoggs)	246	60 (wintered for a third party)	
Set-a-side	-	17	(A hogg is a lamb which has not been sheared)			

Equipment in 1950: three tractors; five horse and two tractor two furrow ploughs; 11 horse grubbers; one tractor cultivator; two horse corn drills; two fertiliser distributors; three mowers; three rakes; one turner; two hay sweeps and sprayer (these all horse-powered); four horse and one tractor binders; one baler; two horse and one tractor potato diggers; one hand and one powered potato sorters; one fixed thresher.

Equipment in 1999: five tractors and trailers; two four furrow ploughs; one 3 metre graindrill; one 24 metre fertiliser sprayer; one John Deere 2254 combine; one small and one large baler and a grain drying plant.

Throughout the parish combine harvesters arrived in the 1950s provided by contractors. Later most farmers bought self-propelled combines as well as installing grain-drying plants. By 1960 tractors had taken over from horses and farm buildings were adapted to house new equipment. New buildings for storing silage when it replaced hay in the 1950s and large cattle courts to enable mechanised winter-feeding then appeared.

Crops

Every farm has grown barley during the last 50 years and most of them have grown wheat as well. In 1945 everyone grew oats, but there was a steady decline in the use of oats for feeding

Economy – Agriculture (cont)

stock. The wartime push to increase yields continued throughout the following 50 years with new varieties of both wheat and barley being developed to provide higher yields and shorter straw. There has been a continuing and expanding use of artificial fertilisers and chemical weed control throughout the period. Specialised firms, such as Crop Chemicals Ltd, at the Fenton Barns Industrial Village, advise on the type and minimum amount of pesticides and fertilisers that should be applied to growing crops. Most farmers carry out spraying, but, in the case of tall crops, such as oilseed rape, contractors are used.

In the last 20/30 years new strains of both barley and wheat have been developed for particular uses. Locally grown barley has been used for malting, whilst wheat is used for bread and biscuit milling and distilling. Yields have also increased substantially. In 1950, barley yields were of the order of 4-6 tonnes per hectare, increased to around 7-8 tonnes per hectare in the 1990s. Post-war yields of wheat similarly rose from 4-6 tonnes per hectare to 10 tonnes per hectare in the 1990s. All cereals produce a great deal of straw. Large round bales replaced the rectangular smaller bales of the early part of the period. In the 1990s large square bales made it easier to transport larger loads of straw to farms in the west of Scotland.

In 1945, every farm grew potatoes and Irish migrant workers were still being employed to gather the crop. The varieties grown at that time were Majestic and King Edward. From the 1960s Majestic, Redskin, Epicure and Maris Piper were the main varieties.

New factory markets for potatoes came into existence in the 1950s. The first was for crisps and, in the 1960s, chips. Suitable varieties were Maris Bard, Nadine and Lady Rosetta. Potatoes grown for the crisp manufacturers usually went to Golden Wonder at Bathgate. The 1960s also saw the introduction of artificial irrigation systems. Water was obtained from watercourses directly or via reservoirs, boreholes and wells, using various types of pumps and sprinkler systems. From the 1960s, some farmers co-operated with a commercial potato growing/buying organisation, guaranteeing a market for the crops; from the 1980s most let the ground allocated for potatoes to these organisations, which provided all the workers and equipment. Maincrop potato yields increased during the last 50 years, from 20/25 tonnes per hectare in 1950 to 40/50 tonnes per hectare by 2000.

In 1950, over half the land growing potatoes was producing early potatoes. Ten years later this had fallen to one third. The decline in growing early potatoes was due to increased competition from other parts of the UK where bigger yields were possible at an earlier date. Queenstonbank grew seed potatoes up to the 1950s and small quantities were grown on a few farms for 20 years from the 1970s. East Fenton grew seed potatoes for most of the period, with Pentland and Nickerson being the varieties provided for the seed trade in England. By the end of the century the growing of both early and seed potatoes had ended.

Old crops, new crops and horticultural crops: since the 18th century turnips and swedes had been a staple crop on all the farms, grown for feeding cattle and sheep in the winter. During the last 50 years the area devoted to these root crops, together with mangolds, fell from 170ha in 1950 to 30ha in the 1970s and to only 2ha in 1999. With fewer sheep and lambs in the 1960s, because of market conditions and silage being used for feeding cattle, the growing of root crops declined and the area devoted to them fell.

Most farmers had grown sugar beet during the war, as it was not possible to import sugar cane. It was a labour intensive crop, from hand thinning and weeding of the young plants through to harvesting. The harvested crop was sent to the processing factory at Cupar in Fife by rail from Gullane, Dirleton and North Berwick railway stations. The factory closed in 1972. The area growing sugar beet varied from 25 ha to 80 ha between 1950 and 1970.

With the impending closure of the sugar beet processing factory, a group of East Lothian and Borders farmers set up a co-operative venture, the East Lothian and Border Association of Growers (ELBA Growers) in 1971. It launched a programme for the growing of vegetables on farms. Pilot crops of peas and sprouts were grown for freezing and canning in 1972. Speedy harvesting was possible because of the availability of mechanical vining machines. Farms which grew peas for the ELBA Growers included East Fenton, Fenton Barns, West Fenton (plus carrots) and Ferrygate (plus cauliflower, broccoli, carrots and leeks). Alastair Miller of Ferrygate was the Chairman of the ELBA Growers, and later Scotfresh Ltd, from 1974-89. Since the mid-1990s, all the pea growers have changed to growing protein peas for animal feed manufacturers, with the varieties grown yielding around 4 tonnes per hectare. There were 70ha of peas in 1980, 45ha in 1990 rising to 84ha in 1999.

In the 1970s a new crop appeared – oilseed rape, with the 'oil' used for the manufacture of margarine and cooking oil. Its yellow flowers and pungent smell in springtime was soon evident within the parish. Initially 14ha were grown, rising to 70ha in 1999. The yield is between 2 ^{1}/2 to 4 tonnes per hectare.

Self-contained Congalton Gardens grew a variety of horticultural crops during the early part of the period, later concentrating on their wholesale business. In recent years they have grown only leeks. On a few farms, cabbages, sprouts and cauliflower have been grown for the last fifty years, and carrots for most of that time. Leeks and broccoli started to be grown about 1980. Changing market conditions were reflected in the area devoted to growing these crops. Cabbages with 32ha and carrots with 15ha, both peaked in the 1960s, whereas cauliflower reached 38ha in 1970. In the early part of the period farmers grew their own crops selling them at the Edinburgh wholesale markets. Increasingly from the 1960s farmers let their land to wholesalers/contractors who carried out the whole cycle from planting to harvest.

Another example of crop diversification was the growing of strawberries at Ferrygate for the retail and 'pick-your-own' trade. This venture started in 1971 with 3ha, increasing each year until 8ha were grown in 1975. Initially, the work involved suited the annual farm routines, but difficulties experienced in recruiting pickers saw a reduction in the strawberry-growing area and an end to the activity in 1984.

Stock

Beef cattle: after the war some farms, including Castlemains and Queenstonbank, were fattening Aberdeen Angus crossed with Hereford bullocks shipped to Glasgow from the west of Ireland. This trade declined in the 1960s. Steve Graham at Queenstonbank then bought Aberdeen Angus-cross bullocks from Orkney, fattening around 200 in the steading and 150 on summer grazing. Other farmers bought store cattle at the autumn sales in Edinburgh, Lanark and Stirling, for winter fattening in the steadings. This released grazing land for more profitable cropping. Additionally, some farmers kept their own herd of suckler cows rearing calves and fattening them as bullocks for eventual sale. From the 1960s, the importation of, usually, French breeds brought changes to the beef herds in the parish. The number of beef

Economy – Agriculture (cont)

cattle kept during the period peaked at almost 2000 in 1970 falling to 1100 in 1999 when only half the farms fattened bullocks.

Dairy cattle: in 1950, there were 227 cows and heifers in milk on seven farms. Two farms, Muirfield and New Mains had kept small dairy herds for a few years after the war. Two farms, Fenton Barns and East Fenton, continued their large dairying operations until 1955 and 1997 respectively.

Fenton Barns operated one of the most successful dairy farms in the country. Established in 1923, it was the first farm to supply certified milk to households in Edinburgh. It had a 200- cow byre, a state-of-the-art-milking parlour and milk processing plant. This enterprise continued until 1955 when the milking herd of 175 cows was sold in order to release space for the growing turkey-rearing business.

By 1960, East Fenton had 250 dairy cattle, which had halved by the time milk production ended in 1997. In 1950 two bulls were kept, but after the establishment of Artificial Insemination Centres the performance of the herd improved significantly. The herd of Ayrshire cows was replaced by Friesian Holstein cows, which resulted in much higher milk yields. In 1950, the average yield was 1000 litres per lactation. This had doubled by the 1990s. A seven-a-side herringbone-milking parlour installed in 1972, meant that one man could milk 120 cows in three hours. New cattle courts were built making it much easier for feeding silage to the cows in winter. The milk was sold to the Scottish Milk Marketing Board, later Scottish Milk, for pasteurisation and processing. A tanker collected it once a day after the morning milking.

Sheep: after the war, ewes and lambs were traditionally fattened in the winter by letting them feed on grass sown after early potatoes, followed by root crops and, where available, sugar beets tops. In the 1950s, Queenstonbank was the first farm in Scotland to fatten lambs inside the steading to gain weight quickly and produce higher quality meat. This activity ended in the 1960s, when there was a decline in market prices, with the meat trade requiring smaller, leaner lambs. Sheep and lambs were bought at markets as far distant as St Boswells and Lairg. However, some farms fattened some hundreds of lambs right through to the late 1970s - the Elders, at Chapel, continuing up to the end of the century. In the last two decades there has been an increase in the number of French sheep breeds seen on the farms.

In the 1990s only a few farms were fattening lambs, with Castlemains and Ferrygate wintering for hill farm friends. During this period Ferrygate has fattened lambs on the residue of the broccoli crop. For much of the last fifty years a substantial proportion of the sheep on the farms belonged to dealers who paid the farmers to look after them - 'a bed and breakfast' arrangement.

Pigs: only Fenton Barns has kept pigs since the war. A significant expansion of the pig unit took place in 1970, with the first environmentally controlled pig-fattening shed constructed to hold 750 pigs. In 1972, the unit was expanded to house 250 sows, with a further 250 catered for in 1974. The fattening of pigs continued up to 1999, when, after weathering severe fluctuations in market prices in the 1990s, the herd was disbanded.

Poultry et al: after the war Ferrygate had diversified into egg production. Domestic straw yards were overtaken by hens kept in 'deep litter' houses, which was a halfway stage to the introduction, in the 1960s, of the intensive battery cage system accommodated in specialised buildings. Laying hens numbered 14,000 in 1970 rising to 45,000 in 1985, falling to 28,000 laying pullets at the end of the century, producing approximately 8m eggs per year.

Economy – Agriculture (cont)

1948 saw the beginning of a new poultry enterprise at Fenton Barns, the production and sale of day-old chicks from a new strain of Danish birds. The chicks were sold to farmers who grew them to the size required by the broiler chicken processors. In 1956, this initiative led to the setting up of Chunky Chicks Ltd, jointly with another poultry farmer, D.B. Marshall of Ratho. By the end of the decade this activity ended at Fenton Barns so that more attention could be given to the expanding turkey enterprise.

In 1947, brothers Rupert and Irvine Chalmers-Watson of Fenton Barns decided to establish a breeding flock of turkeys. Broad-breasted American turkeys were subsequently imported to form the nucleus of a breeding programme. Most of these early developments took place on rented farms elsewhere in East Lothian. In 1962, Rupert Chalmers-Watson joined forces with two of his largest customers in England to form British United Turkeys Ltd (BUT) to develop more widely the turkey egg-hatching business. BUT expanded rapidly in the UK until 1978, when it was sold to an American organisation. The original family farming company, DC Watson & Sons Ltd (DCW), then reassumed the residual turkey business.

The rearing of turkeys continued alongside the egg-hatching activities. Purpose-built sheds were constructed during the 1960s, with two sheds 500 ft x 50 ft, together with a new packing station and canteen for 140 employees being built in 1974. By 1979, 20,000 turkey eggs were being hatched per week and 1million day-old poults were sold. In 1980, $^{1}/4$ million turkeys were reared, two-thirds for the oven-ready market, the remainder for turkey-meat products. An increase in imported oven-ready turkeys saw a move to producing more added-value products based on turkey meat. In 1981, Fenton Barns (Scotland) Ltd. was formed to develop this activity. Live turkey production ceased at the end of 1993, as it became more economic to purchase poultry meat from South America. In 1998, the company was sold to Brown Brothers who employed 80 people in the year 2000.

During the mid-1970s, a crop of partridges was grown in the world war one barrack block at Fenton Barns on a deep litter system. An investigation showed that mushrooms could be produced using the deep litter. Two years later, 5 tonnes of mushrooms were produced per week. Subsequently DCW, joined forces with an Irish company, Monaghan Mushrooms Ltd, (MM) to expand the operation. After four years DCW sold their interest to MM, who continued the mushroom-growing enterprise. By 2000, they had a workforce of 250 and were producing 200,000 lbs of mushrooms per week.

After leaving college in 1966, Keith Chalmers-Watson started a small game bird rearing unit, specialising in grey partridges for sporting release and the table market. Later expansion saw the annual production rise to around 45,000 birds in the late 1990s. During the last 30 years Keith Chalmers-Watson also expanded his hobby, the conservation and breeding of rare game birds. By 2000, the collection had upwards of 60 species, a quarter of the world's game birds, with some of the birds being released in their Asian countries of origin.

In 1950, there were 78 working horses in the parish, an average of five per farm. Ten years later the working horse had virtually disappeared. The most common working horses had been the Clydesdales. However, horses did not disappear from all the parish farms. During the last 30 years, Mrs Eileen Simpson of Highfield has built up and developed a breeding stud of Connemara ponies. Using the farm facilities and a nucleus of two stallions and six mares, she has achieved a high reputation for their progeny. Foals have been sold widely in Britain, with

Economy – Agriculture (cont)

some exported to the USA, Australia and Germany.

At West Fenton in 1973 there were livery facilities for only two horses owners. By 1990, 17 horses were catered for. In that year, on the initiative of Gill Morrison, a group of disabled riders and their helpers moved to West Fenton, forming the Muirfield Group of the Riding for the Disabled Association (RDA). By 2000 the number of horses and ponies kept at livery had reached 40, with a dozen used by the disabled riders. RDA sessions are held on three half days each week with 50 to 60 riders coming from as far as Dunbar and Edinburgh. There are around 45 voluntary helpers. Fund-raising events take place, which, together with support from local businesses and friends, have enabled the group to provide their services without charge to the riders. As the riding arena is outdoors, sessions stop between Christmas and Easter. At the end of the century plans were put in train to provide an indoor riding arena. A major fund-raising campaign was instigated and it is hoped that, if successful in obtaining National Lottery funding, the indoor riding arena will have been built and brought in to operation by 2002.

End pieces

Governmental controls on agriculture have continued ever since 1945. With the entry of the UK into the European Economic Community (EEC), later the European Union (EU), bureaucracy has increased further. Since 1993, all farms in the parish have had to leave fields fallow – set aside – to conform with EU diktats, which have attempted to reduce the amount of cereals grown. In 1999, set aside accounted for 182ha (7%) of the land farmed in the parish. In the 1990s West Fenton and Queenstonbank have used set aside land for conservation purposes.

Of all the changes that have taken place on the farms in the parish since 1945 the greatest has been the reduction in the labour force. In 1950, there were 235 men and 25 women working full-time, and 30 men and 40 women part-time. By 1980, there had been a substantial fall, with 93 men and eight women working full-time and 14 men part-time. However more members of the farming families were then working on their farms - 17 men full-time, and seven men and five women part-time, with a similar number at the end of the century. In 1999, the number of employed people had declined further to 32 men and six women full-time, with nine men and eight women part-time. This represents an almost 80% reduction in the number of people working both full-time and part-time on the farms over 50 years.

Economy – Golf

Golf has shaped Gullane for over 150 years with its influence increasing during each decade of the last fifty years with five golf courses in the parish. These are the three courses of Gullane Golf Club, Luffness New and the Honourable Company of Edinburgh Golfers' Muirfield course. In the second half of the 20th century the number of full-time employees engaged in greenkeeping, administration and catering doubled, reaching almost 100 by 2000. Catering staff and caddies obtain part-time employment.

Over many years local men have been employed in golf and greenkeeping. At the end of the century, the latter in particular has developed a proper career structure with something to offer young people wishing to remain in the parish. The Watt family provides an example. Two brothers became golf professionals, with Hugh Watt being the first professional at Gullane Golf Club. A third brother, Tommy, joined the Gullane greenkeeping staff in 1949 and eventually became head greenkeeper, retiring in 1985. Such long service is not unusual. Luffness New Golf Club has had only three head greenkeepers during the last 63 years and there have been only four men in charge at Muirfield since 1949. At Muirfield the head greenkeeper or course manager and his staff are the key men in maintaining the reputation of the course. Throughout most of the past 50 years there has been a team of eight men carrying out greenkeeping duties. Outstanding amongst these was James Logan. He prepared the Muirfield course for five Open championships, one Curtis Cup, one Walker Cup and one Ryder Cup. He was awarded the British Empire Medal in 1973.

Founded in 1882, Gullane Golf Club has had three courses since 1910. It also runs the children's course at the Smiddy Green. Members are drawn from East Lothian, Edinburgh and beyond, including overseas. In 1950, these numbered around 400, rising to 947 by 1977, and 916 at the end of the century. In the mid-1950s there was no joining fee and the annual subscription was eight guineas, with the cost of a round of golf on course No. 1 being six shillings. In 2000, the joining fee is three times the annual subscription of £311, with a round on No. 1 costing £56 on weekdays and £70 at weekends. 30,000 visitors played over the three courses in 1999. In the 1950s the club's turnover amounted to £13,000, and rose to £1million by the mid-1990s. The business aspects of club management have become increasingly important, manifested in changes in administration and management structures. A clubhouse for visitors and the club's administration staff, built at a cost of £60,000, was opened in 1993. Course development has also taken place and a change in course management in 1993 saw the appointment of an overall course manager with separate foremen in charge of the individual courses.

In 1980, Archie Baird, the historian for both Gullane Golf Club and the Honourable Company of Edinburgh Golfers converted the building next to the Gullane professional's shop into 'The Heritage of Golf Museum'.

At the end of the war the anti-invasion concrete blocks on the No. 1 and No. 2 courses were buried. Sheep had been grazing on Gullane Hill for many years, affecting greenkeeping. However, grazing rights ended in 1950, leaving only the rabbits to cause problems, which were greatly reduced with the onset of myxomatosis later in that decade. Rabbits caused problems again in the 1970s but systematic pest control measures have reduced their damage considerably.

During the last 50 years the maintenance of the courses has become totally mechanised. Until the mid 1950s hand mowers were used to cut the greens. Motor mowers then took over with tractor-drawn gang mowers cutting the fairways by 1960 and increasingly sophisticated equipment being introduced over the following decades. In 1950, the mains water supply had been connected to all 54 greens, these being hand watered until 1983. The original well was brought back into use in the 1980s to supply a distribution system for the new water sprinkler system. In 1993, a new well was drilled to supply up to 5,000 gallons per hour to the greens, and travelling sprinklers were bought for watering fairways.

Gullane golf course No. 1 - the key events: over the years a number of major national and international events have taken place. Since 1966 this has included acting as a venue for the final qualifying rounds for all the Open golf championships held at Muirfield. Other major events for men included the Scottish Professional championship, 1953; the Scottish Open Amateur Strokeplay, 1967 and 1977; the Scottish Amateur championships, 1983 and 1990; the

Economy – Golf (cont)

Open Qualifying... the long walk back.

(Gullane & Dirleton History Society)

seniors' Open Amateur championship in 2000. Ladies' events included the British Ladies' championships, 1947 and 1970; the Ladies' Home Internationals 1947, 1960 and 1984; the Scottish Ladies' Amateur championships 1964, 1979 and 1994 and the Ladies' British Open Amateur Strokeplay in 1993. Events for youths included the Jacques Leglise Trophy, 1965 and 1981; the British Boys' championships 1965 and 1981, and the European Boys' Team championship in 1998.

Gullane Ladies Golf Club

Formed in 1904, Gullane Ladies Golf Club shares the Gullane Golf Club clubhouse, but with its own entrance and separate lounges. It has been involved, along with Gullane Golf Club, in the staging of the major ladies' events mentioned above. Since 1945, the number of members has been in the range of 300 to 400, with annual subscriptions rising from £7.50 in the 1950s to £250 at the end of the century.

A number of members have been highly successful in national and international events. Scottish Ladies' champions were: Jean Anderson (Donald) 1947, 1949 and 1952; Marjory Draper (Peel) 1954; Connie Lugton 1971; Lesley Hope 1975 and Jayne Smith (Ford) in 1999. Lesley Nicholson, in 1999, played in the Vagliano Trophy and in the Home Internationals and European Team championship. Since 1945, five members of the club have been chosen to play in Curtis Cup matches: Jean Donald, Marjory Peel, Marjory Fowler, Margaret Nichol, and Catriona Matthew.

Admission to Dirleton Castle Golf Club has always been restricted to residents of the parish of Dirleton, making it very much a local club. Founded in 1854, it does not have its own clubhouse and plays its golf over the Gullane courses. A legal agreement in 1983 integrated the club with Gullane Golf Club, limiting members to 100 and making membership of Gullane Golf Club a pre-requisite of entry into Dirleton Castle. Amongst its achievements are 11 East Lothian County Cup wins in the past 50 years.

Dirleton Castle Ladies Golf Club was founded in 1921, and all the members must be resident within the parish. Competitions are played on Gullane Golf Club No. 2 and No. 3 courses. Membership is in the range of 40-50.

Other clubs without their own courses include Gullane Comrades' Golf Club. Founded in 1921, primarily for ex-servicemen, membership is drawn from Gullane Golf Club and Dirleton Castle Golf Club parish residents, with trophies played for over Gullane and Muirfield courses, although the latter concession was withdrawn in 1999. There is also a number of clubs within clubs, with membership by invitation.

Young people and golf: golf is very accessible to local children. The children's course is available at no charge and school children aged 9–14 whose parents either live in the parish or are members of Gullane Golf Club can play on the No. 3 course at any time. In 2000, the annual permit cost £18. Gullane Club and Gullane Ladies both have juniors' sections and Dirleton Castle also has junior members. The Peel Trophy, a scratch competition competed for equally by boys and girls of 16 and under, was begun in 1950 and is played for on Gullane No. 3 Course.

Luffness New Golf Club, established in 1894, has an all male membership. For many years post-war Luffness was a second club for Edinburgh golfers, a links course for winter play. As a consequence local members are a small minority, with still a large Edinburgh representation. In 1972, a concerted effort was made to find new members. In 1981 it had 459 members, increasing to 708 by 1999.

After the war it was necessary to undertake a great deal of work to bring the fairways and greens up to good standard. This work was not helped by the presence of the anti-invasion concrete blocks some of which were buried, whilst others, in 1963, were used in the construction of the Cockenzie Power Station. For a few years from 1949 sheep were to be seen grazing on the course.

Starting in 1945, three attempts were made to buy the course from the landowners - Hopes of Luffness. At the third attempt in 1979 the course was bought for £150,000. In 1974/5 improvements were made to the clubhouse, head greenkeeper's cottage and provision of equipment storage, with further additions between 1987 and 1992. In 1991, a watering system of pop-up sprinklers to the greens, tees and fairways was completed at a cost of almost £150,000. From 1966, the Luffness New course was also selected for playing the final qualifying rounds of the Open championships when held at Muirfield.

Muirfield Golf Course and the Honourable Company of Edinburgh Golfers

The Honourable Company of Edinburgh Golfers, a private men-only club, moved to Muirfield in 1891. In the late 1990s, the maximum number of members was 550, with 75 overseas members, paying an annual subscription of £675. At that time visitors were accepted at £85 per round on Tuesday and Thursday provided they had a handicap of 18 or better. Ladies were

Economy – Golf (cont)

allowed to play but not eat in the clubhouse. On the course a hand watering system with some 30 hose points was increased to 51 points in 1993. It was only in 1998 that an automatic watering system was installed for watering the fairways with the greens remaining to be watered manually.

The Open Golf championships

The Honourable Company has hosted seven Open Golf championships since 1945; in 1948, 1959, 1966, 1972, 1980, 1987 and 1992. The 1948 Open is remembered for having been won by the golfing legend, Henry Cotton, whose prize was around £300. (In 1992, Nick Faldo won £95,000). A local golfer, Guy Robertson-Durham, qualified to play in the 1948 Open and was chosen to play in a four-ball match in the company of King George VI, who had spent some time watching the event.

The Open Golf championships at Muirfield make a considerable impact on the area. The 1972 Open was the first to feature a large tented village and a worldwide media presence with television needs to the fore. For the three subsequent Open championships the number of spectators has exceeded 130,000. A local firm, J. & R. Hay, first employed in 1972, has undertaken the joinery work, not only at Muirfield, but at all the Opens since.

At Muirfield car parks and hospitality tents are located in nearby fields with a bridge over the main road providing access to a temporary caravan park. There is a helicopter base at West Fenton farm. A bus shuttle service to and from Drem station connects with Scotrail's 'Golflink'

Reception at Dirleton Castle for Open Golf Championships, 1980.

Economy – Golf (cont)

services. There is an augmented bus service to and from Edinburgh, but most people come to Muirfield by road. Car-parking restrictions in the village not only inconvenience residents but also affect trade for local shops.

There is also a credit side. All hotels are fully booked well in advance and upwards of a quarter of the homes in the district have visitors to stay, many as paying guests, and well over 5% of residents let their houses. The extensive media coverage highlights Gullane as a tourist destination. A large proportion of people living in the parish attend the Open on one or more days, with many obtaining work at Muirfield or jobs resulting from the Open. These jobs include teenage litter pickers, through to the members of local golf clubs who act as stewards around the course.

Other major golf events at Muirfield

Muirfield also hosted other international and national events. Since 1948 these have included the Ryder Cup 1973; the Walker Cup 1959 and 1979; Home Internationals 1948, 1956 and 1976; the British Amateur championships 1954, 1974, 1990 and 1998; and the Scottish Amateur championships 1949, 1955, 1962 and 1968. Ladies' events: the Curtis Cup 1952 and 1984, and the Vagliano Trophy 1963 and 1984.

Local Government

The local community council covers the villages of Aberlady, Dirleton, Drem and Gullane. Main subjects of concern are vandalism, the state of the roads and road safety in all its aspects. The consideration of the community's views on current planning applications, particularly for larger developments, is a very time-consuming issue. In the 1990s the installation of masts for mobile telephone networks has caused concern.

Dirleton Village Association is concerned chiefly with amenity and planning issues. The main topics in 1999 were the planning applications made by Scottish Heritable and Rocco Forte pertaining to Archerfield estate. It also distributes the Dirleton Flyer at intervals to keep residents aware of progress on local issues and it organised the Millennium Hogmanay event.

The only political parties to have local groups are the Scottish Conservative Party, which has a Gullane branch and the Scottish Labour party with a joint North Berwick / Gullane branch.

Miscellany

Events

The first major celebration of the second half of the century was the Coronation of Queen Elizabeth II on Tuesday 2 June 1953. The day was commemorated in Gullane by a full-day's programme beginning with a United Open-air service on Goose Green at 9.30 am, family sports in the afternoon followed by the official opening of the Gullane War Memorial Playing Field. The evening saw an old folks' entertainment in the public hall and a torchlight procession and bonfire on Gullane Hill at 11pm. The week continued with a Grand Free-to-All Coronation Celebration Dance in the public hall on Wednesday, a special 'Coronation' mixed foursomes on No. 2 course on the Thursday and late-night and all-night Coronation revels (10pm till 4am) in the Queen's Hotel on the Friday.

Miscellany (cont)

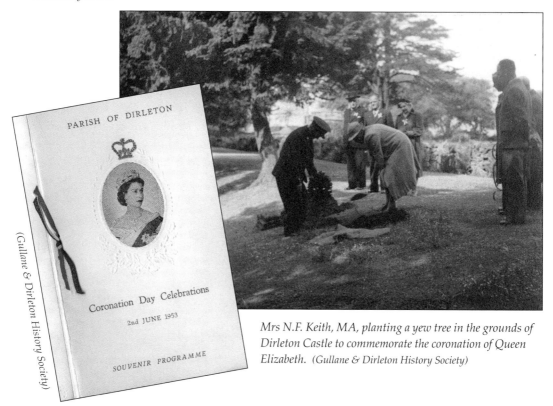

(Gullane & Dirleton History Society)

Mrs N.F. Keith, MA, planting a yew tree in the grounds of Dirleton Castle to commemorate the coronation of Queen Elizabeth. (Gullane & Dirleton History Society)

Twenty-five years later to celebrate the Queen's Silver Jubilee a fair, opened by Lady Anne-Louise Hamilton-Dalrymple, was held on the Smiddy Green. A variety of village organisations had stalls, providing a mixture of games and merchandise. This event, along with a number of other money-raising ventures, provided funds for the installation of a clock on the wall at the Goose Green bakery. The local authority took on its maintenance and pays for the electricity used. The local group of the National Housewives' Register produced *A Glimpse of Gullane,* describing the village at that time.

Each village had its own Millennium celebrations on Hogmanay 1999. In Dirleton a procession with candles and flares went from the church to a bonfire and fireworks display on Dirleton Green. In Gullane a torchlight procession made its way to the Bents car park where an estimated turnout of over 2000 people also enjoyed a fireworks display, the whole event characterised by a great spirit of friendliness and good humour. On January 1 a ceilidh was held in the village hall. Other Millennium-related events in Dirleton included a Rock Nativity presented by the school children and a celebration of traditional sports and games in the castle grounds.

In Gullane the schoolchildren planted the first of 2000 trees for the Gullane Millennium Woodland project. A village calendar was produced, as was a video of events of the year 2000. A viewfinder was planned, and subsequently built, on Gullane Hill as was a plinth and descriptive plaque in the grounds of the ruined church. Another plan, which was later implemented, was the restoration of the Blue Stane, a traditional meeting place for the village youth.

People

Sir Jamie Stormonth Darling (1918-2000), CBE, MC LLd lived in Dirleton from the mid 1960s until his death in 2000. He was the Director of the National Trust for Scotland from 1949 until his retirement in 1983 and was instrumental in its growth from small beginnings to a large and influential organisation. He was very supportive of the Dirleton community.

Garth Morrison CBE, born 1943, retired from the Royal Navy in 1973, having seen service in submarines. New to scouting he was appointed Area Commissioner for scouting for East Lothian in 1973 and for Scotland in 1981. His appointment as Chief Scout in 1988 continued to 1996. Since 1983 he has attended five Scout Jamborees. From 1994, he has successively served as Chairman of three Lothian National Health Service Trusts. He has served as a Deputy Lieutenant of East Lothian since 1984, and was due to take over as Lord-Lieutenant from April 2001.

Robert Sinclair (1909-85) followed his father in the village pharmacy, retiring in 1980. Throughout his life he served the community in many capacities. He was a member of the county council for over 20 years, until the demise of that body in 1975, then Conservative District Councillor. He was also secretary and chairman of Gullane Community Association. He had been a scoutmaster; founder member of the Gullane tennis and badminton clubs; stage director for pantomimes and dramatic shows for 30 years; a church elder for 40 years and Session Clerk from 1967 until 1978. He was a keen local historian and preserver of many records.

This account of Dirleton Parish was compiled by the Gullane and Dirleton History Society, and edited for the Society by Anne McCarthy. Research and essays were provided by the following:

Archie Baird   Mike Fraser
Dr W.L. Blackett   Anne McCarthy
Michael Cox   Bill Nimmo
Gillian Dick   Beryl Robinson
Russell Dick   Maurice Timson
Liz Fraser

And the farmers in the parish

Information has been drawn from library sources, the Gullane and Dirleton History Society's archive, its own publications of members' researches and specially commissioned contributions.

Notes

[1] The content of this work is as specified by the Gullane & Dirleton History Society. There has been no input by the project editor, Sonia Baker, except to ensure that the order of material is consistent with the overall style of the publication

North Berwick
Parish Representative: *Norman Hall*

Introduction

North Berwick, the most northerly of all the county's parishes, covers some 2198 ha (5431 acres), and is largely agricultural, with extensive farms. While the location of the parish can be pinpointed from miles away by the conical outline of North Berwick Law, the fortunes of the burgh - the main settlement - have been, for many years, moulded by its coastal location. Its long history as a fishing town and seaside resort changed considerably between 1945 and 2000: the fishing industry petered out, and the decline of the town as a holiday venue and the rise of the day visitor placed new pressures on North Berwick.

Tindall admits that the decision was made to expand the town as a 'high class residential town, rather than a tourist resort', and that 'tawdry shops selling beach trash' were not to be allowed (Tindall, F. 1998 p34). And so it was; North Berwick attracted tourists almost by default, and of all the East Lothian burghs, it emerged as the most affluent - a desirable place to live. This in itself attracted a certain type of visitor - who appreciated the natural beauty of the town and the area for itself, rather than what entertainment was on offer. This focus culminated at the end of the period in the development of the North Berwick Seabird Centre; the three offshore islands of Craigleith, Lamb and (especially) the Bass Rock were being utilised as tourist attractions in their own right.

The town had long been attractive to retirees, and from the late 1980s development here was directed towards attracting new residents from Edinburgh and beyond. The result has been an increase of the building of modern houses targeted at the upper end of the housing market. Meantime, the needs of the local population are widely felt to have been ignored; few houses have been built for the first-time buyer, and the right-to-buy scheme combined with changes in public housing provision mean a long wait for the less affluent who wish to remain in their home town.

In 1945, the effects and shortages of war were still being felt. For instance, in the schools, for a short time slates were again brought into use to save paper. A number of male teachers were still serving in the armed forces so several over-age teachers remained on the staff. From 1941, North Berwick's secondary pupils (12+ years) were taught in the High School in Grange Road and, for many years after 1945, the 'new' school retained its camouflage paint! The radar station at Castleton (Canty Bay, also known as Tantallon), established in 1944 by the Air Ministry and Admiralty, was manned by a detachment of the Royal Navy until the early 1950s.

At the end of the war, there was a chronic shortage of council houses for rent and this was perhaps one of the most serious problems. There were several reasons for this shortage, not the least of which was returning servicemen and women; many had married when in the forces and had lived temporarily with relatives or in rented accommodation. They now wanted to set up homes of their own. There were many cases where a serviceman had married a local girl and had chosen to live here. In other cases children had arrived so bigger accommodation was required. In addition, the Polish service men and women based in the area could not return to their homeland, and many settled in North Berwick.

Environment

Farmers Bill McNicol of Castleton and Andrew Miller of Bonnington comment on wildlife changes that have been noticed by both of them.

Environment (cont)

Aerial view of North Berwick, 1946
(RCAHMS (RAF Air Photographs Collection))

Environment (cont)

Aerial view of North Berwick, 1988. (Crown Copyright: RCAHMS (All Scotland Survey Collection))

'Hares are much less common than formerly. In the mid 1970s you could shoot 50 hares in a night at Bonnington but now they are scarce. However, rabbits have returned in numbers as they have recovered from myxomatosis and now live and breed above ground in buildings and straw bales. Up to ten roe deer frequent Castleton as well as about five herons, which feed on the shore.

Partridges have also declined greatly though they are still present in small numbers on both farms where set-aside has probably helped. House sparrows have disappeared completely from Bonnington for unknown reasons. Lapwings used to nest prior to the 1960s but have not done so since - the increased extent of winter cereals, which mean the crop is too tall in spring, and the spraying of weeds is thought to be the explanation.

On the plus side buzzards have returned to both farms - part of the recolonisation of the Lothians in the last ten years thought to result from less persecution in game rearing areas. Pink-footed geese occur in winter on both farms with increased numbers at Bonnington, perhaps because of milder winters. They are attracted to winter cereals in the autumn where they may cause some damage but are not regarded as a serious problem. At Castleton the very large flocks of wood pigeons that used to be of concern have largely gone.

Fields have got larger over the years and the few remnant hedgerows at Castleton have now gone. At Bonnington, one and half miles of new hedgerows of native species were planted in the 1970s as well as 1000 sycamores'.

While the coast boasts most of the natural interest in the parish, the lakes at Balgone support a sizeable colony of swans (SNH, 1994, p5).

Environment (cont)

North Berwick Law

There are three Sites of Special Scientific Interest (SSSI) in the parish, and one that straddles both it and Dirleton. The volcanic plug of North Berwick Law is noted for its botanical interest. Additionally there is a group of rather straggly beech trees *(Fagus sylvatica)* huddled together on the northeastern slope that were purportedly planted to commemorate the Act of Union in 1707.

The second SSSI is the complex dune system that extends from the west of the town, to Gullane (Dirleton parish); this area is of botanical, ornithological and geological value. The Forth Islands – Craigleith, Lamb and Fidra (in Dirleton), are an SSSI because of their seabird colonies.

And finally there is the Bass Rock; this is another former volcano, and is designated for its geological and ornithological interest. Bass Rock supports one of the largest breeding seabird colonies in the Forth.

The Bass Rock is woven into the Atlantic gannet's scientific name Morus bassanus. Famous for centuries, this durable plug of basalt, barely 3 km from the fretted East Lothian coast, is one of Scotland's most spectacular seabird haunts and probably the most accessible. It is, and for centuries has been, a mecca for the seabird enthusiast and the roll-call of the distinguished ornithologists who have scaled its modest height (350 feet) is long, and includes such luminaries as Ray, Willoughby, Pennant, MacGillivray, Peterson, Fisher, Tinbergen and many more.

Its most celebrated denizen, the gannet, has increased vastly in number since the last war. In 1949, the total number of nesting pairs was about 4,800 and had changed little from pre-war years. The birds were concentrated mainly on the east and west cliffs with little overspill onto

Environment (cont)

the slopes above. Consequently the rock appeared mainly green, covered with fine turf, and in places with tree-mallow. Now in 2000, the rock appears white all-over right up to the summit cairn except (from the south) for a narrow strip where the path winds up. The population is now of the order of 35 to 40,000 pairs; the uncertainty is due not only to the difficulty of counting but to the presence of several thousand pre-breeding birds who have no nests and whose precise status is unclear. The increase has been at the rate of about 3% to 5% per year and could have resulted from the colony's own output, although there have been some (probably only a few) immigrants.

The main reason for the increase is simple. Formerly, gannets were heavily persecuted and protection has allowed them to realise their natural level of productivity. If anything, their natural food supply has decreased. Herring stocks have collapsed, mackerel are fished commercially and the Danes hoover up millions of tons of sand eels from the Wee Bankie in the North Sea, one of the gannet's fishing areas. Whether discards from trawlers have provided a significant supplementary source of food is a moot point. Nevertheless, the gannet's productivity has remained consistently high since at least 1960 – about 80-90% of all hatchlings survive to leave the Bass.

The populations of the other nine species of seabirds have fluctuated over this period. Kittiwakes have declined from a maximum of more than 2000 pairs to around 400. As the gannets have spread onto the slopes on which many hundreds of pairs of herring gulls and some lesser black-backed gulls nested, these have decreased and now total less than 350 pairs, mainly herring gulls. A recent and unwelcome addition has been three pairs of the predatory great black-backed gull.

Guillemots have lost some breeding areas to the gannets and now number some 1,100-1,500 individuals. There are fewer than 50 pairs of razorbills. Puffins are restricted to the walls of the battlements and seem to have decreased to around 30 birds. Shags have decreased markedly from a high of more than 200 nests in the 1960s and 1970s to the current population of, in some years, fewer than ten nests. Fulmars have increased slowly but steadily to some 60-70 pairs, mainly on the sides of the gully.

Bass Rock and Tantallon Castle, photographed from the south near Auldhame, 1989. (David Moody)

A helicopter pad, built in 1974, expedited relief for the lighthouse keepers who, previously, were taken off by boat. Although there is a brackish-water well near the garrison garden, not far below the summit of the rock, drinking water used to be piped ashore from a lighthouse vessel and stored at the base of the tower. In 1988 the light became automatic and the keepers departed. Occasional visits are made to maintain equipment but nowadays the Bass is mostly left to the seabirds.

The islands of Lamb and Craigleith lie between Fidra and the Bass and are the nearest to North Berwick but are the most difficult to land on, with calm weather and an obliging boatman essential for a visit. The Lamb is really just a large rock, home to sea birds and occasional resting seals but too small to be of much interest otherwise. The Lamb is an RSPB reserve by agreement with the owner. Craigleith (or the 'Craig' as it is known) is larger but again the principal interest is the nesting seabirds. The large and invasive tree mallow has colonised the Craig from the Bass since the war and now forms an impressive jungle over a significant part of the island, which is used as a roost in winter by thousands of starlings.

Land Ownership

Development in the burgh continued right through the period, eating up vacant lots and farmland closest to the town. While it is difficult to follow every transaction, some of the most important changes included the following. In the 1960s, North Berwick Town Council purchased large parts of North Berwick Mains from owner Mr Muirhead. Other parts of the Mains were sold off in the mid to late 1960s to private developers, such as the ground where Lady Jane Gardens is now. Mr Muirhead sold off the one field adjacent to the farmhouse - now Macnair Avenue. Anderson's nursery became Abbey Court. Littledean was sold and was developed as Marmion Crescent; in 1972 he released land to the west of Glenorchy Road, and in 1985 he sold land to the west of Ware Road - the largest area ever to be developed in the town.

The North Berwick Trust was established when, prior to the North Berwick Town Council being disbanded, the councillors were concerned that the remaining North Berwick Mains land would fall, like all the other town amenities, into the ownership of the new East Lothian District Council in 1975. It was therefore decided by the town council to appoint a group named the North Berwick Trust and transfer the ownership of the remaining land on the Mains to the North Berwick Trust for the then development value of the land. The land south of Grange Road continues to be managed by the North Berwick Trust for the benefit of the community. If the ground is ever sold the original value of the land in 1975 has to be paid to the East Lothian Council and the remainder spent in the community (several millions).

In the parish (according to the 1945-46 valuation roll) post-war land ownership still rested to a degree with the historic landowners, in particular the Grant-Suttie family. In 1945, they owned Balgone, Sheriffhall (the home farm), Balgone Barns, Carperstane, Redside, and Rockville; the farms were all tenanted.

The Hamilton Dalrymple Trust Company owned Blackdykes (tenant D.C. Watson & Sons), and Leuchie.

With the exception of Rhodes farm (North Berwick Town Council), the remaining farms in the parish were owner-occupied: Highfield (W.D. Simpson); East Craig (Jeffrey Ritchie); Wamphray (J. & A. Fleming); North Berwick Mains (Dundas & Mary Thomson); Horse Crook

Land Ownership (cont)

& Heugh (W.J. & D.P. Wright); Bonnington (James Mitchell & Son); Castleton (J.H. McNicol) and Gleghornie (Thomson Shepherd).

The Rhodes smallholdings (nos 1-5) were owned by the Secretary of State for Scotland, and still occupied by smallholders - Thomas Somerville, James Fergusson, John Black, William Thomson and James R. Inglis.

By 2000, the Grant-Suttie family had sold Balgone House and garden (1989), and moved to Sheriffhall, retaining the estate. The Hamilton Dalrymple Trust Company still owned Leuchie and Blackdykes.

William Evans purchased the cluster of buildings on the shore at Canty Bay from Sir Hew Hamilton Dalrymple in 1923. In 1936 ownership was transferred to the Evans Trust, and remained with the trust in 2000 (see Miscellany).

Townscapes, Buildings, & Landscapes of Distinction

The burgh's townscape is enhanced by a number of fine buildings, many of which have been listed by Historic Scotland; of particular note are Bunkerhill, Westerdunes, and Carlekemp and Carlekemp Lodge, all grade A listed buildings in Abbotsford Road. The policy of the council in recent years has been to retain the character and overall attractiveness of North Berwick. This keenness to preserve the character has benefited from parts of North Berwick being designated a conservation area in 1969. The original conservation area included the original 18th and 19th century core of the town, to the south of the harbour, and this was later extended along Westgate and Beach Road. In 1981, further areas of the town were scheduled.

The architecture is mainly traditional with the use of turrets, crow stepped gables and elaborately carved bargeboards. Materials such as stone, red sandstone, natural slate, clay pantiles and harling cladding are used all of which are compatible with the locality. There has been the occasional deviation from the norm and at Fowler Court one suspects the designer has seen work by Le Corbusier, one of the more famous architects of the 20th century with a distinctive suggestion of the chapel at Ronchamp, France in its design!

The first proposal to pedestrianise the High Street was made in 1965; in 2000, the High Street remained full of traffic, though only bearing down on unsuspecting pedestrians from one direction.

Outwith the town, almost as prominent as the Law is the curtain wall of the 14th century Tantallon Castle. Still owned by Sir Hew Dalrymple, Tantallon was handed over 'in care' to the then Ancient Monuments Board in the 1920s. Tantallon is now in the care of Historic Scotland, and is a major tourist attraction in the county.

Fenton Tower, on Highfield Farm near Kingston, was for most of the last century a ruin.

The Simpson family bought Highfield farm in 1920. In 1998 Ian Simpson and John Macaskill decided to restore the tower and convert it into a comfortable modern residence for the 21st century.

Scattered about the parish are the old farm buildings - steadings, cart sheds and granaries - that enhance the landscape. Fortunately, while some have been superseded by the larger structures essential to modern farming, many of these rather winsome buildings have merely been abandoned, not demolished. Latterly there has been an increasing trend to convert some of them into homes, for example the steadings at Redside, at Rockville and the farm complex at Heugh Farm.

Townscapes, Buildings, & Landscapes of Distinction (cont)

Balgone Barns, East Craig, Rhodes, Sheriffhall and Wamphray all have cart sheds and granary buildings of note. Sheriffhall also has a horse mill and a chimney; Heugh Farm also has a horse mill, as does Blackdykes.

The 'big' houses at Balgone and Leuchie serve to remind the parish of earlier times, when the large estates were the norm; both estates now are much reduced in scale, and their surrounding landscapes and policies add much to the general amenity of the parish.

The 17th and 18th century Balgone House is set in the remnants of an 18th century formal park, overlaid with a 19th century picturesque garden and lakes (SNH, 1994, pp22-50). The Grant-Suttie link with Balgone ended in 1989, when Balgone was bought by Alan Dean. His son Marcus Dean removed the large Victorian extension in 1992. Balgone House, the North Lodge and the Coach House are all B listed.

From 1699, Leuchie was the ancestral home of the Dalrymples (LUC, 1987, pp143-149). It is thought that, 1800-04, John Claudius Loudon worked on designs for the estate. The estate was reduced in size c1922 and, during the war years, the woodlands and parks to the north were utilised. The timber was felled and the parks used for agriculture.

Leuchie House (1779-85) is A listed. In 1960, the family moved to a house in the walled garden (designers Law and Dunbar / Naysmith). Leuchie House was then used as a convent (by two different orders of nuns, 1961-70), then a Richard Cave holiday home, and a hospice, both for the Multiple Sclerosis Society (1970-date). Leuchie remains in the ownership of Sir Hew Hamilton Dalrymple.

Population

By parish, from the General Registrar's office
By burgh, from the General Registrar's Office

1931	4083	1596M	2487F	*By locality – census –*
1931	*3473*	*1292M*	*2181F*	*ie North Berwick itself*
1951	4580	1983M	2597F	
1951	*4001*	*1687M*	*2314F*	
1961	4470	1877M	2593F	
1961	*4161*	*1731M*	*2430F*	
1971	4604	1991M	2613F	4581 2008M 2573F
1971	*4414*	*1892M*	*2522F*	
1981	5260	2414M	2846F	5162 2360M 2802F
1981	*4684*	*–*	*–*	*By Small Area Statistics - census*
1991	5638	2578M	3060F	5329 2417M 2912F
2001	6553	3044M	3509	-- -- --
By parish, from ELDC				*By settlement, from ELDC*
1991	5400			5555
1997 (est.)	6119 (sic)	2805M	3316F	6097
2001	--	--	--	6223 (ELC)

Population figures are difficult to compare, as no two sources extract data in the same way.

The data reveals that throughout the period North Berwick has had some 500 more females than males. This is perhaps because of its popularity as a place for retirement, and the fact that generally, women live longer than men.

Belief

In addition to the North Berwick Christian Fellowship (1991) and the more recently established Baptist church (1994), the traditional churches are well represented in the parish. There are two Churches of Scotland (three until 1989: Abbey, St Andrew's, Blackadder); one Roman Catholic church; and one Scottish Episcopalian church. All are located in North Berwick burgh.

The Churches of Scotland

In 1950, the Abbey church introduced the weekly Freewill Offering scheme, and consequently abolished seat rents for pews. No longer could parishioners claim that 'this is my pew'!

On 11 June 1954, the large window above the gallery (facing on to the High Street) was dedicated to Rev Robert Small (minister 1903-37) by his son Rev Dr Leonard Small. The stained glass depicts features associated with the church and community, and Mr Small's ministry.

Ministers

1937-49	A.T. Mackenzie
1950-56	Arthur G. Gunn
1956-64	E. Stanley P. Heavenor
1965-74	R. Nichol Bell
1975-84	James G. Lees
1985-98	P. Hamilton Cashman
1998-date	Dr David J. Graham

The congregation's constitution was changed in March 1986, from the United Presbyterian constitution (with a board of managers and preses to order the financial and property affairs) to the model constitution of the Church of Scotland, with a congregational board. The current board constitution states that the board should have twelve members who are elected from the congregation, and twelve elders.

In 1989 Abbey was linked, with the same minister, to the neighbouring parish of Dirleton to the west. This situation retained each separate Kirk Session and individual responsibility for worship and property, but the costs of the ministry were shared on the basis of Abbey $^2/_3$ and Dirleton $^1/_3$. In 1990, the church hall was renovated. The previous large stage area, which had been used for concerts and drama, was removed. In its place was left a very small raised platform, thus giving more floor area. In 1993 an Allen digital organ was installed, to replace the ageing pipe organ. The original organ pipes were retained however, and at present are still a feature behind the pulpit.

The ecclesiastical parish boundaries were readjusted in 1991, after the union of the other two Church of Scotland congregations in the town, which formed the parish of St Andrew & Blackadder. The previous boundaries had applied since 1931. It was agreed by Lothian Presbytery that the boundary between the two parishes in North Berwick should run from the sea, along Balderstone's Wynd, High Street, Westgate, Abbey Road, Nungate, Trainer's Brae, Grange Road, and Haddington Road, then out into the country.

Belief (cont)

St Andrew's 1945-89

Ministers

1928-51	R.D. Lyon
1952-88	W. McGill Ferrier
1989	vacant

November 1989 union with Blackadder under new minister E McKenna

In 1955, a complete redecoration of the church took place; a service of thanksgiving and rededication took place on 12 June 1995. In 1956 St Andrew's, along with Abbey and Blackadder churches, carried out a joint visitation of every home in North Berwick under the auspices of the 'Tell Scotland' campaign.

In November 1959, under the will of Miss Winifred Grey, money was bequeathed for the installation of a stained glass window. This was duly installed in the central circular space in the east gallery.

A memorial for the Rev R. Doughty Lyon, subscribed to by the congregation, took the form of an oak communion table and matching minister's chair. A stained glass window donated by Mrs Lyon and her two sons was installed in the central position in the west gallery. Mrs Lyon unveiled the window and the communion table and chair on 30 December 1962.

In 1965, two members of the congregation were training for work overseas under the Church of Scotland - nurse Rosemary Blair and lecturer Helen Bee. A service of dedication was held for them on 6 June and 26 June respectively.

At the beginning of 1966, discussions started on whether St. Andrew's (whose affairs had been overseen by one body - the Kirk Session) should adopt what was then known as the 'model constitution'. As a result the congregational board was instituted in 1967.

A thanksgiving service was held on 5 November 1967 to commemorate the diamond jubilee of the North Berwick scouts in St Andrew's church. On 13 July 1969, the BBC televised the morning service from St Andrew's; in the afternoon they recorded Songs of Praise (shown on 27 July). At the morning service in St Andrew's on Sunday 26 March 1972, the first North Berwick Scout Troop was presented with new colours.

By 1975 the General Assembly had removed the barrier excluding women from the eldership. Rosemary Blair, who had returned from overseas, was ordained elder on 13 November 1975 - the first woman elder in North Berwick. A second, Alison Dickson, was ordained on 20 September 1981.

In May 1975 a joint visitation of North Berwick by the three Church of Scotland churches took place. Mr Ferrier was the guest of honour at an evening in church in October 1977, conducted on the lines of 'This is Your Life', to celebrate his 25 years' ministry in St Andrews.

In 1982 a parish development programme was embarked upon. In 1983, celebrations to mark the centenary of the present church took place. In addition, a service of thanksgiving was held in June in the ruined church in Kirk Ports.

In 1989, agreement was reached regarding the union of the congregations in St Andrews and Blackadder. The service of union took place on 5 March that year, in Blackadder church. It had been agreed that with the union, the place of worship would be St Andrews.

Belief (cont)

Blackadder church until 1989

Blackadder church continued its evangelical tradition when Rev Crichton Barr went to the Scots' Kirk, Melbourne in 1946. Rev Charlie Stewart, an ex padre, was called in 1947. He was instrumental in leading a team of mainly returned ex-servicemen who stripped and polished the pews transforming the appearance of the sanctuary. This tradition of maintaining and looking after the church was a feature right up to the union with St Andrew's in 1989.

In 1951 Rev Andrew Gray was appointed but returned to his native South Africa in 1959. Rev Donald McAlister came in 1960 and his long ministry continued until 1989. Highlights at this time were a building-up of the strong missionary tradition with several going out to the mission field. Church of Scotland summer missions were an important aspect of the home mission effort of Blackadder church and were to play a very important role is bringing many people over the years to a belief in Christ as Saviour and Lord.

The illness of the minister Dr McAlister and the impending retiral of Walter Ferrier meant that in 1987 discussion began to take place regarding the future of the churches in North Berwick. It was hoped that the distinctive witness of Blackadder might continue in some form or other and after lengthy discussions, with Dr McAlister's retiral it was finally agreed to unite with St Andrew's in March 1989, thus ending a distinguished era of service for Christ.

Ministers

1938-46	A. Crichton Barr
1947-51	Charlie Stewart
1951-59	Andrew Gray
1960-89	Donald McAlister

1989 union with St Andrews

Lynne Turnbull shares some memories of Blackadder church during her teens (1970s-80s)

'The song 'If I had a hammer'; the youth fellowship (a youth club / Christian group for teenagers); the seaside mission, with summer Sunday school on the beach; and Christmas presents – donations of toys still in good condition to give to deprived children – labelled 'boy/girl' and age'.

On courtship

'You might meet at the under-18s disco at the Pavilion, the Gullane Games disco. In the 1980s, perhaps in Edinburgh bars (eg Harry's Bar, the Piano Bar, the Penguin), and in the 1990s, Indigo Yard.

Places to go were Yellowcraigs car park or Daisy Island car park. Courtship occurred at 'the Shows' – the funfair in the recreation park in July, especially to meet holidaymakers. In the 1980s, courtship occurred at 18th birthday parties – everyone had one held either in the rugby club or Old Clubhouse, Gullane. An older friend brought you the alcohol - Martini Rosso or Lambrusco.

Often you were engaged for years before getting married. It was not usual for man to surprise woman with a ring he had chosen; more likely they'd go to a jeweller together. The man asked her father for permission, as a formality, after he'd asked the woman'.

Lynne Turnbull

And on marriage

'[Popular] places to get married included Dirleton church, as well as Dirleton Castle, Lennoxlove and Green Craig Hotel. Often a bus was laid on to transport guests from the church to the reception.

Belief (cont)

Receptions in the 1980s were held at the Elizabethan Suite, at the Marine Hotel. The format was usually a meal, speeches then a ceilidh band. In the 1990s, the speeches came before the meal. The woman and her mother organised the whole thing, and the man did not have much say (or want any role) in the organisation. If people had lived together for years (common), they often had a registry office wedding for fear of being hypocrites or false.

In the 1980s, the man might wear a kilt, the woman a 'meringue' dress; by the 1990s, the man favoured tartan trews, the woman, a tight bodice with a straight skirt and tiara. The first dance (1990s) was often a well-known pop song (like Eric Clapton, Elvis, etc.) The bride's family would pay for 70% of the wedding; the groom's family 20% and 10% from the actual couple. Average cost £10,000.

A typical wedding menu: starter - haggis parcels in filo pastry in a whisky cream sauce, main course - salmon steak, dessert - summer fruit cheesecake'.

Lynne Turnbull

St Andrew Blackadder Church of Scotland from 1989

The formation of the new congregation was greeted with both the congregation's determination to make it work, and a sense of unease. In August 1989, the vacancy committee began the process of choosing a new minister for the new charge, proposing the Reverend Eddie McKenna as sole nominee. At 30, the new minister was young and untried and soon began the work of uniting the two traditions together. Growth in the worshipping congregation and an increase of young families was soon in evidence and together with the Kirk Session, a long period of consolidating the buildings began.

St Andrew's manse was sold, as were the Blackadder church and halls. St Andrew Blackadder church was totally re-roofed. In 1999 the congregation voted to proceed with proposals to redevelop the St Andrew Blackadder church.

In early 2000, Sir Hew Hamilton Dalrymple laid the foundation stone of the new premises. On 16 December 2000, the congregation met for the first time in the refurbished church. An exciting scheme, the redevelopment soon attracted national attention and has provided a wide range of facilities for the church and town. The congregation adapted well to the new facilities and junior church and youth clubs and the youth fellowship soon grew to record levels for the union.

Other churches in the parish

The Catholic Church of Our Lady, Star of the Sea

In 1945, with the end of the war, two noteworthy events occurred, both of which contributed to the life of the local Catholic population. Firstly, many of the Polish service men and women based in the parish, who had sung their sad hymns and songs in the church, settled here. In 1946, Luffness House, Dirleton was used as a Polish convalescent home, and Mass was celebrated in various rooms there, latterly in the converted furniture store. This ceased in 1982. Secondly, in 1945 the Benedictine monks of Fort Augustus opened a junior school at Carlekemp. The monks became well known in the town, until the school closed in 1977. The games field was often used for pre-match practice by visiting international rugby teams.

From 1961, Leuchie House was used by nuns of the la Sagesse congregation as a training establishment. In 1970, the nuns of the Servite Order, who ran it as a holiday home for the Multiple Sclerosis Society, succeeded them. The nuns left in 1998, but the house is still in use by the society. Mass is still said there on occasion.

Belief (cont)

In 1954 the parish hall was begun and opened on 25 September 1955. In 1979 the centenary of the building of the Star of the Sea church was celebrated. The parish priest was Father Kevin Rafferty, later to be ordained bishop. The present parish priest is Father John Barry, who was appointed in 1989.

St Baldred's Episcopalian Church
The centenary of St Baldred's was celebrated in 1962, and the church was linked with St Adrian's, Gullane in 1976, becoming St Adrian's & St Baldred's Scottish Episcopal Church.

Ministers

1937-48	Hector B. Gooderham
1949-55	A. Lawrence Wilson
1956-62	Kenneth W. Kennet
1963-68	Fred Drake
1969-80	R.J. Denholm
1976 linked to St Adrian's, Gullane	
1981-87	Æneas Macintosh
1988-date	John Lindsay

The building was improved over the years: the west doors were gifted in memory of Mrs Grant Suttie (1948); a replacement organ was installed from Chalmers Church, Anstruther (1983); in 1991, the high altar was moved forward and the reredos removed to restore the original apse; and in 1994, the bell tower was removed to ease the pressure on the chancel arch.

The North Berwick Christian Centre
This began in 1988 as a small homegroup, meeting in a basement flat in the town. The group was led by William and Sally Nisbet who at the time were based in a large Edinburgh church where William was one of the full-time eldership team. Over time the homegroup grew and in October 1991 became known as North Berwick Christian Fellowship, obtaining charitable recognition in November 1994 and financial independence from January 1995.
The church is non-denominational, adheres to the basic tenets of the Christian faith and would be classified as one of the 'new churches' which have sprung up in the UK over the past 30 years. The church spans all ages and meets in the local High School each Sunday and during the week in various locations and contexts. There is a core congregation of some 60+ adults and 20+ children. The centre offers a creche, children's church (5-10), 4YP (11-14) and teens. The church has good relationships with other congregations in the town and William meets regularly with other church leaders in North Berwick.

The North Berwick Baptist Church
This was established in 1994, based at the old Blackadder church building, Victoria Road. As part of the reformed theologians, North Berwick Baptist Church practises baptism by immersion of believers. There are about 30 in the congregation.

Homes

During the period 1945-2000, extensive change took place in the burgh, driven jointly by North Berwick's attraction as a retirement location and the steady rise in population levels.

In 1951, the burgh population was just over 4000, rising by about 10% by 1971 and thereafter reaching a settlement population of 6223 by 2001 (*see* Population). Of households in North Berwick in 1951, there were three main categories: owner-occupier, private rented, and accommodation rented from the local authority. At this time the figure for each type was approximately 33%. In 1981 the figures were just over 20% for owner-occupiers, about 17% for private rented accommodation and over 60% rented from local authority. By 1991, these figures have reversed and we have over 50% for owner-occupiers, just under 10% for private rentals and just under 40% for rentals from the local authority. It can be seen that the trend has become to own rather than rent.

With bigger and better salaries in the 1960s, purchasing property was the order of the day and the town council introduced a new fixed-rate mortgage to first-time buyers working in the town. It was said that North Berwick set the highest rents in the county, using the additional revenue to maintain and upgrade the town's amenities. In 1975, burgh councils were disbanded and newly formed East Lothian District Council spent large sums of money bringing other areas up to the standard set in North Berwick. As a result the town suffered from a lack of investment.

In later years the trend was for more and more private housing to be built, but even these developments became smaller as land was less available. There was a growing need for rented accommodation and for sheltered accommodation to meet the needs of the high numbers of retired residents. With escalating costs of housing in Edinburgh, North Berwick with its excellent amenities and travel facilities, also provided the solution to private housing requirements. On the other hand, it has been said that North Berwick in the 1990s had the worst homeless record in East Lothian, which has continued to the present day. The waiting list for council housing is said to be about 17 years, a situation which, when one studies the trend in housing availability, does not seem solvable.

Public provision

In a summary of the year's events the *Haddingtonshire Courier* reported that in 1946 there was an acute housing shortage. North Berwick Town Council stated that housing was priority number one, and asked the Department of Health for temporary houses. The government allocated 35, which were erected throughout the year. The town council planned to extend their housing scheme with the development of the area between Dunbar Road and Law Road, north of the Law and to the south of Lady Jane Gardens and Dundas Avenue. In July that year, 76 permanent houses were erected adjacent to the prefab site. In 1947 housing progress was reported as slow but steady; more temporary houses were allocated by the government. A block of four larger houses was commenced in August on the old bowling green site in the Lodge grounds. In 1948, the temporary housing was completed and the houses at the Lodge completed. A scheme for the Lochbridge site of 76 permanent houses commenced with ten houses and a further ten allocated to tenants with larger families. In 1952 further houses on the Lochbridge site were completed with some allocated to old people. In 1953 further housing was

Homes (cont)

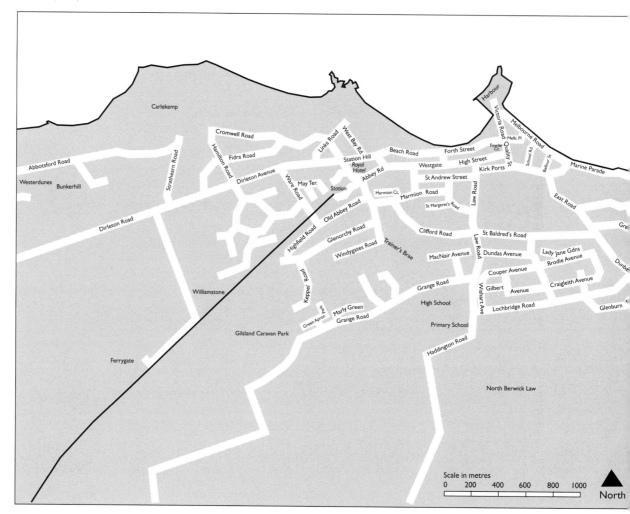

North Berwick Burgh   *This map is reproduced from Ordnance Survey material with the permission of Ordnance Survey on behalf of the Controller of Her Majesty's Stationary Office. © Crown copyright. Unauthorised reproduction infringes Crown copyright and may lead to prosecution or civil proceedings. OS Licence 100023381*

completed with site preparation for more housing to be started in 1954. North Berwick was regarded as progressive in its approach to housing, having completed 200 municipal houses in the post-war period.

In 1964, the council and the National Trust for Scotland worked together on a redevelopment (designer W. Schomberg Scott) of the Lodge into eight flats. In 1966 private house building featured strongly, while the council continued to carry out further schemes at Lady Jane Gardens and Forth Street, but work was hindered by a government credit squeeze.

In 1967, prefabricated houses in Craigleith Avenue and Dundas Avenue were demolished and rented accommodation was built on these sites. In the 1960s the council had purchased large parts of Mains Farm and in 1970 houses were built in Gilbert Avenue and Couper Avenue. Wishart Avenue was also built with stone from the re-opened quarry at the Law, this development receiving an architectural award. The streets were named after former provosts of the town.

Homes (cont)

Rhodes Park

Tantallon Road

Lochbridge Road with North Berwick Law behind. (*Valentine & Sons Ltd*)

The Lodge, North Berwick, before redevelopment. (below) (*National Trust for Scotland*)

Homes (cont)

High Street, North Berwick, 1960s. Florence Bates ladies' outfitters, run by Mrs Elspeth Waghorn, is the first shop on the left, next to John Aitken's sweet shop. The Playhouse Cinema was demolished in the 1980s and in 2000 the Cancer Research charity shop occupied the site, along with Victoria Wines. Carr's shoe shop on the corner of Balderstone's Wynd (right) had become Readmore bookshop.

Homes (cont)

Looking east along Forth Street from Balderstone's Wynd, North Berwick. The buildings on the right have been demolished. The white building in the distance was the Co-op store on the corner of Market Place, now replaced by shops and luxury flats.

Homes (cont)

In 1973, the council built flats at Brodies yard and in Forth Street. In the 1980s, new housing for the elderly was proposed in Forth Street and on the former site of the Ben Sayer's factory.

As part of the Lothian Structure Plan 1994, local authorities were instructed to sell off any land they owned that was not being used to its full potential. The Rhodes Caravan Park, having declined in its use, was sold by the council c1991 for private development, which began in 1999.

Development of a site in Quality Street for East Lothian Housing Association's scheme for 14 flats was proposed in 1996 but delayed for nine months while an archaeological dig was undertaken. The building proceeded, with a tower on the corner, an internal courtyard and a harled finish decorated with a piece of artwork.

Private development

Post war, there were a lot of large houses in the town that were far too big for servant-less families; architect G.E. Shackleton began to purchase a number of large properties to the west of the town, and converted them into apartments. Two examples of his work can be seen at Hyndford House and Anchor Villa in West Bay Road.

In the burgh, as in towns everywhere, land was recycled over and over again as the need arose, and extensive demolition was undertaken to allow for necessary redevelopment. This included cottages in Law Road, Tantallon Hall, shops and garages in Westgate, the fire station, and tenements in Forth Street. Other buildings demolished were houses in East Road, and stable yard in Kirk Ports, the Playhouse Cinema in the High Street (a victim of the popularity of TV, closed in the mid 1980s), blacksmith's premises in Forth Street, the Pavilion at the harbour, a plethora of garages, Glasclune in Greenheads Road, Tantallon Hall, Vale Hotel (Forth Street), Globe Lemonade Works (Forth Street Lane), Hunter Brothers' haulage yard (Imperial Car Park), Ben Sayers' factory in Forth Street and the Royal Hotel to name but a few. Some of the buildings had been allowed to fall into disrepair prior to demolition, their original purpose no longer of relevance; examples included the Pavilion, the granary, the old Co-op building and Tantallon Hall.

In almost all instances, in North Berwick, redevelopment took the form of housing. Glasclune, in Greenheads Road, was a large imposing house built for J.B. Balfour in 1889 and had been the home in more recent years for Dr Barnardo's children. In 1979 there was a fire and the building was badly damaged. Was it an electrical fault or was someone smoking in a cupboard? The building became derelict, the whole site being redeveloped between 1985-87 with private housing in Glasclune Gardens and private flats in Glasclune Court.

The Royal Hotel remained empty for several years and was not helping in appeal to the main approach to North Berwick. After much debate, permission was given to proceed with redevelopment of the site. The building was demolished and in 2000, luxury flats were built on the site with private sheltered accommodation on adjoining land. Many outraged cries were to be heard of other residents' inability to see the sea any more but the main approach to the town had been brought up to standard!

Tantallon Hall was built originally as an hotel for golfing visitors. It was situated overlooking the burgh golf course and stood out as one of the burgh's main features. In 1921 it became a holiday home for St Dunstan and in 1925 a Friendship Holiday Association home.

More recently no use could be found for it and it was demolished in 1966 to make way for a private housing development.

The 19th century granary at the harbour, formerly known as Harbour Terrace, was home to the fisherfolk. This building fell to the hands of the developers and was redeveloped in the 1970s into luxury flats (designer Mary Tindall). The design won a Civic Trust Award in 1972.

The Douglas Court development in 1998 consisted of the refurbishment of the old Co-op building on the corner of Forth Street and Market Place. The building had been empty for at least four years and was causing much concern as it marred the appearance of the town. The building was gutted and three shops and a restaurant were formed on the ground floor with luxury flats above. The finished exterior decor of the building caused quite a stir, being of a violent reddish hue.

Expansion

From the 1970s, new developments mushroomed all over North Berwick. These included: Marmion Crescent; Abbey Court; Macnair Avenue; Clare Court in Old Abbey Road; Milsey Court in School Road; Marly Green; Macnair Avenue was extended northwards, and Springfield Gardens (Cromwell Road).

In 1972, land to the west of Glenorchy Road had been released by Sir Hew Hamilton Dalrymple where the Keppel Road and Green Apron Park developments were built, the former being named in honour of Lady Anne Louise Hamilton Dalrymple.

By the late 1970s, all large areas of land available for housing had been developed and smaller plots were sought by the developers, including plots in Forth Street, Brentwood Hill, Fidra Road and numerous sites in St Andrew Street, Strathearn Road and Easter Ferrygate. In 1985, land to the west of Ware Road was sold to Walker Homes (Scotland) Ltd, which then constructed Lord President Road and the various adjacent cul-de-sacs. Since then, developments have continued apace, despite local objections. In the 1990s, large areas of land were developed: to the east, a large private development bordered by Tantallon Road, to the south a four ha site bordered by Windygates Road and Grange Road, and to the southwest, an area bordering the railway and the rear of Dirleton Avenue. In 1999, permission was given for 32 houses and bungalows at Trainer's Brae, and the same year the development for 140 private dwellings at the old Rhodes caravan park went ahead. Although the proposal had been passed around 1991, building work here had been delayed until the schools were extended to cope with more pupils. Smaller developments occurred to the extreme west of the town.

In spite of this amount of housing expansion, the overall appearance of North Berwick has changed little over the last 50 years. There are houses peeping out above East Bay but the well defined large spaces afforded by the two golf courses and the putting green at West Bay provide an open and spacious landscape. All these areas are well maintained and add to the general pleasing ambience of the town.

North Berwick has always been a special place and continues to be and those of us who live here feel very privileged.

Lynne Turnbull recalls standards of living

'In the 1970s, we lived in a three-bedroom house. The other rooms were an office/study; piano room; utility room. The kitchen had lino tiles on the floor, a gas hob and oven, with a grill above the hob used for

Homes (cont)

toast (no toaster). The sitting room was carpeted; there was an electric bar fire, TV (no video), and a record player (45 and 33 rpm records). Mains electricity was used for cooking, heating, lighting. There were oil radiators in bedrooms in the 1970s. Wet clothes were hung over these to dry, or dried on a clothes line in the garden.

The bath had a rubber tap hose, which was detachable for use as a 'shower'. I used to wash my hair in the kitchen sink three times a week, especially on a Sunday night using Vosene medicated shampoo and Pears soap.

In the 1980s, popular perfumes were: Anais Anais, Impulse (women); Drachar Noir, Hi Karate and Givenchy (men). Sachets called 'toners and shaders' – non-permanent colour for a Saturday night – were popular.

We had three meals a day – breakfast 7.30am, lunch 1pm, tea 5pm. Breakfast – father ate alone at 7am. Kids ate at 7.45am – Coco Pops or Weetabix. First up got the cream at the top of the glass milk bottle (delivered daily). School dinners comprised sausage rolls, chips, beans and cheese, praline/tiffin bar. Or lunch at home – Heinz tomato soup, plain loaf, white bread, Ambrosia creamed rice. Dinner – meat (eg liver and bacon, pork fillet, meat loaf), potatoes and vegetables. Then toast and marmalade. 1970s drinks - Cremola foam, Five Alive, red cola, ice cream float. The woman and children cleared away afterwards.

In the 1990s I lived in a flat; 'two-bedroomed' meant merely one bedroom, plus a boxroom with no window. In the kitchen, there was a microwave, TV, dishwasher, integrated hob and oven. The sitting room had a DVD player, stereo for CDs, and a wooden polished floor.

Modernisation of homes in the 1980s to gas central heating meant we no longer needed to remember to put on immersion for hot water as it was now on a timer switch - we woke up to a hot house and hot water. There were mixer taps on all sinks, electric or power shower above the bath or as a cubicle. Many houses had two bathrooms, one of which was a shower room. Shower and hairwash daily or at the very least four times a week, or sometimes twice a day, using Body Shop fruity shower gels, scrubs and shampoo, and other makes of shampoo – Neutrogena, Organics. Essential oils are very popular to put in bath or to burn. 'Bath bombs' popular – rose petals in bicarbonate of soda. Both men and women used Calvin Klein, Tommy Hilfiger.

Clothes were dried on a whirly-gig in the garden, tumble dryer or clotheshorse in airing cupboard. The washing machine goes on at least once a day and many woollens can go in a wool cycle. People who work in offices in Edinburgh (living in East Lothian) have more clothes that need to be dry-cleaned and use a local dry cleaner in Edinburgh in their lunch hour.

We still eat three meals a day – breakfast 7am, lunch 2pm, tea 7pm, and at the weekend it would be two meals – brunch at 11/12, usually in a café or as a takeaway – and dinner at 8/9pm. Breakfast – Special K with skimmed milk; lunch – sandwich (Emmental cheese, pastrami, humus, sundried tomatoes, ciabbata bread or focaccia, Muller yoghurt corners, left over tea microwaved from previous evening). Dinner - chilli con carne, pasta with pesto sauce, 'Chicken tonight' casserole, fish kebabs, Linda McCartney's vegetarian frozen meals, fresh pasta and sauce, frozen curry from supermarket, fish pie (popular dinners from Ainslie Harriot's Cookbook).   Drinks included Pepsi Max, fresh orange, bottled water. The woman made meals at home – wife or mother, rarely the male; the husband and wife took turns to load dishwasher.

I see a change from the 1970s; by 2000, men were having more of an input into meal preparation and clearing. However, it is still mostly the female who plans the week's meals, writes the shopping list etc.'

Utilities

For many years the town council continued to maintain the burgh water supply, at a time when other councils had transferred responsibility to the County Council Water Board. Following the construction of the Whiteadder reservoir (open 1969), Kingside pumping station and the chemical filtration plant at Whittingehame by the county council in the 1950s, the water tanks and sand filters at the Whisky Bottle (a lake at the foot of the Law) were closed, and the tanks at the Heugh were used for water storage. In 1975, the supply of water was under the authority of Lothian Regional Council and in 1996 this passed to East of Scotland Water Board.

The Ferrygate Gas Works closed in 1972, when the town's gas supply was produced at Granton.

In 1958, North Berwick Town Council installed electric street lighting for the first time, under the supervision of burgh surveyor James Dalgleish. This meant the services of Joe Armstrong the 'lamp-lighter' were no longer required, but he continued as 'town-crier' on official occasions. Two of the original decorative lamp standards presented to the town by the gas company in 1905, with the burgh coat of arms engraved on the glass, still exist. One lamp was erected at the foot of the stairs leading to the council chambers and the other until 1975 was outside the provost's residence. This was traditionally moved each time a new provost was elected.

For the new system, the town council decided to use warm white fluorescent light rather than the more efficient and economical sodium filament. The fluorescent light gave a pleasing warm glow and was so popular with residents and tourists that the street lighting was switched on during the summer evenings. The town was unique in East Lothian in using this system and the town council continued to maintain the street lighting until 1975, when Lothian Region Transportation Department took over operations and standardised the system to sodium lighting.

Domestic waste was collected in two separate metal containers, food leftovers and household refuse. The food waste was fed to the pigs at the Rhodes farm, a very profitable venture which reduced the rates. The town council purchased Rhodes farm in the 1940s and used the outbuildings as workshops and stabling for a pair of sturdy Clydesdale horses, which were in regular use until the early 1960s. The agricultural land on the Rhodes farm was rented out, new council houses built forming Lime Grove, and a pig farm established on ground where later the burgh caravan site was laid out, now Rhodes Park (housing). The household refuse was deposited in the former lime quarry at the Rhodes farm.

The area west of Strathearn Road including Westerdunes was not part of the burgh and all services in that district were under the jurisdiction of East Lothian County Council. In the 1960s, when the refuse site at the Rhodes was full, the household rubbish was transported to the quarry on the south of Berwick Law where it was incinerated to minimise the waste, then used to in-fill the old quarry. In 1975, East Lothian District Council, as the new local authority, took over the management of refuse when it was processed at the baling station at Barbachlaw, Musselburgh.

Introduced in 1990, the green 'wheelie bin' became a common sight. The amenity household refuse disposal site in Heugh Brae was opened in 1992, offering recycling facilities for bottles, cans, clothes and shoes.

The town council financed the costs of all services in the burgh until 1975, through the

Utilities (cont)

household rates. For large projects like the new street lighting, the town council borrowed the capital, which was repaid over several years, under the prudent management of town chamberlain William Simpson. Each year at the 'legendary' ratepayers' meeting held in the Pavilion, the town councillors faced the community, and many a colourful debate ensued, when the locals took the opportunity to express their opinion on how effectively their money was being spent by the town council - old fashioned democracy at work.

With the population increase in the 1970s and the rapid growth in house building, the town council realised that the practice of discharging increased amounts of raw sewage into the Firth of Forth was not environmentally acceptable, and they commissioned a feasibility study by civil engineers into the building of a sewage treatment plant and upgrading the drainage system.

Over ten years would elapse before Lothian Region came up with an imaginative plan in 1986 to construct a sewage treatment plant in the steeply sloping gully bounded by 'Jacob's Ladder' in Haugh Road. The building, which resembles a secret bunker from a James Bond movie, was constructed in such a confined space the engineers had to design a unique filtration system using chemically assisted primary settlement rather than traditional techniques. The treated effluent is then discharged via the twin long sea outfall pipes off 'The Leithies' at a depth of 16 metres. The sludge remaining from the primary treatment is transferred to road tankers for subsequent disposal.

The waste was gathered from the west of the town, incorporating a pumping station in Fidra Road, then forced by gravity through the 1200mm collection pipes along Milsey Bay to the treatment plant. Unfortunately the concrete pipes in the West Bay were not laid deep enough and continue to form an unsightly scar. Three new rainwater outfall pipes were cut through the rocks to the sea, and the old barnacle-covered Victorian sewage pipes removed. The fully automated and unmanned sewage treatment plant with a capacity for a population of 16,000 was opened in 1995, and received a Saltire Award for civil engineering design.

High Street look east, 1970s, wit James Hunter's grocer's shop on corner of Law R and his coal merchant's offic next door (55, F St), now occupi by 'L'Argenette jewellers.

Shops & Services

In the post-war period, North Berwick served its community with a range of shops seen in other towns of similar size. The East Lothian Co-operative Society had three premises in the town: Dunbar Road (grocery); Lochbridge Road (grocery); and Market Place (grocery, household goods, electrical supplies, furnishing, and a footwear department). The Dunbar Road store ran from the same site until the 1960s, and later became two private houses. FW Woolworth opened a branch in 1955.

Similarly, local trades people necessary for maintenance of properties and suchlike serviced the burgh.

In addition, it had the tourist facilities of the period: 'six licensed hotels, seven restaurants, 30 private hotels, and an ever-changing and increasing number of boarding houses'. However, even in the 1950s, the pattern of the tourist trade was changing, with an increase in day visitors, and a decline in the longer-staying guests (Snodgrass, C.P. 1953, pp362, 363).

In the 1960s, North Berwick was seriously affected by the so-called package holidays to Spain and the like which turned out to be cheaper for a fortnight than two weeks in a North Berwick boarding house. Over a period, many of these were sold and split into flats, and the seasonal tourist activities on offer declined. With fewer visitors, shopkeepers found life less prosperous and empty shops began to appear; these numbered over a dozen at one point.

While we once had the services of a post office (long established in Westgate) and a sub-post office (Dunbar Road) we now have just one which, when the Post Office privatised the service, won the franchise. The post office is now in the eastern High Street. Other changes to the town meant two of the three fish shops closed with four out of five butchers, and five out of six grocers following suit. These were replaced by two small and one large supermarket.

By 2000, the town had two supermarkets - Rasul Brothers in the High Street, and Safeway in Dunbar Road. The Dunbar Road site became a Safeway c1998, having formerly been run as Presto (a Safeway subsidiary), which had moved from its High Street location to the new site in 1994. Presto had been in the High Street for about ten years, operating from what had been Galbraith's.

Interior Fabrics took over the old High Street Presto shop, and provided a badly needed local outlet for furnishings. Several of the empty shops in the town were taken over by charities, and by 2000 there were three – the Heart Foundation, Cancer Research and the Red Cross.

In 2000, there were five pubs, and six hotels - Blenheim House Hotel; County Hotel; Golf Hotel; Harbour House Hotel; Nether Abbey Hotel; Point Garry Hotel, and nine restaurants - Bella Italia; The Folly; The Grange (Scottish); Millennium Spice (the Joypur Indian Restaurant (Balti) which was renamed in 2000!); Lucky House (Chinese); Miller's Bistro; Poonthai's (Thai); and the Tantallon Inn (Scottish).

Lynne Turnbull looks back at shopping

'[In the 1970s] we bought in all the food – none of it was produced at home; a big grocery shop on Fridays, but most days bought one or two items as necessary. The wife or mother (ie the female in the family) bought it and walked home with it from the High Street. We shopped at Beck's grocer's store in the High Street and Patersons green grocer, and at the local fish shop and local butchers, Struths; all High Street bought in the 1970s.

Shops and Services (cont)

(above) East end of the High Street, 1950s. The Co-op shop on the extreme left is now Anderson's butchers. Wilson's grocers (No. 34) was later occupied by W.A. Scott Ltd., paints & wallpapers. Fowler's garage, long demolished, is now the site of a supermarket and the Imperial Hotel, Quality Street, in the distance, has been converted into flats.

This is the rear of East End garage in 1950s, which extended from High Street back to Forth Street. This site is now occupied by Creel Court. The building on the far side of the garage is the 'Auld Hoose' public house, built 1898 and still standing on the corner of Forth Street Lane.

Shops and Services (cont)

In the 1990s on Saturday morning – a weekly big shop; couples went together to buy food with the car. 80% of food bought in one go at a supermarket, either Safeway's in North Berwick, Tesco's in Haddington (they have a café!), Asda in Edinburgh (sell clothes, music, garden supplies etc.) During the week if you ran out of eg milk, it was purchased in the local Asian shop or in the chip shop while buying a fish supper.

Alcohol purchased mostly at the local off-licence (Threshers or Victoria Wine and sometimes at the supermarket). If going to a party or Christmas time – bought alcopops (eg Bacardi Breezers, Moscow Mule etc) and bottles of beer such as Bud Ice or Molson Dry. A box of wine for the fridge to allow a daily glass at evening meal – it doesn't go off'.

On clothes' purchasing
'The ski jackets, drainpipe jeans, tukka boots and donkey jackets of the 1980s came from a John Moore or Littlewoods catalogue, or Princes Street. Under these we wore such as a ra-ra dress, drainpipe pinstripe stretch jeans. Under these were M&S twin sets, vest and shorts, pants (polka dot).

In the 1990s, the duffel coat, flying jacket, fur coat, knee-high boots, body warmers, cargo/combat pants, and bootleg trousers came from Princes Street, Next Directory, or shopping centre – like the Gyle. Underwear was Sloggi knickers, Calvin Klein knickers, M&S white bra, pop sox, hold-ups. Underwear came from Marks & Spencer, Jenners, and John Lewis'.

Hairstyles were important:
'From the 1970s young people were rarely seen in a local salon. It was prestigious to get the train up to Edinburgh on a Saturday morning or late night Thursday to get a hair cut at a named salon. Hairdressers in Edinburgh – Ian Cameron, Cheynes, Brian Drum.

The 1970s [style was] a pageboy cut or short cropped – often looking like a boy! By the 1980s, a 'shake' cut – long hair feathered on to the face. They would serve a coffee in the hairdressers. By the 1990s, it was a straight bob, and the hair was worn up with crocodile clip; [the hair stylists] offered a glass of wine and a 'Hello' magazine. Haircuts every 8-12 weeks, and the average haircut cost for a woman £25-£40'.
Lynne Turnbull

Following the closure of the library, which was part of the service offered by Boots the chemist at 33 Westgate, the community-spirited Miss Dow persuaded the town council to establish a library in the Hope Rooms. In the 1950s, Mrs Annie Buckingham was asked to supervise the new service and was appointed the first town librarian; she was often to be seen riding her bicycle around town, and retired as librarian in 1964 at the age of 71 years. As the population increased in the 1970s the library became too small and the facility moved to the former public school in School Road, where it remained in 2000, offering cassettes, CD's, videos and free internet access as well as books.

Healthcare

In the 1940s General Practitioners worked from home either alone or with a partner, their wives answering all the telephone calls and acting as receptionists. With the emergence in the mid-1950s of a group practice (five doctors) working under one roof, a secretary and receptionist were employed, and only out-of-hours calls were taken by the doctor at home. They were helped by one district nurse and one health visitor working in the community and sometimes in the doctors' surgery. The Health Visitor held clinics for children and also helped the school doctor. Children with orthopaedic, eye and ENT problems could attend local clinics.

Healthcare (cont)

The Edington Cottage Hospital, North Berwick has nine GP beds available to any GP in the area. It is linked to North Berwick Health Centre but manned by Health Board staff. North Berwick GPs could also use the facilities at both East Fortune and Roodlands hospitals. The Edington usually provides beds for patients with illness not requiring specialist care, post-op cases and is sometimes used for respite care. From 1983, the doctors could do minor ops there; minor injuries too were dealt with there, more severe injuries being sent by ambulance to Haddington or Edinburgh.   Occasionally a helicopter would transfer more inaccessible casualties to Edinburgh. There was a Flying Squad, which transported mothers requiring emergency maternity care, and by the late 1980s ambulances also had paramedics.

By the 1970s practice nurses were helping the GPs, and in 1983 all the doctors and nurses came under one roof at the new health centre and there were facilities for dentists, physiotherapists and chiropodists to work. Visiting pediatricians and psychiatrists also held clinics. All patients with serious illness such as cancer, multiple sclerosis, AIDS, VD, ME, etc. are treated in specialist hospitals in Edinburgh.

When the accident and emergency department in Roodlands closed all cases were sent to Edinburgh. As TB was becoming rare the respiratory wards at East Fortune were closed and with the closure of that hospital, geriatric and handicapped patients were moved. Now more ill elderly patients are cared for at home with nursing and home help services, and some handicapped patients are looked after with help in the community.

Dr Jean Walinck, North Berwick GP 1958-90, comments on health in the parish

'As antibiotics in the form of penicillin only became available in the early 1940s, the main illnesses that people worried about were infectious illnesses. TB was the main worry as drugs to treat this only became available in the 1950s – patients being treated in East Fortune Hospital. Before immunisations became available there was also concern about polio, diphtheria, scarlet and rheumatic fever, rubella and measles. Before joint replacement became available in 1960s many worried about arthritis. Many patients with heart disease and heart failure suffered chronic illness before drugs for failure were used in the 1950s and coronary bypass was performed.

As far as I know, mothers in East Lothian did not encourage their children to visit others with infectious illness, as measles and whooping cough could leave long-term side effects. Girls may have been encouraged to get rubella. [There] were fears about smallpox vaccine and polio injections (before oral vaccine was used). Recently there have been fears about MMR giving autism.

Polio vaccine was started in the late 1950s and during my time in North Berwick from 1958 I did not see a confirmed case. There was however quite an epidemic in 1947. As this is an agricultural area we did see occasional cases of brucellosis and orf.

Before 1948 some poorer families might not call a doctor because of the cost, and might try some home cures instead. After 1948 there was no rush of patients to be seen. Minor bumps and scrapes were treated with iodene, Germolene (antiseptic ointmant) and later with TCP. Splinters might be treated with a bread poultice and infected wounds with eusol or mag sulph and glycerine dressings.

The doctor, helped by the health visitor, routinely did eye tests in primary school. Adults consulted an optician. When free eye tests were introduced I think parents then had the option of taking their child to an optician of their choice.

Both adults and children had to pay for dental care but I believe they could have their children's teeth

Healthcare (cont)

looked at by the school orthodontist who, until 2000, held clinics in the health centre. After free dental care was introduced, all who wished it could choose a dentist who offered free care.

Foot care was available privately from a chiropodist in North Berwick. An NHS chiropodist saw people in a clinic in the health centre, or visited frail elderly at home. Some people were referred to the foot clinic in Edinburgh, if they required special footwear'.

Pre-school children

'All children up to school age were checked regularly by the health visitor giving them advice about feeding and immunisations. She held clinics to distribute powdered milk, orange juice and vitamins and folic acid to pregnant mothers. Any problems could be referred back to the GP or the paediatrician who held clinics in the health centre. In the 1990s the GPs assisted by the health visitor held child health surveillance clinics. Contraceptive advice was given either by the GPs or at a family planning clinic for all women in the area and held in the High Street'.

Babies were delivered at home or in the Vert, Haddington, complicated births going to Edinburgh. When the Vert closed (1971) all babies were delivered in Edinburgh.

'Until pregnancy testing came in (possibly early 1970s), diagnosis of pregnancy was done by the doctor examining the patient. The test usually took several days to be reported, and was superseded by a test the patient could buy from the chemist which gave instant results.

Pregnant women were given antenatal care by their own GP for delivery at home or in the Vert Hospital. Because all the doctors were trained in midwifery shared care was done with the hospital obstetricians for mothers having hospital delivery. In the 1980s the district midwife also did shared antenatal clinics.

Up until the Vert Maternity Hospital closed in 1971 a mother could choose (provided her GP agreed) to have her baby at home, in the Vert or in one of the Edinburgh maternity hospitals. After that all pregnant women had their babies in Edinburgh, but could decide to take 48 hour discharge. (With mothers who took a 24-48 hour discharge there was usually help from the husband or a close relative, especially if there were other siblings). Should a mother decide to have her baby at home she would have to find a GP willing to do that. In the North Berwick practice we decided not to do any home deliveries. She could however decide to be looked after antenatally by her own GP and have the district midwife supervise her delivery, the doctor only being called in in an emergency.

Fathers did attend the birth of their babies in the 1960s but this did not become common practice until the 1980s'.

Dr Jean Walinck

'Babies were born in the Simpson's and the Eastern (Edinburgh) until 1994, then Simpson's or St John's Hospital in Livingston. Birthing pools were very popular. Antenatal classes – usually six (three including partners) which involved breathing exercises, watching videos of birth, and breast-feeding workshops. It was an accepted norm in the 1990s that the father should be present at the birth. It is his job to use his mobile phone to call friends and relatives with the good news. Father usually gets drunk that evening with close friends to 'wet the baby's head'. Mother stays in hospital average three days. Breastfeeding in the 1990s – on demand not four-hourly. Commonplace myth to give formula bottle as the last feed of the day to make the baby sleep through the night.

Midwife visits mother at home daily for first ten days, then health visitor visits once a week.

Healthcare (cont)

> *Aqua-natal exercise classes at local swimming pool both before and after the birth.*
> *Tradition - ladies put a 50p or £1 coin in the pram of a newborn for luck'.*

Lynne Turnbull (1990s)

On care of the elderly, and of older people with one or more heathcare needs

'Over the years 1945-60 fewer married women worked and were able to look after older members of their family, either by giving them support in their own homes or by having them to live with them. With more mothers now working, they are unable to give this support. Some families however do cope with older family members by having a granny flat attached to their house, and grannies (if fit) have always and still do play a great part in looking after their grandchildren. However with families now living in different parts of the country this is not always possible. More families - with no near family and mothers now working - are having to rely on other forms of childcare.

With early discharge from hospital, fewer beds for chronic illness, more elderly people are looked after at home helped by home care assistants, meals provided at home and help from the getting up and putting to bed carers. In general now more young people do not always feel they should be responsible for their elderly, often frail, relatives.

Even with the inherent problems, there is still a proportion of families who will try to look after elderly members of their family in their own homes. If they do this, respite care for an elderly ill relative is very necessary. Respite care in North Berwick can be arranged in the Edington Hospital, although this is now only for a limited period. Three generations living in one house can cause quite a strain on the family, but provided the older person is still mentally active he/she can be an asset. Increasingly, with the split up of family units, more young people feel that the care of the elderly should rest with the government.

With the increase of home helps, care of the elderly in day care centres, and other care services for elderly, more people are continuing to manage to look after themselves at home. Only when either severe physical disability or deteriorating mental ability is present do they need long-term nursing home or hospital care. With the closure of many nursing homes and the decrease in hospital geriatric beds this is becoming more difficult'.

Jean Walinck

St Baldred's Tower (built 1885) was for many years a nursing home for the elderly; it closed in mid 2000 (to be converted into flats). The Abbey closed in 1995 for refurbishment; it re-opened in 1997, and took in people from Redcroft Nursing Home. There were fewer beds in the Abbey, so not everyone from Redcroft could be accommodated there. Redcroft itself closed in 1997.

Long- or short-stay beds for people needing nursing care are now being provided in Copper Beech and Fidra Nursing Homes (both in North Berwick). Nursing care is also provided in Muirfield Nursing Home in Gullane, and Hilton Lodge in Haddington, both taking North Berwick patients.

Disability

'Up till the early 1970s there was very little provision for either children or adults with physical disability, and most of them were looked after at home. Most parents felt they got very little support. Some disabled children over the age of twelve were admitted to adult wards in East Fortune Hospital. Deaf children were taught in Donaldson's Hospital and blind children in the Royal Blind School after the age of five.

Healthcare (cont)

Up till the 1970s mental illness was regarded as something to be ashamed of and was often not fully understood or discussed. Although tranquillisers were used in the 1950s drugs for the more serious psychotic illnesses had not been discovered. With the coming of TV and more recently the internet, mental illness is more discussed and understood. Also more chronic mental illness is treatable provided you can persuade the patients to take their medicine. This can sometimes be a problem with psychotics who have no insight into their illness.

People with Downs Syndrome, learning difficulties or mild brain damage could often be kept at home but older children (say with incontinence) would be too much for parents to cope with and could be admitted to East Fortune Hospital. Some older children might be admitted to Herdmanflat Hospital, Haddington.

Adults with mental health problems who needed hospital admission (either going in voluntarily or under certificate) were admitted to Herdmanflat Hospital or one of the Edinburgh psychiatric hospitals.

In the 1970s because there were no facilities for children with special needs some mothers with handicapped children started a handicapped play scheme in North Berwick Community Centre and organised a toy library, initially based in Tranent. A swimming class for disabled children and adults was started in Haddington swimming pool and took anyone living in East Lothian. All these activities were mainly run by volunteers with support with transport from the Round Table and scouts and guides raising funds. By the 1980s much more support for these disabled people was given as they were more accepted into the community. In the 1990s parents got help with speech therapy, occupational therapy, music therapy either at home or at school; there is now also a special needs class in North Berwick school'.
Dr Jean Walinck

Education (*see* CD-ROM for additional information)

An important and comparatively recent development has been provision for pre-school age children. In 1945 there were no facilities for this age group. It was the changing social patterns (eg more working mothers) and new ideas of the 1970s, which led to the opening of North Berwick Nursery School. In September 1974 a mobile unit was set up in the grounds of the Community Centre, Law Road, to which the first children were admitted a few weeks later. The present premises, at the rear of the Community Centre, opened in January 1977.

By 2000 a private nursery school (the Beehive) had also started, on the site of the former Brentwood Hotel at the corner of Marmion Road and Clifford Road.

Primary

Most primary age children in the town attended the local authority school. In 1945 this was located in Law Road, in the building that had been the High School from 1894-1941. Both primary and secondary departments shared the same rector (headteacher). This arrangement continued until summer 1973. On the retiral of rector Tom Davidson, the primary school was separated from the high school. Jack McKay was appointed as first headteacher of the primary school.

In January 1975 the school (now called Law Primary School) moved into new purpose-built accommodation near the foot of the Law. At the same time staff and pupils from Kingston Primary School joined them. The single-storey building was organized in semi-open plan teaching bases. In June 1998 an extension was added, made necessary by growing pupil

Education (cont)

Law Primary School, North Berwick, built 1975 (above)

Carlekemp Priory School, south elevation, main building (above)

North Berwick High School, c1955. (left)

numbers. Latterly some pupils had been taught in mobile units in the adjoining high school grounds.

The General Inspection of 1948/49 recorded that there were 137 infants and 246 primary stage pupils in the school. In 2000, the school roll was 646. Average class sizes are about 30 pupils. From 1957 there were two classes for every primary year group. Now the average has risen to three, with four P7 groups.

Inevitably there have been many changes in the education delivered by the primary school. In the earlier times, much learning was by rote, yet the 1948/49 General Inspection reveals that both individual and group methods were used with infants.

In recent years primary curricular change has been rapid, in line with national policies. Target-setting, the 5-14 Programme and the spread of IT have all had major effects on the curriculum. For example, since the late 1990s pupils from P6 have been taught French. In English equal significance is attached to reading, writing, talking and listening. The timetable has been influenced by the need to balance pupils' time in the elements of language, science, mathematics, environmental studies, expressive arts and moral/religious studies. IT provision in particular has grown very fast. It is now possible to timetable whole class groups to use laptops and have access to the Internet.

Testing pupils' ability has undergone transformation. In 1945 pupils were tested at the end of their primary schooling in arithmetic, English and verbal reasoning. The 'Qualifying Examination' [1] of P7 was used to 'stream' them for progression on to secondary school. Testing is now done at various stages throughout primary, according to national 5–14 guidelines, to ascertain levels of attainment. From P4 some classes (eg mathematics) are 'set' but most subjects are studied in classes arranged in several ability groups.

Mention must be made of primary pupils with special needs. They are now catered for very differently from the early days of the period under review. Then they might have attended Tyninghame school (until its closure in 1961) or struggled along in class. A few years ago East Lothian's inclusion policy led to the setting up of a support base for the North Berwick cluster of primary schools. Most of the pupils concerned spend the majority of their time in the classroom, with the help of a support-staff teacher or an auxiliary; the rest of their time is spent in the support base, where they receive individual help.

There was also the private sector. Miss Walker and Miss Rhind both ran private schools, which were joined together in the late 1940s. St Baldred's School, as it was called, was based in a house of the same name at the corner of Dirleton Avenue and Hamilton Road. Later Miss Rhind joined forces with Mrs Airs, who ran the school at Springfield in Fidra Road.

Carlekemp Priory School, run by the Benedictine Community at Fort Augustus, was another private school. An earlier Abbey preparatory school, St Andrew's in Canaan Lane, Edinburgh, had been evacuated to Fort Augustus during the war, when its buildings and grounds were taken over by the Royal Signal Corps. In September 1945 the school faced a predicament - the Canaan Lane building was still not available, and too many boys had been enrolled for Fort Augustus to accommodate. Lord Carmont's house in North Berwick presented the solution. Carlekemp Priory School opened on 9 October 1945. In 1977 Carlekemp closed its doors because it was no longer paying its way.

Education (cont)

Secondary

North Berwick's secondary pupils (12+ years) were taught in North Berwick High School in Grange Road; this had first come into use in September 1940, and was fully open from autumn 1941. In 1948 the school roll was 324; in 2000 it stood at 765.

Two major building phases extended accommodation at the high school. In 1960/61 a technical block, new science and art rooms, a homecraft flat, an extra domestic science room and a new gymnasium came into use. Growing numbers led in 1973 to the delivery of the first three mobile classrooms that mushroomed on the edges of school grounds until the late 1990s. From the 1970s the school and the PTA kept up pressure for new, purpose-built accommodation to replace these mobile units. This bore fruit in the late 1990s, with the addition of a new music suite, library, teaching block and a programme of refurbishment throughout the school.

In the post-war years special needs pupils aged 12+, stayed on in the primary school or were schooled at Tyninghame school *(see page 154)*. When the latter closed in 1961, a special class (ten pupils at the start) opened in the high school. Its pupils were mainly taught by a single teacher, Miss McNeil, but joined with their contemporaries for music, gym, etc. The special class closed in 1978, on Miss McNeil's retiral. This decision was taken because the intake had dropped to less than one pupil per year, and because modern education theory had moved against segregation. Instead, remedial support was provided, to individual pupils and within class groups. In 1985 Lothian region introduced a policy of co-operative teaching whereby learning support departments worked directly to support teachers in the delivery of courses to pupils with special needs. This was implemented in North Berwick High School in 1992. By 2000, special needs pupils were integrated within classrooms, with the help of classroom auxiliaries as well as specialist learning support teachers.

The demand for adult education has also had to be met. Evening classes were available for adults from the post-war years. Early courses were mainly work-related (commercial courses, technical/craft courses) or leisure-orientated (art, crafts, local history, conversation in modern languages). Certificate courses and, more recently, IT and personal development courses have been offered, both at the high school and the community centre.

For a few years after 1989 a small number of adults studied certificate courses within the classroom, alongside senior students. This has been overtaken by the availability of both day and evening classes run by East Lothian's Adult Education Programme, in North Berwick, at other centres through the county and at the East Lothian Centre for Lifelong Learning at Haddington. Another opportunity is the University of the Third Age; the East Lothian U3A was founded in April 1999. It is one of ten separate U3As in Scotland. Occasional lectures and meetings are held in North Berwick.

Changes

Parents now have greater involvement in the running of schools. In the past fifteen years PTAs and school boards have encouraged this.

Pupils' experience of school has been affected by other changes too. The school day, week and year have been modified. In 1945 school opened at 9am and closed at 4pm. Now the day starts and closes a little earlier, with shorter breaks. Pupils do not attend school on Friday afternoons (to facilitate staff in-service training). There is a full week's holiday in October.

Education (cont)

The large classes (perhaps as many as 40+) of the 1940s and 1950s no longer exist. A national teachers' contract of 1976 fixed maximum class sizes, according to school-stage and subject, at between 20 and 33.

In the 1950s two valuable additions to the education service appeared. From 1950 youth employment officers have worked with and advised pupils in the secondary school. Library provision was extended. The reorganized high school library was opened in 1951, to acclaim as a model of good practice. In 1979 the first school librarian was appointed to the school.

When considering more than half a century of education in the parish of North Berwick, it is clear that a number of key developments have made a particular impact over the years 1945 to 2000. Among these the raising of the school leaving age (twice) has had major consequences on the need for accommodation and on the design of the curriculum offered to senior pupils. Highers and Lowers, which were targets for only a minority of pupils in the 1940s and 1950s, have been replaced by a national examination system that includes a much larger proportion of young people. In the 1950s in North Berwick, S6 comprised a handful of students who in S5 had achieved sufficient certificate passes to qualify for university entrance. In 2000 the number staying on to S6 is approaching 100.

The impact of technology has been huge. In the 1940s and 1950s filmstrip projectors (later slide projectors) were the only technological aids, and radio schools programmes had to be taken 'live'. Now all classes have access to television and video. Contrast this with the situation in 1970 when the director of education and an architect visited the primary school to decide on the placing of a television set. Computers have had an even greater impact. Since 1988 courses and rooms have been dedicated to computer-based studies. Computers are key tools for staff, pupils and library, supporting study, research and production of materials. In 1986 SCAMP (Schools Computer Administration and Management Project) was introduced.

There is now greater uniformity in courses taught, both in the primary and secondary schools. Largely this has been the result of national legislation, the 5-14 Programme and new certificate examinations. There has been a corresponding decrease in schools' autonomy in designing their own teaching programmes.

Equality of opportunity for girls and boys is now the policy of East Lothian Council. This means, for example, that there are no longer separate entrances and play areas for boys and girls, nor are there gender-restrictions in subjects studied.

Here, ex-pupils share their memories of their school days

Primary

'… *The subjects covered included arithmetic, composition, spelling, dictation, history, geography, nature study, mental arithmetic, music, drawing and gym. Physical exercises took place in the gymnasium with games outdoors such as rounders in the playground in summer. Sports day was held at high school sports field. Grass was always newly cut and I would suffer hay fever.*

We had one or two teachers for each year plus one or two specialist teachers, eg PT, music. In primary 2 (1941-42) our teacher was a Miss Cameron who was strong on teaching arithmetic. She did this by using strings of beads in groups of 2, 5 and 10, which could be strung together in any number up to 1000. Another favourite was to do multiple addition and subtraction sums with all members of the class, taken in rotation to take one's turn. This meant one had to remember whether or not your preceding neighbour

Education (cont)

had any tens or units left over and when your time came you incorporated the appropriate number. This of course was all written up on the blackboard, and if you managed to get it wrong you were chastised, not with the tawse for six-seven year olds, but with a thick blue correcting pencil she marked jotters with, across the knuckles. I was not bullied: it was very rare.

The senior class was in the art room in the primary school, which had a magnificent view north over the town and the Firth of Forth, especially in the summer of 1947 when the US Atlantic Fleet lay offshore for about a week'.

P.E. Rooney - primary 1940s

'In Infant 1, reading was taught by a mixture of Look and Say and Phonic (sic) work using the Radiant Way Reading Scheme. In the infant department number work was taught with the help of counters (blue and red cardboard disks) and coloured beads which were threaded with wire.

In Primary 1 we were delighted to be taught 'real writing' (joined script) and in P2 we had ink writing lessons which were rather messy as the ink (from a well in the desk) was very watery and the pens which had scratchy nibs were difficult to hold as the metal nib attachment jabbed one's fingers.

From P3-5 we had five to six 'spelling words' to learn at home from the Schönell Word Lists and by P4 we regularly had dictation when the teacher dictated a short passage which we had to write down. The 'learnt' spelling words were also written (on dictation, usually daily). Spelling mistakes for the 'learnt' spelling words and the dictations had generally to be written out correctly three times underneath the work with the mistakes.

Much number work was done by rote learning, particularly the learning of multiplication tables and from P3-P5 each day had a short period of mental arithmetic.

In P4 an intelligence test was sat and in P5 we had the dreaded 'Qualie' – the qualifying exam, which consisted of three papers, English, arithmetic and another intelligence test. These tests were taken in March and the results were used for grading in Class I of the secondary school'.

Barbara Montgomery – North Berwick High School Primary Department, 1943-50

'Classrooms smelt of chalk, plasticine, and on wet days smelt of damp coats. On the walls were maps, pictures from educational magazines and some pupil-work. Windows tended to be set higher on the wall in primary school (an older building). We got $^1/3$ pint of milk at morning break, and took an apple or biscuit. Sometimes I took school dinner.

We studied arithmetic, reading, history, geography, drawing, nature study, music. On Friday afternoons we had drawing and stories were read. There was also sewing and knitting for girls. Music and PE were taught by specialists. In summer we went outside for nature study, to the Lodge grounds. We did exercises in the gym, and in summer we played rounders outside.

Teachers: Miss Watt, who first led me to see I could do well. Miss Ross – very firm discipline; I had the belt every day for a year (at the so-called 'wailing wall' - blackboard) for talking, but she made learning great fun and brought me on enormously by her encouragement. She could really motivate pupils. Mr Lonie who taught P7 was the only male teacher. Admin took up a lot of his time - we heard a lot about sailing round Canada!

At playtime I played endless games and varieties of 'tig'. Hide-and-seek and skipping were also popular.

I was bullied in primary school. I had long hair (plaits), and a brother and sister in my class waylaid me regularly on my way home and one jumped on my back while the other pulled my hair.

Education (cont)

Even though we were streamed before entry to high school we still kept up friendships formed in primary school. My experience of school was a very happy one'.

Margaret Costa - North Berwick High School Primary Department, 1945-53

'Maps and pictures on walls. Single desks and chairs in infant dept, from P4 desks and chairs were for two pupils. Ink wells and pens. Windows too high to look out. Stale smell. I enjoyed playtime. We played skipping and peevers, high-tig and low-tig, singing games, two balls against the walls, sometimes one ball against wall with two, three or four girls in a line singing Mrs Dunlop (sic) and jumping over the ball at end of song for other girl behind to catch it.

I was bullied in primary for a short time by a girl in my class who was much larger than myself. She sat beside me in class, would dip the silver top of the milk bottle in the inkwell and put it down my back. Would nip me or push me off the seat when the teacher wasn't looking. However, with a push from my gran telling me to stand up to her even if she was bigger than me, we had a real go at each other and ended up the best of friends'.

Anon - North Berwick Primary School, 1946-53

'I remember the smell of primary school as old dusty wooden floors. The classrooms were furnished with old oak desks. The walls were sometimes covered in art works but mostly it was a barren type of room and a bit dingy. I always wore school uniform, and always walked to school.

In Primary 6 I had a Mr Johnston. He used to have us run a parliament and we had a debate on a Friday against an opposing team. I always remember setting a question to our top classmate and he couldn't answer it. I thought, well lady you really aren't as stupid as you think. I did not enjoy primary school and felt that teachers didn't encourage us enough. I think the teachers thought I was a dimwit. I don't think I was bullied and I would have retaliated if I had been. I was a wild child but I don't remember bullying anyone'.

Bernice Graham, nee Woodburn, primary 1953-57

'The old primary was a law unto itself. In torrential rain it closed at one. If it snowed, playtime could last 40 minutes to let us all go round to the back for snowballing and making slides. In class we sat at wooden double desks. Walking up in twos to the high school to go to the library or see a play was a highlight. Corporal punishment was administered using the tawse. In Primary 4, I was once belted for reading "Bruce and Wallace" instead of "Wallace and Bruce". However, fortunately, in Primaries 5, 6 and 7 I had a new young teacher, Miss Draffan, and an older lady, Miss Walker, and I loved school.

In earlier classes I had been glad to be able to do the work, as life had been hard for those who could not keep up. They were given rows and at times ridiculed. Also there had seemed to be a less caring attitude towards poorer children. Childhood here wasn't all tennis lessons, horse riding, Aertex shirts and Boots' library tickets.

Today, 50 years on, one of the things most evocative of my primary school days is hearing the Radio 4 United Kingdom Theme if I'm ever awake at 5.30am, that is. We must have learned the words of its every song from "Early One Morning" to "Rule Britannia". They encapsulate the feel of those times in such a way that I can almost smell the wood and chalk dust'.

Anne Cowan – primary in the 1950s

'I remember all classrooms in the primary school had very high windows with frosted glass on the lower panes – impossible to see outside. School uniform was a pinafore dress – navy, shirt, cardigan and

Education (cont)

red/black striped tie – in winter navy blue nap coat. I took my own snack for 'playtimes', and came home every day for lunch. I walked to and from school.

I have very little recollection of subjects taught! We had one teacher for each year: a two-stream school. I specifically remember P2 teacher physically rubbing her knuckles over my cheeks when I made a mistake with oral maths!

Sports days were a big event with both primary and secondary schools combining events in high school playing field. I remember skipping/chanting games and 'tig'. No recollections of any bullying'.
Jacqueline Dillon, primary 1955-60

'My first day at primary school still sticks firmly in my mind almost 42 years after the day in question. Unlike our children who have had the benefit of playgroup and nursery school, I was not really prepared (at the age of five) for being separated from my Mum and Dad and I well remember being in floods of tears for most of my first day at school. My teacher (Mrs Kerr) tried to console me by getting me to use a toy telephone but my memory suggests that her efforts failed. I did know some of the other children in my class as they lived near to our house but some of them had been attending Dunedin (a private nursery on Fidra Road) and they seemed to be much more confident than I was. Happily, those initial apprehensions soon passed and I went on to enjoy my seven years there.

The primary school was situated at that time in what is now the community centre but which had previously been used (in my father's time at school) as the high school. In many ways I don't think the building had changed much since Dad went there in the 1930s and indeed today, it is still possible to see what the building was like with its tiled walls in several parts.

In the playground at the front, there were a couple of concrete air raid shelters, which had presumably been used during world war two. While these were 'blocked off', it was possible to get in and to play in the narrow corridors. These were eventually demolished (possibly to make way for the first mobile classrooms which I believe appeared in about 1966).

The playground also had a boys' shed and a girls' shed where we could shelter during inclement weather. I have no recollection of ever being allowed to stay in at playtime when the weather was bad.

Each morning we were provided with a glass bottle [of milk], which was usually warm and not very palatable. I believe, however, that we were expected to drink it. The smell left by the dregs of milk, slowly going off in the bottle in a crate in a corner of the classroom, lingered on.

Travel to school was only ever by foot, as my parents did not own a car until I was well into secondary school. The walk was not too far although the journey had to be done four times each day as I never had a school dinner during my entire time at school. School dinners in those days were generally only taken by those who stayed in the country and came to school by bus and also the children from the Dr Barnardo's home in the town (of whom there were a number in my class throughout primary school).

Most of the desks which I remember were large, quite old, wooden affairs with fixed seats on a metal frame. These desks also had ink wells. I recall a comical occasion one day when one of the clowns in the class (other than me) drank ink from his ink well. We all thought that this was hilarious.

I recall that several teachers operated a type of points or rewards system which were wonderful incentives to work hard. Rewards typically included sweets. Physical exercise was not terribly frequent and was usually led by a visiting gym teacher who would take the class for about 30 minutes or so. The exercise usually involved hula hoops, benches and climbing ropes.

In my years at primary school I had seven teachers (one a year) and most of them had taught at the school for many years. Almost all were still there when I moved on to the high school. Only one of my *teachers was male (in Primary 7) and I believe that there were never more than two male teachers in the school at any time during these years. There were two classes for each of the years (Primary 1A, 1B, 2A, 2B and so on)'.*

Robert D. Burgon, North Berwick Primary School, 1960-67

Secondary

'In first year there were four graded classes A, B, C, D, the more able pupils being in 1A and studying French and Latin. The B class were taught French, while the C and D classes were given a basic education with the boys also being taught woodwork and technical subjects and the girls were taught domestic science – cooking, sewing and laundry.

At the end of third year, leaving certificates were presented to all pupils as they could legally leave school at age 15. Those of us who were continuing our studies had to choose at the end of third year which subjects we were going to take for the higher leaving certificate, commonly called 'The Highers'. These exams were sat in March and in June the headmaster called the fifth year to their form room and read out the results to the candidates. The actual certificate with the results was sent out later'.

Barbara Montgomery, North Berwick High School, 1950-55

'Classrooms – all wood panelled to a height of approximately 1200mm, as were the corridors. The plastered walls above were generally painted a mustardy colour. All had blackboards. The walls only had the odd notice pinned up but the geography room had the scroll type maps of the UK and the world hanging on the walls.

Science labs – all had benches with lab sinks with standing wastes. Bunsen burners were attached to the gas outlets. Stools were provided – not very comfortable. Fume cupboards were present. Small brass scales sat on the bench next the windows. The rear wall had glass-fronted cupboards containing bottles of chemicals, etc, even 100% proof spirit (tasted by one 5th year pupil).

Windows – you could generally see out of them, the most interesting view being over the adjacent field when the bull was let loose among the cows.

School wear – school uniform was worn every day consisting of long grey flannels, grey shirt, school tie, grey pullover in winter, black blazer and black shoes or boots.

Refreshment – I recollect that milk was provided ($^{1}/3$ pint bottles). I suffered school meals for I think a year then carried sandwiches. The food provided for school meals was generally pretty awful – Irish stew where the grease floated on top of the container several inches thick, watery mince with greyish mashed potatoes, bricks, ie shortbread with chocolate covering (you almost needed a hammer and chisel to break it into pieces) with lumpy custard, and other 'delights'. I think the pigs did well considering the amount of waste scrapped into the bin.

During the year there were a number of special events, the main ones being the leisure work exhibition and the Xmas dance; country dancing was taught in preparation for the Xmas dance

The exhibition took place not long before the summer holidays. Pupils displayed items they had made, painted, knitted, etc. in their leisure hours throughout the year. The items were judged and points awarded to your house (either Law, Glen or Craig).

Each year a painting was awarded to the house gaining the most points from the leisure exhibition, from inter-house rugby, hockey, cricket, netball, etc. matches and from sports day events. Each picture was hung in the school corridors with a little brass plaque attached inscribed with the year and winning house.

Education (cont)

There was an annual cricket match and hockey match against the staff each year. It gave the boys a chance to bowl body-liners at the members of staff you did not like and a chance for the girls to whack them with their hockey sticks. Sometimes, of course, the tables were turned.

Other memories that come to mind are pranks pupils got up to on their last day at school.

Two involved the music teacher's car, an Austin 7 if I remember correctly. One year it was lifted up the steps and deposited in the entrance vestibule of the school and another year taken to the far side of the playing fields where it was covered in grass cuttings from the cricket square etc.

I personally was involved in a prank on my last day at school. During the staff meeting (we always thought they extended the playtime to have a glass of sherry) four or five of us sneaked into the science room and concocted a stink bomb. This was then hidden behind a ventilator in the ladies staffroom. Unfortunately, unknown to us, we were spied by the janitor and later summoned before the head and given a lecture and told how we should act as responsible people now we were going out into the big wide world.

After school hours some of the teachers gave up their time to hold leisure activities for pupils who wished to attend. You could take part in drama, photography, etc, and also various sports activities'.
James Walker, North Berwick High School, 1952-58

'I think what I remember from primary and secondary was the discipline. The belt was used in both schools – sometimes the whole class would get it if there was talking when a visitor came into the room, sometimes for homework that wasn't done in time.

In secondary we went for a trip down the Clyde. We got an early train from North Berwick to Glasgow. Walked from the station to the river Clyde where we boarded the ship "The Duchess of Hamilton". We sailed down through the dockyards (John Brown was only one of many) and into the Firth of Clyde to Rothesay, round the Kyles of Bute, having both lunch and tea on board, then returning in the train in the evening. A most enjoyable day was had by all, teachers and pupils alike'.
Anon - North Berwick High School, 1953-1956

'I walked to school. Some pupils came by school bus; Drem children came by train and got out a few minutes early (we all envied them for that!) I can't recall any coming by car though some cycled.

Teachers: Hector Macpherson was very neat and particular in his habits, but he was a most caring and encouraging teacher. He had excellent relationship with pupils. He ran the library. Douglas Stenhouse was an absolutely inspirational teacher of English and history. John Marshall (rector) and Wallace Monaghan (depute) worked hard to ensure a liberal education was experienced as well as the first-rate delivery of their own subjects. Miss Mackenzie made Latin fascinating. I never heard her raise her voice to a pupil, and none thought of being cheeky to her. Bill Brown - his Latin classes (S6) were extraordinary. Music, philosophy were as much in the agenda as Ovid. I was walked round the playing field because he believed Cicero should be declaimed out of doors. My confidence in myself grew a great deal from the level of discussion he encouraged.'
Margaret Costa - North Berwick High School, 1953-58

'At High School, the smells I remember were of young girls trying out different perfumes. At high school PT was usually a double and single period. In the double we would play hockey or badminton. In June we had track sports; I liked sport at school.

I sang in the choir at school and remember Miss McIntyre taking us to the Usher Hall and we won first place. I also liked taking part in gymnastic events'.
Bernice Graham, nee Woodburn, secondary 1958-64

Education (cont)

North Berwick High School, March, 1955. Pupils studying in the library. (Margaret Costa)

Pupils in class at North Berwick High School, 1995 (Margaret Costa)

Education (cont)

'School uniform – still 'school uniform' but always tried to interpret this in a fashionable way. I particularly remember art and dress and design teachers – smaller classes and practical. I enjoyed the camaraderie – especially enjoyed 6th year at secondary when I was made a prefect. I was part of the secondary school drama group – good memories of putting on plays in school hall'.
Jacqueline Dillon, secondary, 1961-68

'I remember that the biology lab always smelt funny, when I was about 14 or 15 and taking my standard grades. The smell in the lab came from the skulls and bones of animals on the rack down the left hand wall as you walked in. The smell gave me migraine attacks.

When I was twelve, I started at North Berwick High School. My parents bought me a school uniform – when I got to school I discovered that hardly anyone else except the 'geeks' were wearing blazers. I got a severe 'slagging off', verging on bullying, for wearing a blazer. I had many arguments with my parents about refusing to wear it. They didn't understand that I badly wanted to fit in and be invisible.

When she was old enough my sister joined me in the walk from home to school. We lived in May Terrace. To get to school we had to walk through the railway station, past the fire station, up Trainer's Brae (surrounded by fields of cows and sheep at that time) with an endless stream of other kids and then we would come out at the playing fields and the school. We only got a lift in the car if we were horribly late, but that hardly ever happened. Mum was strict about waking us and sent us to school even if we felt unwell. She wasn't mean, she just didn't encourage us to 'skive' off school.

The mobiles that we were taught in were as cold as ice in winter (we had to keep on our coats) and like a furnace in the summer. I loved it there despite the conditions.

I didn't realise how hard the teachers worked until I had left. I was quite fond of some and despised others.

I did not enjoy my school days. There were good times but I spent most of my teenage years feeling paranoid, unpopular and terrified. I don't think I had such a bad time really – there were just some injustices. I didn't feel listened to by teachers sometimes and I made stupid mistakes because I was young. I wouldn't go back!

The most exciting part of high school was the school dances. Every year around November in PE instead of normal sport, we would learn Scottish country dancing for the school dance at the end of term. This was very nerve-racking and exciting at the same time. All the girls would line up one side of the hall and all the boys along the other side when the games teacher told us we had to pick each other to dance. Most of the time the boys had to do this. Sometimes it was ladies' choice. It was always very humiliating for both sides. Everyone was dressed to the nines for the school dance and sometimes romance blossomed but most of the time we just tormented each other; I was once dropped on the floor in my new dress!'.
Gillian E. Lindsay, North Berwick High School, 1988-94

Muriel N. Shiel muses on changes – she was a high school pupil (1939-45) and then teacher (primary 1955-90) in North Berwick
'At the high school the majority of the girls wore blazers, white blouses and gym costumes or navy skirts. The boys wore blazers, white or grey shirts and grey trousers. Many of the boys wore short, grey trousers up till 3rd or 4th year.

I did not enjoy primary school at all but the high school was heaven by comparison. We were streamed and in small classes therefore we could assimilate appropriate knowledge at an appropriate rate.

There was also very little peer pressure at school as, quite simply, there were no designer brands. Home discipline was excellent. If one misbehaved at school then one received a second helping of punishment at home. Very few parents ever set foot in school to complain about their children's punishment.

Also up till decimalisation (1971), long multiplication and division of money, weight, measurement and capacity were a nightmare. If you made a mistake in the farthings of a long multiplication of money that was it! Also just imagine nine year olds being expected to cope with long multiplication of weight when you had to divide your totals by the then 14. My schooldays were not the happiest days of my life as my experience of primary instilled a fear of punishment for making unintentional mistakes. However I have very happy memories of my years at the high school'.

Transport

In 2000, North Berwick was served by an hourly train service to and from Edinburgh. However, the service was nearly lost when in 1963, the 'destruction king' of British Railways, the infamous Dr Beeching, placed a closure order on our branch line from Drem (Tindall, F.P. 1998 p272, Hajducki, A. 1992 pp140-143). Fortunately, three commuters and a retired British Rail employee formed a committee and working very closely with North Berwick Town Council placed an appeal before the Transport Users' Consultative Committee. Their decision, after a public hearing in the Pavilion at which the town council evidence proved critical, was to retain the line, albeit with a reduced service of three trains per day either way. This proved inadequate for many commuters who had to resort to the much slower and less comfortable bus service. Happily, the train service is now much improved and is used extensively by commuters, whose numbers have increasingly swollen thanks to a buoyant jobs' market in Edinburgh and the supply of new housing in North Berwick. However, while these trains do not now bring in hordes of summer visitors of the 'stay-for-a-fortnight' variety they deliver a goodly number of day visitors.

Once in the town, the volume of traffic causes severe problems, especially during the summer. The one-way traffic system in the High Street / Forth Street began as long ago as August 1934, initially during the summer months, and was then extended to apply all year round. The first traffic warden in North Berwick was appointed in 1974.

Police

The laws relating to *bona fide* travellers affected social life in the 1940s; it was an offence to drink alcohol in the area in which you resided on a Sunday, so to overcome this problem the would-be drinkers had to travel a distance of at least three miles to licensed premises in order to get a drink. A visitors' book for that purpose was by law, kept on the premises for all travellers to enter their names and addresses and it was regularly checked by the local police. It was an offence under the Licensing (Scotland) Act if this law was contravened.

The regular mode of transport for the police at that time in North Berwick was pedal cycles and public transport - ie buses. The police were entitled to travel free whilst in uniform. By the 1950s, the force was becoming mechanised and the local police took delivery of a Norton 500cc motorcycle, which meant that those officers not in possession of a motorcycle licence had to take a test.

North Berwick then progressed to a mini van, then the first of the Morris 1000s and so on. These vehicles are known as pandas due to the two-tone blue and white colour. The public in

Police (cont)

the 1980s were becoming concerned about the lack of police officers patrolling the streets and in 1984, the pedal cycles were re-introduced. This allowed an officer to patrol a larger area in the burgh, while a panda could cover the outlying district. The total beat area in the North Berwick section is approximately 23,000 acres, stretching to Gosford (near Longniddry) on the west, to Ballencrieff on the south and Whitekirk on the east, and bounded by the Firth of Forth on the north.

The average strength of North Berwick police was approximately twelve officers with at least two being on duty at any one time. There were also two civilian typists who worked either a day shift or back shift. Three working shifts provided the manpower, ie day shift (6am-2pm), back shift (2pm-10pm) and night shift (10pm-6am), and of course there were always two officers on two days off per week. The two sergeants also worked shifts, ie 9am-5pm and 5pm-1am.

As North Berwick police station was badly in need of refurbishment at that time, it was decided to close the station while work was in progress for approximately six months. Temporary accommodation was acquired at 26 Dunbar Road at the unoccupied premises of the East Lothian Co-operative Society (now a dwelling house). The policing certainly improved thereafter with the introduction of more reliable and efficient communications. With a new radio mast on the roof of the police station, personal radio reception was greatly improved.

There were originally four cells in the station, and one was made into an interview room, one a storeroom and two left for prisoners. Later the community constable was introduced. He, or she, was (and remains) a very high profile officer whose duties include visiting schools, giving talks to various organisations, attending council meetings etc.

Until the 1970s a regular job for the police was to visit the local abattoir to ensure that the slaughtering of animals was done in a humane manner. A register of animals for slaughter also had to be examined. The abattoir was where the Safeway supermarket is now situated.

Another unusual job for the county police was to visit farms in the area and supervise the dipping of sheep and again to check registers. If there was a suspected outbreak of any notifiable disease on any farm, ie anthrax, swine fever, foot and mouth etc then the police were responsible for the issuing of the appropriate forms governing the movement of livestock and prohibiting entry to premises.

In the 1940s the crime rate was not so high as it is today and any crimes were usually committed by locals. The crime pattern has changed dramatically in the past few years mainly due to the travelling criminals. Highly mobile, they usually target holiday resorts, similar to North Berwick, where even families and gangs would operate. It has been known for organised criminals to travel from the Newcastle area and further afield to commit crime in the burgh. The most frequent crime carried out regularly, summer and winter, is theft of golf clubs and equipment usually from unattended parked cars. As North Berwick area is a Mecca for golfers with two courses in the burgh and a further 15 in the county there is ample opportunity to steal from the careless golfer.

Now that supermarkets are in most towns a large percentage of crime is by shoplifting.

Another type of theft, OLP (Opening Lockfast Places) occurs regularly in the summer when visitors' cars are broken into and articles, which are visible, ie handbags stolen. Intruder alarms are now being fitted as standard to new houses and similarly older houses in the burgh have been updated, which has caused a drop in the number of housebreakings.

116

One main factor is the shortage of police manpower. This is often due to long-term sickness, officers attending court, or courses, or for other reasons. This often means that there is only one police constable on duty. Then, if available, a constable from either Dunbar or Haddington will assist, likewise it is quite common for a sergeant in North Berwick to be responsible for Dunbar and Haddington, during his tour of duty. As each station is approximately ten miles apart then at least 30 miles is covered each shift. At weekends, usually the busiest, the two-man night shift is supported by the back shift officers, working two hours overtime, until 1am.

The only other method of increasing the station strength is by the use of special constables, but this is not always practical. The use of drugs in the burgh is on the increase, and cannabis is easily obtained, and the most widely used. Most drugs change hands in local public houses. The drug squad based in Dalkeith regularly attends and visits licensed premises.

The consumption of alcohol by the under age group is very much on the increase, and youngsters can be seen drinking in public parks and on the beach, most weekends. One of the reasons is that children have far more money to spend. The situation has got out of hand, so much so that the council is preparing a byelaw prohibiting drinking alcohol in public places at weekends.

Until a few years ago the station was constantly manned during the day shift and back shift but this was usually a waste of manpower. The new system operates much more efficiently, for instance if a member of the public telephones the unmanned station, the call is automatically transferred to divisional headquarters at Dalkeith. The officer or clerkess receiving the call immediately contacts the local officer by means of personal radio and the matter is attended to. Similarly, if someone calling at the station finds it closed, then a free public police telephone situated outside the office can be used to the same effect.

Uniforms and equipment worn by the police have changed over the years. In the 1940s a basic uniform was issued along with a notebook, whistle and baton. Nowadays, the police officer has a navy blue jersey with the police logo, replacing the tunic, and the equipment now includes notebook, handcuffs, personal radio, larger baton and CS spray (no whistle!)

Fire Service

The war years saw a radical change in fire fighting and the structure of the new fire service which would change from the National Fire Service (NFS) to regional brigades throughout the country.

A strict but cohesive regime existed after the war, usually of 48 hours on and 24 hours off duty. There was and still is a 'family' bond within modern shift systems; this is essential for a working emergency team to operate efficiently and successfully.

Fire appliances have evolved over the 50 years, for the better of course, so have the methods of tackling fires, the equipment used and uniforms as well, all now oriented towards safety and protection.

The fire station was what is now the Bass Rock Garage outdoor showroom. This was once the site of the old gas works, then a pump house was built, which eventually housed two fire engines until a new station was built on the former railway shunting yard adjacent to the rail station. This was formally opened on 18 March 1982 and is a purpose-built operational fire station with two engine bays, a muster room, a workroom and male & female wash facilities and also a large lecture room.

Fire Service (cont)

North Berwick has at present one female firefighter but has seen four pass through the station who have left because of other commitments, and one female left to enter the full-time service. She now serves at the busy Newcraighall fire station. There are now 15 retained fire fighters at North Berwick that form an efficient team trained to deal with everything from a litter bin fire to major structure fires or road accidents or rescue work at height.

HM Coastguard

The long history of the coastguard service in North Berwick continued through the war years when coastguard duties multiplied and included coast patrols, reporting of mines and explosive objects, possible landings of German agents etc.

In 1952 it was considered unnecessary to maintain a station and the station was closed. The station living quarters were a row of stone-built, coastguard houses between School Road and Balfour Street. Here, too, was the stone-built 'rocket house' where the cart and breeches-buoy equipment was kept.

North Berwick remained without a coastguard station until 1969 when it re-opened as an 'auxiliary' station only. Some of its early members had served in the 'rocket' crew.

From fairly primitive beginnings (telephone, binoculars and little else) the station has progressively been upgraded. A succession of vehicles from Hillman Imps to Landrovers has extended the station coverage eastwards as far as the river Tyne, and west to Port Seton. Vehicles are fully equipped with VHF radio, search equipment, mobile searchlights, cliff rescue gear, etc.

It was fitting that, when vehicles arrived, the station moved away from the look-out back to the old 'rocket brigade' house. The look-out is now used by East Lothian Yacht Club for racing control. It is also very fitting that frequently, when lifeboat crew retire from duty, they transfer over to coastguard, ensuring that their skills continue to be utilised.

HM Coastguard acts as search and rescue co-ordinators. Coastguard teams investigate 999 reports and report to Forth MRSC who decide the appropriate response, activate launches of boats, or search teams for shore work, and control the rescue procedures. Forth MRSC is manned 24 hours a day, and monitors VHF channels 16 and 67.

Lifeboat

The first lifeboat station operated from 1860 until 1926 when it was closed. In 1967 it was necessary to re-open the station to deal with the growing number of incidents involving sailing dinghies, motor boats, air-beds etc. An inflatable inshore lifeboat was provided (one of four sponsored by the Blue Peter TV programme) and housed in the old granary until 1990. The R.N.L.I. then re-acquired the original boathouse (the Victoria Cafe) including additional land, which enabled a major upgrade to be undertaken in 1997 to house the lifeboat and provide a well equipped and modern station. The present lifeboat is the fourth generation and all have been paid for by Blue Peter. This is manned by a crew of three volunteers but at least 15 volunteers are required to ensure it can be called out whenever required. The average launch time is six minutes from the time the crew is alerted by ringing their electronic pagers.

Helicopters have increasingly taken over rescue work in recent years but they are not always available and at best it takes 40 minutes for a helicopter to reach the area from Northumberland. The inshore lifeboat can operate in poor visibility and go into shallow water areas more easily

Lifeboat (cont)

North Berwick harbour on Life Boat Day, 1950s. East Lothian Yacht Club is still based in the building in the middle of the picture but this has been refurbished, as have the other harbour buildings. The Seabird Centre offices and Education Centre are now housed in the building on the left. (A&J Gordon)

than a conventional lifeboat. Equipment carried includes a navigation system, night-vision scope and oxygen to give to divers if they have had problems with the 'bends'. Since 1967 there have been 262 launches with 108 lives saved and many others given assistance.

Leisure (*see also* Economy)

With North Berwick's dual role as a residential centre and tourist attraction, both groups were attracted to many of the leisure services. Local interests were looked after in the winter by numerous clubs and associations with the still popular scouts and guides catering for the youngsters. Entertainment of a different kind was provided by the North Berwick & District Operatic Society that produced a variety of musicals such as *The Desert Song, Carousel* and *South Pacific* to name but three. The North Berwick Drama Circle began in 1976 as the St Andrew's Drama Circle; their two shows a year play to full houses, and make a lot of money for charity. There is a core of some 15-20 members. Lady Skrene's St Andrew's Drama Club, with Roberta Greig as producer, ran between 1956-65.

The present North Berwick Pipe Band was formed in 1957. Its immediate predecessor - the scout band - had run from 1950-c54, having itself been just another in a long tradition of bands in the town, dating back to the 19th century. The new band was built around the membership of the scout band, using their equipment and adopting the McKenzie (Seaforth) tartan. Between 1967 and 1974, the band organised a successful annual contest in the town; 54 bands competed in the final contest. Since 1995, with annual British Energy sponsorship, the North Berwick Highland Games Association has organised a pipe band contest, in which the band participates.

Leisure (cont)

North Berwick outdoor swimming pool closed in 1998 and has been filled in. The Pavilion was demolished in 1997. The harbour buildings beyond are still intact, as is the tiny black and white half-timbered building in the middle distance. This is the Lifeboat House on the corner of Melbourne Road. (A&J Gordon)

The beaches and open-air swimming pool were very popular as were, needless to say, the east and west golf courses.

Of the numerous facilities on offer, a few stand out.

The outdoor swimming pool next to the harbour was always tremendously popular with numerous events during the day and the evening including galas and celebrities to attract people. Huge crowds would attend these events and the end of season party in September included a big firework display. The pool was allegedly heated but swimming could still be a chilly experience! In winter, north-east gales used to sweep waves across the pool, which acted as a kind of safety valve protecting the rest of the harbour area. The pool was just short of its centenary when it was closed in 1998 despite a vigorous local campaign to save it; the council was blamed for neglecting the pool until they claimed it was uneconomic to restore it.

'The pool lay for some years in what could only be described as a filthy pond filled with green stagnant water; it was a disgrace in a tourist town'.
Anne Cowie

For many years the centre of North Berwick's social life – for both locals and visitors – was the Pavilion at the harbour (built 1930). The Pavilion had many uses, with regular dances all year round; in the 1950s, 1960s, and 1970s with live bands on stage it was packed with dancers (although troublemakers from elsewhere forced the ending of the Saturday dances).

'In the 1960s and 1970s, Jim Johnston and his band played the Pavilion – Scottish country dance music… The Saturday night disco and dance with a live band – there was no drink, so we were in the pub until ten, then went to the dance; they were well attended, especially after ten! The age group was about 16-22 ish. I think the last bus out was about twenty to midnight – to Haddington and along the coast'.
Robert Gray

Leisure (cont)

Public meetings were held here with, perhaps, the most popular being the annual ratepayers meeting when the local population had the chance to verbally criticise the council or air complaints such as the length of the council housing list or one's position on it.

The Pavilion had become derelict and was vandalised for several years prior to the eventual decision to demolish it; consideration was given in 1996 to its possible use as a seabird centre but this was considered to be too expensive and so the treasured building which had become an eyesore was demolished in 1997 (despite the protests). This left the town with no hall capable of hosting a meeting of any decent numbers of townsfolk.

'Like many other traditional Scottish coastal resorts North Berwick lost much of its tourist business in the 1970s and 1980s. By the late 1980s this had affected the former busy High Street with 20 shops lying empty. Even the picturesque harbour area was blighted with its old outdoor swimming pool and harbour Pavilion both in need of repair and a sad reminder of happier days'
Bill Gardner

The harbour has not changed much over the period but its use has altered a little. Until the 1960s, pilot cutters used North Berwick as a base in suitable weather conditions when waiting for ships to pilot up the Forth. The harbour has been principally used for pleasure craft over the period but yachts and sailing dinghies have become larger and are not made of wood as they all were until the 1950s. The harbour is now completely full of small boats with a lengthy waiting list.

The granary (the large building by the harbour) was converted into flats in the 1960s. Before that it was a fishermen's store as well as being used for storing the rowing boats, which were hired out to visitors in considerable numbers up to the 1950s when safety regulations brought that to an end. The outdoor swimming pool is now filled in and the space used for storing dinghies and as a diver's preparation area.

The yacht club started in 1928 and has been based in the same building by the harbour ever since – and owned by the club since 1995. Its membership has grown steadily over the period and is now 275, mainly young people but including all ages. Sailing is mostly in dinghies with relatively few larger boats. After the war, boats of all sizes would compete with each other in races but now races are restricted to the specific classes. The club runs a training scheme leading to the RYA certificate.

Other water-based activities that have become popular in recent years are canoeing, windsurfing and diving.

Sports centre

Prior to the formation of the National Health Service, a town fete was held each year (on Cow's Green, East Links) to raise funds for the Edinburgh Royal Infirmary. In the 1950s and 1960s, the fund raising continued and it was decided by a sub-committee of the traders' association (later constituted as the North Berwick and District Community Association) to finance a worthwhile project.

The decision was to build a sports centre. Limited by the funds available, the design was based on use of a prefabricated grain barn with an attached squash court. Princess Margaret opened it in 1971. In 1977 the building was sold to East Lothian District Council who extended the facility. In May 1996, after a £2.6 million refurbishment programme, sporting a new swimming pool, a health suite and a cafe, it was opened to the public.

Leisure (cont)

Other sports too were popular, although support varied over the period; in 1952, the North Berwick Rugby Club was established and it attracted many youngsters new to the sport. The Bass Rock Football Club was also going through a successful period in the Lothian's Amateur League.

Anne Cowan recalls growing up in the 1950s

' *We were free to roam right to the edges of the town, up the Glen, down Trainers Brae, along the beaches and all round the harbour and rocks. You went out with your pals and came back at meal times. Five shillings bought a season ticket for the outdoor pool, which was the most wonderful place to play. A car on the Law Brae was a rarity. We could play ball diagonally across the road on the way to school.*

Later, Miss Middleton's teenage dancing class in the Hope Rooms was popular and the dancing, three nights weekly at the Pavilion, packed them in. The trades holidays and Glasgow Fair brought fresh talent to these local hops. Late buses left shortly before midnight to take revellers to outlying farms and villages'.

And Alastair McKay recalls North Berwick in the 1970s

'When the sports centre opened on 8 June 1971, I was there without a flag to see Princess Margaret plant a tree. I overheard someone describe the building as a "white elephant" which was strange, but now seems like a literal description of the architecture. In 1972, Arnold Palmer and Tony Jacklin helicoptered in to play the 15th hole on the West links. The Open was at Muirfield that year, followed by the Ryder Cup. I watched both tournaments through a cardboard periscope. …

For 224 days, the local MP was a Conservative. In the two elections of 1974, Michael Ancram won, then lost East Lothian and Berwickshire to John Mackintosh. The seat was so important that News at Ten filmed Ted Heath speaking at the Harbour Pavilion.'
Alastair McKay

Economy – Tourism
During the earlier part of the period, this played a major role in North Berwick life

'In the early years, many competitions were organised by the town council on the golf courses, on the beaches where children built all manner of things in sand competitions, in the yacht pond where model boats were judged and raced and in the pool where there were regular galas. The putting courses were kept in top class condition and were arguably the finest in Scotland thanks to the efforts of two burgh course greenkeepers transferred one to each green for the summer from their usual duties.'
Anne Cowie

The previous statistical account covered the period in North Berwick which saw the end of the London society annual relocation to North Berwick, but the large mansion houses which they had built to the east and west of the town remained more or less intact until the 1970s.

The immediate post-war period, say from 1950-65, saw North Berwick as the annual holiday Mecca for the city dwellers of Edinburgh and Glasgow. The first two weeks would find the town full of Edinburgh trades holidaymakers and the second two weeks their counterparts enjoying the Glasgow Fair. In 1953 there were 39 hotels and boarding houses providing full board, three meals per day interspersed with the healthy pursuits of golf, walking and bathing in the sea or outdoor unheated swimming pool. 3000 would attend a children's swimming gala and 700 would pack into a Saturday night dance in the harbour Pavilion. So many passengers

Economy – Tourism (cont)

*Royal Hotel,
North Berwick, 1949,
demolished in 2000.
(Valentine & Sons Ltd.)*

thronged the outbound trains at the end of Edinburgh and Glasgow holiday that it took two steam locomotives to pull them up the incline to the gasworks.

The landlady played a pivotal role in the tourist industry; here Douglas Seaton summarises his interview with Mrs S. Skwara, formerly Miss Young, proprietor of Fairhaven, 20 Melbourne Road, for 53 years.

In the 1950s, the summer season in North Berwick lasted from late May until September, and the guesthouse landlady with her welcoming smile, attention to detail, and friendly manner was an integral part of the success the town experienced during its heyday as a holiday resort.

The landlady was part of a team, normally supported by her family, working from 6am until midnight during the season. The elderly visitors arrived in June to enjoy the peace and quiet, before the Edinburgh trades fortnight in July. By the time the Glasgow accents could be heard during the second half of July, the summer season was in full swing. August was the period when the factory workers from Paisley arrived, and the English school holidays began.

In the 1950s, full board was the standard fare, which included breakfast, lunch, 'Scottish' high tea, and supper. The guests stayed for a week or a fortnight and the majority booked family rooms. The glossy brochures enticed the visitors with slogans such as 'H&C basins in every bedroom'. It worked, they came in their thousands from all over Britain.

The landlady's day started at 6am in Brodie's bakehouse situated in the courtyard through the close at 13, High Street. There, the freshly made rolls and bread, still warm from the ovens were collected. On the way home she would pass the horse and cart from the Bass Rock Dairy delivering milk with an inch of cream on top, and the freshly laid eggs from the Heugh Farm.

In the days before frozen vegetables, the meals had to be freshly prepared, including homemade soup, pastries and plenty of apple pie for the guests to have a second helping. All the provisions were supplied daily from the local butcher, fishmonger and greengrocer, delivered by a message boy on his bike. Sometimes the menu was hastily altered as produce was unavailable, but the landlady was accustomed to shortages following years of rationing. On Friday fish was available for those with a particular religious persuasion, and the bacon was discreetly removed from the breakfast plate. The guesthouse linen was sent

Economy – Tourism (cont)

to the laundry in Dunbar Road, and returned the following day. During the busy part of the season, the laundry helped out by offering a three times weekly service.

In the evening the guests would gather on the wall in Melbourne Road enjoying the last of the day's sun, as they waited for the sound of the gong from their respective guesthouses. The children all wanted to strike the gong, and jelly and ice cream was their favourite.

With fewer motor vehicles around, the children could safely cross the road to the beach. The activities organised for them included sand castle and model yachting competitions, and swimming galas in the outdoor pool. The Seaside Mission encamped on the beach opposite the Victoria Cafe was always a good sing-a-long, and fishing off the harbour entrance for a 'podlie' or two, filled an afternoon. Few guesthouses had a television, and the families enjoyed the twice-nightly pierrots' variety show at the harbour Pavilion. Mr. Halkett's bus trips were popular when granny stole 'forty winks' travelling round the countryside. No holiday was complete without a sail round the islands in one of David Tweedie's boats, or hiring a rowing boat in the West Bay from Mr Pearson. With the putting greens, children's golf course and tennis courts, there was plenty to keep everyone occupied, and on a rainy day the cinema opened especially for the visitors.

During the 1950s, the guests were mainly working-class families from all corners of Great Britain. Later the number of families visiting from Europe, America and Canada increased. A family from the Rockies arrived in North Berwick and, having never seen the sea before, was not convinced when told by the landlady that the sea rises and falls with the tide. They were given the room with a balcony overlooking the beach, and the family stayed up all night just watching the sea ebb and flow.

The story of the German couple that booked in for one night, and stayed for a fortnight is typical of the friendly manner in which the visitors were received. Many families came back year after year to the same guesthouse and the landlady watched as their children grew up. Often Christmas cards were exchanged, and these friendships lasted long after the landlady retired.

By the time of the Glasgow holiday weekend at the end of September, the gas street lighting had been switched on. The lamplight dipped and spluttered as the pressure fluctuated when the guesthouse cookers came into action. This was the end of a long but rewarding season'.

The mid 1960s saw a substantial change and though visitors still came they were now tourists with cars who stayed for a shorter period and drove on to the next attraction. Their children, the post-war baby boom, had already found the delights of European package holidays, the dependable Mediterranean weather and the freedom which social changes engendered.

North Berwick soldiered on oblivious or unwilling to change, or see the need for change. Bed and breakfast, bar meals and other down-market developments were shunned and the season contracted as the post-war parents eventually joined their children in European resorts. But the writing was on the wall and fire regulations in the 1970s gave a lucrative exit for those hotel and boarding house owners faced with the substantial expense of complying with the fire regulations or the escape route of converting their large properties into saleable flats. Many took the conversion alternative, many of them were anyway of an age to retire.

Bed and breakfast came eventually of course, although perhaps more by change of ownership than change of practice among the traditional owners. By 2000 there were only six hotels left, no boarding houses and only a handful of bed and breakfast establishments. There were a few self-catering units but relatively few compared with the demand and the much larger provision 50 years previously.

Economy – Tourism (cont)

Looking north along Quality Street, North Berwick, 1960s, with Melbourne Place in the distance. Tucked in beside the cloak room and toilets was a tourist information centre. Gilbert's was one of three garages in the town and the site is now occupied by flats.

The July peak has gone; indeed many local traders now take their holidays in July because the town is so quiet. The business comes now principally from golfers in May, June, September and October, and from English holidaymakers in August. There is a steady trickle of European and North American visitors throughout the year and any major event in Edinburgh, for example the Edinburgh Festival, will cause substantial demand for accommodation in North Berwick by virtue of proximity and the 30-minute train service to the heart of Edinburgh.

It would be hard to argue that North Berwick is any longer a holiday resort. It is essentially a retirement town and a commuter town for Edinburgh. The bulk of building in recent years has been new housing and although there has been some infill of shops, there have been no new hotels built for many years and a steady disposal or conversion of the old ones.

'After the end of the second world war, serious attempts were made to restore the pre-war holiday resort image the town had gained with, it has to be said, some success. Our population around this time was about 4000 and the months of July and August in the fifties saw this at least double with summer visitors mainly from Edinburgh and Glasgow. Boarding houses, hotels and private houses all catered for these summer arrivals. The grocers – Edingtons and Cowans acted as agents to try to satisfy the needs of

Economy – Tourism (cont)

the visitors and those prepared to let their premises complete or in part. Trains (still steam) arrived loaded with these holidaymakers to be met by numerous taxis from Gilbert's, Russell's and Fowler's Garages plus a taxi firm of Bertrams. All provided at least three cars which could deliver one hire then swiftly return for a second. The fare for an address in town was two shillings and sixpence and to the Rhodes or Gilsland caravan sites three shillings and sixpence (12.5 and 17.5 pence)'.
Anne Cowie

Caravan and camping
Bill McNair recalls the growth of Gilsland from its small beginnings before the war

'Pre-war, the Heugh was a dairy and poultry farm at the top of the Heugh Brae. It had a field adjoining the Law with a 'doocot' in the middle and on the periphery of that field were several holiday huts and buses where people enjoyed their holidays. The Abbey farm was a dairy farm at the telephone exchange and its field lay to the west. One field was called the Mason's Apron or the Green Apron field, and in that field adjoining Grange Road were two holiday abodes. One was a wooden hut owned by George Woodburn and four other chaps, and the other was an old bus body, turned into a caravan owned by the Stewarts, Mr and Mrs Stewart, Jim, Alan, Terry and their two sisters. These were used faithfully at all holiday times.

One day in the early 1930s, my father was driving along Grange Road and noticed that the old fever hospital looked as though it had been abandoned. He contacted the county council and asked if he could buy it. His idea was to convert it into a holiday home for his patients in Leith. The council sold him it and not long after the Abbey farm came up for sale so he bought ten acres opposite to keep hens and ponies.

My grandfather looked after the place and the holiday home took shape. It was so successful that they started to copy the Heugh and the Abbey by putting old buses, single and double deckers, trams and even railway carriages on the chicken field. Then the second world war came along and Gilsland was used for evacuees. They soon went home, so the place was filled up with airmen.

My father and I went to war and on demob we started up where my grandfather had left off and instead of old buses, trams and huts, people started to turn up with huts on wheels, vans converted into caravans, and tent trailers. Everyone wanted holidays, weekends and now two weeks in the summer. There was a lot of animosity against this in North Berwick and the town council tried to stop it. But Gilsland was outside the burgh and the county was quite happy with it and Gilsland got busier. The town council then thought they would get in on the act and started to take in caravans on the car park next to the rugby pitches. This was a great success and we both did well as more and more people could afford a few days off work to relax. Then a Mr Muirhead bought the Mains farm at the top of the Law Brae. He saw all the caravans going along Grange Road to Gilsland. He started showing them into his field next to his house. By this time, the town council had moved their site from the rugby pitch to Lime Grove.

Caravanning got busier and busier and, in 1959, the government introduced the Caravan Act and minimum standards were set, ie number of toilets, roads, fire points etc., etc, which we all had to comply with and cost a great deal of money. Yet caravanning became so popular all over the country and especially at North Berwick, the government raised the minimum standards 100% within two years, and in the 1960s, 1970s and early 1980s it was hard work catering for many caravanners' every needs. Then the cheap air fares to sunny places and package holidays took over and the touring caravans started to

126

decline, and the people changed to static holiday caravans. They took their main holiday abroad in the sun and had their weekends and any other free time at their static caravan.

This trend seems to be the norm nowadays. Most if not all of our clients go abroad for the sunshine at least once a year and for the rest of the year they like to pop down to North Berwick for golfing, walking or diving etc., at weekends or short stays. They want to be able to drive down or come by train or bus and pop into their caravan that has all the mod. cons. without the harassment of towing it. So the caravan is now their country home where they can get away from it all and relax without too much hassle or stress'.

Boats

There has been a long tradition of boat trips to the islands near the town, particularly to the Bass Rock and Fidra. After the war this started up again with at least three boats in regular use. These were the *Britannia, St Baldreds* and *St Nicholas* which each took up to 40 to 50 passengers. They had been commandeered as picket boats in Scapa Flow during the war but survived to provide peacetime service for over ten years, run by Alec Hutchinson, his son Ronnie and David Tweedie. In suitable conditions during the summer there would be a trip round the Bass every 30 minutes as well as frequent trips to Fidra.

Since about 1960, only Fred and Chris Marr have run regular boat trips to the islands, and they continue to do so using their second generation Sula, which takes up to 72 passengers. As package holidays abroad developed in the 1960s, fewer visitors stayed in North Berwick and the demand for boat trips also declined. However, there continues to be substantial numbers each year for whom a trip to the Bass to see the gannets is an unforgettable experience. Most boat trips go round the Bass (and sometimes Craigleith) with only a few visits to Fidra nowadays where a short landing is only possible in the right sea conditions. Landing on the Bass requires permission from the owner and is usually restricted to organised parties.

Getting visitors on and off boats can be a tricky business especially when they are elderly. With the harbour dry at low tide it is necessary to use the exposed outer jetty (the old pier) a lot of the time, while landing on the Bass can be difficult even in calm conditions. Weather can deteriorate rapidly so good planning is essential. It is a great credit to the different boatmen who have operated over the years that none of their many tens of thousands of passengers have been lost or suffered serious injury.

Local boats serviced the lighthouses on the Bass and Fidra until these went automatic in 1988 and 1971 respectively. This would typically involve two or three visits a week, taking out food, fresh water, equipment etc as well as conveying the lighthouse keepers. Wives and families of the three keepers lived on Fidra, which was designated as a 'shore rock' but not on the Bass (a 'sea rock') where only the keepers resided. A Mrs McFie is remembered for providing teas and scones for visitors who landed on Fidra.

The Scottish Seabird Centre

This has proved to be a success for the town. In 1992, East Lothian District Council launched a Harbour Area Study. Partly in response to this, Bill Gardner, then vice-chairman of the North Berwick Community Council, suggested that the spectacular Pavilion site should be the location for a Scottish Seabird Centre, using new technology to interpret the life cycles of the twelve species of nesting seabirds (over 350,000 birds) on the nearby islands, including most

Economy – Tourism (cont)

importantly the vast gannet colony on the Bass Rock. He envisaged using remote TV cameras and transmitters on the Bass Rock and other islands together with multi-media and other facilities to create a world-class visitor centre. With the help of a small grant he compiled a comprehensive feasibility study setting out how such a centre could be created.

After several false starts, a small group consisting of Bill Gardner, Sir Hew Dalrymple (whose family has owned the Bass for almost three centuries) and David Minns of the RSPB investigated the possibility of obtaining lottery funds. In 1995 an application was submitted to the Millennium Commission and followed by a full bid in 1996. This was well received by the commission and the project then took off with the formation of a charitable trust, later chaired by Rear Admiral Neil Rankin. Financial help from East Lothian Council and Lothian & Edinburgh Enterprise enabled the design and business planning to be undertaken and the further funding needed for the construction and equipment was raised from a wide variety of sources. Local help included a major landfill tax contribution from Viridor and donation of cement from Blue Circle at Dunbar as well as a local quarry company which provided the stone for the external cladding free of charge.

An innovative and attractive building has been constructed and fitted out at a total cost of £3.7 million and was opened on 21 May 2000 by HRH Prince Charles. The centre includes a shop, cafe and small cinema as well as extensive interpretation about the natural history of the offshore islands. As originally envisaged there are close-up pictures of seabirds from remote cameras on the Bass and Fidra as well as a viewing platform with telescopes looking out to the islands and along the coast.

The Scottish Seabird Centre is a charity that aims to increase awareness and appreciation of Scotland's natural environment. It has proved to be a great attraction to visitors and is a tremendous asset for North Berwick, East Lothian and Scotland.

'It has more than lived up to the hopes for its popularity and continues to provide much pleasure to both locals and visitors alike. The building design, by Simpson & Brown, has been well received and has had much acclaim architecturally'.
Norma Buckingham

Economy – Industry
In spite of proposals (1960s, 1970, 1972) to build factories and expand small industrial estates in North Berwick, only a few industries persisted.

In March 1958, it was announced that Ranco Ltd. was to take on a seven-year lease of the former Admiralty buildings at Castleton/Tantallon (Canty Bay). The following month, Ranco Ltd 'makers of thermostatic controls … and rotar units for refrigeration etc' was advertising for senior and junior engineers for the design and development of small rotating electrical machines in the FHP range, to work at the company's development laboratory at North Berwick (*Haddingtonshire Courier* 1958 April 18). At this time Ranco was the largest producer of motors in the United Kingdom. In 1962, the production moved to Haddington while the development work continued at Castleton. Due to American trade restrictions in the 1970s, the UK division became Lothian Electronic Machines (LEMAC). The development and research work stopped at Castleton in the 1980s and the company operations were consolidated in Haddington and Livingston.

Economy – Industry (cont)

The site was again listed as vacant in 1983; by this time, it was the Ministry of Defence that was listed as the owner. In 1984, the council extended the planning consent to include light industrial research and development purposes, and Ferranti took over the site (*East Lothian Courier* 1984 September 7), purchasing it outright from the MOD. By 1991, following a fall in the amount of defence-related work available, the GEC-Ferranti testing plant (employing 23) was to close (*East Lothian Courier* 1991 October 11). In the early 1990s, DERA (the Defence Evaluation Research Establishment) a part of the MOD, leased the site for a few years from Ferranti, (later GEC-Marconi), who retained ownership.

In 1964, the long-standing Ben Sayers firm – manufacturers of golf clubs – moved to their new factory in Tantallon Road. The business was sold to Grampian Holdings, then in 1998 to the Caledonian Golf Group.

There were few other industrial developments of any size: Robertson Textiles built their factory in Heugh Road (designated an industrial park). KEX, then Initial Towel Co Ltd – a large employer – moved to Tantallon Road.

Wilco Sports manufactured fishing tackle; they closed in 1999.

Old Ben Sayers factory, Forth Street, North Berwick. By the time this photograph was taken in c1983, the factory had been relocated for nearly 20 years (left)

New site in Tantallon Road, North Berwick, 1964 (below)

Economy – The Sea

The period since the last war has seen the continued slow decline of fishing as an important part of the local economy, a decline that started towards the end of the 19th century. Before the last war, fishing with long lines was widely used – this involved baiting perhaps 600 hooks on a line which was left on the sea bottom for about two hours before being hauled in. Haddock, whiting and cod were the main catch. This continued for a while after the war but it became increasingly uneconomic and after a few years there were insufficient fish left to catch in this way. Bigger boats operating further offshore took over the catches of white fish. For some years visitors were taken out in small boats to fish for mackerel but there have not been enough fish for that to be worthwhile in recent years. One factor, which is thought to have contributed to the decline of fish stocks, is trawling for prawns - the small mesh net that is used scrapes along the sea bottom and can kill a lot of small fish. This started after the war and still continues, though not from North Berwick.

After the war there were six boats fishing out of North Berwick each with a crew of two. At least eight fishermen made a full time living out of crabs and lobsters using about 80-90 creels each and there were additional part-time jobs as well. Nowadays there are only four boats operating with 200 creels or more each, providing part time employment only for up to six fishermen – an indication of the decline in crabs and lobsters. In the 1950s and 1960s it was not unusual to find three or four lobsters in one creel – which would be unheard of nowadays. Mechanical winches have made it easier and quicker to haul in and check the creels so that more can be handled; the result is that there is now more fishing pressure on stocks even though there are less boats operating. Lobsters are less abundant than in the past and crabs have become very scarce in the last few years. Creels are put out all year round when the weather allows but catches are less in the winter though the catch is then more valuable. Lobsters and crabs go to holding pools in Dunbar before being sent abroad to France and Spain. Only a few are consumed locally.

A sad reminder of the dangers of fishing occurred in 1965 when Jim Pearson's brother Benjie was drowned. He was trying to enter the harbour on his own when his boat was turned over by a huge wave.

Economy – Agriculture

This remains an important part of the parish economy. John Hunt interviewed two farmers for this summary: Bill McNicol whose family has farmed Castleton Farm (145ha) since 1908, his grandfather buying the farm in 1921 for £11,000, and Andrew Miller whose family has farmed Bonnington Farm (100ha) since 1912, his grandfather buying the farm in 1922 for £7,000. Mr Miller was brought up on a farm near East Linton and took over Bonnington from his uncle in 1967. (*See also* Environment, where both comment on the changes in wildlife on their farms).

Both farms are predominantly arable though Castleton has a little coastal grassland plus 4ha of woodland. Some additional ground is rented elsewhere (about 30 ha) by both farmers for grazing or cropping.

After the war, mixed farming was practised with a wide variety of crops grown including wheat, barley, potatoes, turnips, sugar beet and hay (silage from the late 1950s). Sheep and cattle were bought in during the autumn and over-wintered, being fed on turnips and hay, with the muck produced then spread on the fields.

Economy – Agriculture (cont)

Horses were in use on both farms for a period after the war - these were Clydesdales, huge horses used in pairs to pull the plough and for other work. At Bonnington, Mr Miller's uncle bred Clydesdales preferring them to tractors. Four pairs were used and were only replaced by tractors in the 1950s. At Castleton tractors came in a little earlier but one pair of Clydesdales was still in use in the early 1950s. On this farm there were 18 pairs of horses before the war. One pair of horses could plough one acre a day in good conditions but the early small tractors could manage three acres a day (nowadays much larger tractors plough considerably more).

Until the 1950s all tasks on the farm were labour intensive. Harvesting corn was by binder with the cut crop then formed into stooks to dry before being brought into the stackyard and piled up into large stacks. The corn would later be threshed in a mill - either a static mill on the farm or a travelling threshing mill - in order to produce the grain, which was then put into sacks. Since the late 1950s, combine harvesters have done all this in one operation with the machines getting progressively larger and faster. The grain now goes into an electric and diesel fired grain dryer and large silo before eventually departing for the grain merchant.

Potatoes also demanded a lot of physical work with squads of temporary workers planting, weeding and gathering by hand with the crop stored in outside clamps (layers of straw covered by soil) before being sorted and bagged during the winter. The 'tattie squads' provided a lot of employment up to the late 1960s when potato harvesters came in.

Haymaking was another busy time in the farming year with the cut hay turned by hand until dry and then made into ricks before being brought in on carts and built into a huge stack. Hay was mainly used for feeding livestock in the winter. Haymaking stopped on Castleton in the mid 1950s but continued until later at Bonnington.

Both farms bought cattle each autumn for over-wintering and fattening. At Bonnington, over 100 three-year-old Irish store cattle were purchased at Haddington or East Linton markets - both markets closed in the 1960s. They were kept inside, fed on hay and turnips and sold for slaughter in the summer after fattening outside on grass. Some animals were slaughtered for local consumption at the North Berwick slaughterhouse (where the Safeway supermarket now stands) up to the 1960s when it closed. Recent closures of other local slaughterhouses mean that today animals have to travel big distances to Aberdeen or elsewhere.

Hoggs (young sheep) from Orkney, Caithness or elsewhere in the Highlands were also bought for wintering on the farm – either to be fattened for slaughter or in the case of ewe hoggs for sale on to other farms for breeding. Other livestock on the farm included a few pigs, chickens and a farm cow for milk.

Inevitably, farming changes have had a huge impact on the employment provided. In the 1970s Castleton employed 14 people some of whom were part time, giving the equivalent of about eight full time jobs. They mostly lived in six farm cottages. Other temporary work was provided at peak periods such as harvest time. The number employed just after the war is not known but would have been a little higher than in the 1970s. Nowadays all the work is done on the farm by Mr McNicol with help from his son. No temporary work is provided any longer.

It has been a similar story at Bonnington, which employed four ploughmen up to the 1950s. Their sons also worked on the farm in various capacities as well as the ploughmen's wives on a part-time basis. All were housed in four farm cottages. Between them about eight full time job equivalents were provided in addition to the farmer's family. There were also four bothies,

Economy - Agriculture (cont)

three for men and one for women, which provided very basic accommodation for up to some 20 temporary farm workers who helped at peak periods - these were often men from county Mayo or Donegal in Ireland. They fought each other so it was important not to have both at the same time! Today only Mr Miller works the farm with some part time help from his son and son-in-law.

Cropping on both farms is now largely restricted to winter wheat and spring barley (equally split between the two) with some silage also made at Bonnington. About 10% of the land is in set-aside - in grass with no crop produced. Castleton used to over-winter cattle and sheep but this stopped in the 1960s when a large chicken egg rearing enterprise started. That continued until 1997 when it became uneconomic. When the old steading was demolished, the stone which was thought to have come originally from nearby Tantallon Castle, moved on to a third existence in various building developments in North Berwick.

Bonnington continues to over-winter about 100 suckled calves (bought at ten to twelve months of age), which are kept in a huge shed erected in the 1950s to replace the old farm buildings. This shed is large enough to also house a silage pit plus all the straw bales, machinery, fertiliser etc.

The vastly reduced need for labour on the modern farm has been made possible by enormous advances in farm machinery. Each farm has two large tractors (about 90 HP, four-wheel drive), a small tractor for odd jobs and a combine harvester plus a small number of specialised machines such as a forklift truck. Tractors are now very comfortable - fully enclosed, air conditioned and equipped with hi-fi. Simplification of the farming crops has also helped to reduce the number of different tasks required and thus makes it feasible for one highly skilled and well-equipped person to do everything.

Machinery may have displaced jobs but it has eased the physical demands of farming. The ploughmen who toiled behind their Clydesdales were rarely able to continue after the age of 35 because the work was so demanding. If they were lucky they then got lighter work on the farm such as looking after the livestock, but if that was not available they could lose both job and home.

Farming technology has improved enormously and continues to do so. Better varieties of seed, improved chemical weed and disease control plus the use of inorganic fertilisers have resulted in big increases in yield. Two tons per acre of spring barley was exceptional after the war but now three tons per acre is normal. In the 1960s one and a half tons per acre of winter wheat was the norm, now four tons per acre is achieved. With potatoes, ten tons per acre after the war was thought to be phenomenal, now up to 30 tons per acre is expected though irrigation is used today.

Some personal reflections from the two farmers indicate the huge changes over the period:

'The continuing innovation in farming practices and technology has been a challenge and source of satisfaction. Mobile phones, faxes and computers are now a vital part of the job.

Life for farmers has become rather lonely and more stressful, and they miss the many people (including the characters) that used to be around the farm. Visits to the market are now a rare event instead of the frequent business and social occasions of the past.

Since 1996 farming has become less profitable despite the long hours that have to be worked (typically over 70 hours a week at peak periods with holidays a rare event). Farmers believe that government does not care about them and they feel besieged by bureaucracy and paper work.

The future of farming seems very uncertain with the average age of farmers now 58 and a reluctance by the younger generation to take on the long hours, stress and rather solitary life that is involved'.

Economy – Golf

This has a dual role in the parish - as an important part of the tourist industry, and as an employer. There are two courses - the East course (also known as the Burgh course and originally owned and administered by North Berwick Town Council) and the West links.

In 1950, the East course at North Berwick was played by the Glen Golf Club, Glen Ladies' Club and the artisan Rhodes Golf Club. The West links was played by the North Berwick Club, Tantallon Golf Club, North Berwick New Club, North Berwick Ladies' Club and the artisan Bass Rock Golf Club.

Prior to the war, both courses attracted thousands of visitors but during the following decade with so many other distractions, interest in golf declined and the membership of golf clubs fell dramatically. In 1947, the town council held a plebiscite of all the municipal voters to decide whether playing golf on a Sunday should be permitted on the East course. On that occasion the majority voted against, and golf was not played on a Sunday until 11 March 1958.

Part of the West links (Elcho Green to the March Dyke) is common land, protected by the National Trust for Scotland. The remainder of the West links was purchased by the town council in 1954. Following local government regionalisation in 1975, all the town assets including the East course were administered by East Lothian District Council and the local authority now own the land. Glen Golf Club successfully negotiated a long-term lease for the East course.

By 1962 the membership of the North Berwick Golf Club had declined to a point that the North Berwick New Club was approached to take over their assets including the trophies. On 1 January 1963 the North Berwick New Club adopted the name North Berwick Golf Club and took over the lease of the West links.

Bass Rock Golf Club was the first in the county to offer junior membership in 1961 and by the end of the decade interest in golf had increased, mainly due to the exposure of golf on television. During this period James Watt, the last of the traditional clubmakers retired from his business at the foot of Station Hill. In 1967, North Berwick Golf Club appointed David Huish as its first golf professional, a position he has retained for over 35 years. That year the town council installed electricity to the professional's shop for the first time. In 1972, the last of the Scottish Boys' Championships was played over the West links. This event had been played annually at North Berwick since 1935.

Visitors to the area have always been more aware of the town's golfing heritage and the late 1960s saw an increase in the number of golfers from around the world wishing to experience the West links. The popularity of the course was boosted in 1972 when Arnold Palmer and Tony Jacklin played the famous 15th hole Redan, with legendary golf commentator Henry Longhurst during the filming of an '18 holes at 18 different courses helicopter round'. The West links was used as a qualifying course when the Open Championship was played at Muirfield in 1959, 1966, 1972, 1980 and 1992, which added to the profile of the area and the West links became an integral part of the 'golf package tour'.

In 1978, Tantallon Golf Club celebrated 125 years since its formation, and is now the oldest club in North Berwick. In 1981, the PGA Senior's Championship was played over the West links, which was won by Australian Peter Thomson. That year the dry spring weather left the course burnt golden brown, and the competitors described the links 'like playing golf on the

Economy - Golf (cont)

Sahara desert'. Ten years later an automatic watering system was installed and since then the rainfall in this district has been the highest on record.

Despite the new golf equipment, the East course and West links continue to be a formidable challenge. The golf clubs have a full membership, some with a seven-year waiting list. The courses continue to attract prestigious tournaments including the Vagliano Trophy played over the West links, and the British Blind Society that held its International Match over the East course in 1997.

Local Government

In 1945, the governance of the parish had not changed for many years, but the next 55 years were to see many changes. Then the royal burgh was controlled by a town council with East Lothian County Council supervising some functions in the town as well as being the controlling body for all local government functions in the landward area of the parish and other landward areas in the county.

In 1945, North Berwick Town Council was the most significant part of the system governance as far as the Royal Burgh of North Berwick was concerned, with provost George C. Gilbert as leader, town clerk J.W. Menzies of lawyers Wallace & Menzies, Andrew Robertson as burgh surveyor and pond master, J. McCracken. Local traders dominated the council, and the council was striving to keep the economy of the town strong by supporting tourism with a considerable degree of success.

Schools, roads, planning and other functions were controlled by the county council, otherwise the town council dealt with functions from housing to gas supply. Decisions on extension of council housing, electrification of street lighting, heating the pool, supporting the retention of the railway and Harbour Terrace together with demolition of Tantallon Hotel and creation of the council caravan site, and running events to support tourists – all of these were the bread and butter of council business. The tower of strength in all the minor as well as major issues was the burgh surveyor, Andrew Robertson, and later Jimmy Dalgleish. It was this 'local' force and leadership that was swept away in 1974 by regionalisation. Control went to Haddington and Edinburgh where staff had neither the knowledge nor incentive to make things happen in the same way. There were however two mitigating factors. Tourism by this date had reduced in importance and commuting with employment in Edinburgh was more dominant. Nevertheless the local had gone out of local government despite the efforts of the community council under its first chairman, Ben Miller and has not returned by the end of the millennium.

The same of course happened with the post of town clerk, with Robin Wotherspoon seeing out the old structure. There was however in 1974, at the initiative of the last provost John MacNair, the town treasurer Norman Hall and the town clerk, one last act of significance of the parish council – the formation of the North Berwick Trust (see Land Ownership) which was given control of 103 acres of land adjacent to the high school, with a limit on the repayment to the succeeding local authority, any surplus on the later sale of the land to go to the benefit of the town.

Equally the town lost its other servant William Simpson as chamberlain whose responsibility was financial control of the town's affairs and the control of expenditure based on rates set by the town council with few problems about non-payment.

East Lothian Council has made some efforts to recreate a degree of local initiative through the North Berwick Community Council formed at the demise of the town council in 1974, and the community council has the statutory power of consultation on some issues and developed its own role as protector of local interests. Most of these changes have not been to the benefit of identity or governance of burghs like North Berwick, though it has to be said that the increasing functions and regulations would have put a small burgh under considerable pressure.

Revisiting the Past

North Berwick Museum

North Berwick Town Council, funded with the help of a grant of £650 from the Carnegie Trust, opened the North Berwick Museum in 1957. The prime mover behind the venture was Dr J.S. Richardson (*see* Miscellany), who became the first honorary curator.

In 1975, on the reorganisation of local government in Scotland, responsibility for the museum was taken over by East Lothian District Council. A management committee was formed locally with representation from the local authority, the community and the secondary school. The responsibility of the committee was to develop the museum and to present the display of its collection.

The museum is housed on the upper floor of a former burgh school - a grade C listed building - with static displays in the smaller rooms and changing displays and exhibitions in the corridor and the large spaces beyond, created when storage was relocated in 1996 in the new facility in Haddington. The museum is open from April to October. The collection consists of items of national importance ranging from Scottish pottery to regalia of the Ancient Order of Foresters. Items of local significance include pewter communion vessels, communion tokens, documentation on the history of the burgh, and archaeological finds from local sites.

Expansion and reorganisation of the museum was identified as needing consideration in 1983 when a report on museums was prepared by the Council for Museums and Galleries in Scotland, now the Scottish Museums' Council. Subsequent plans were prepared for alteration and extension of the building, housing both the museum and the library, but as funding was not available these remain thoughts on paper. The East Lothian Museum Service was formed in 1990 with its first museums' officer, the late Sue Jenkinson.

The Friends of North Berwick Museum

In 1984, this group was formed by a group of enthusiastic supporters. The object of the friends was to promote interest in the museum by arranging a programme of meetings and events, organising visits to places of interest and lastly, raising funds for acquiring items for the collection and helping to arrange exhibitions. The friends won support from both the management committee and the district council. Their major fund raising event each year ranged from an antiques evening to lectures and film shows. Further talks were held monthly throughout the winter months. The enthusiasm is still there today although the funding requirements have changed. The friends still flourish as a small group of dedicated people with the interests of the museum in their hearts. Each week a small band of volunteers meet in the museum to continue the work. Funds continue to be raised and recently they have equipped the newly formed education room on the ground floor.

Revisiting the Past (cont)

The future of the friends may be uncertain with talk of a possible merger with a proposed new history society.

Miscellany

Working with the Scottish Refugee Council, the town accommodated two separate groups of refugees. Bosnian refugees were accommodated at Chaylesmore Lodge (that had closed in May 1991) between 1993-95.

In 1999, a group of 59 Kosovan refugees (including 15 children) aged four weeks to 84 years were welcomed to the former Redcroft old people's home.

In 1997, North Berwick was the first town in the county to have an Internet presence, and has a couple of dedicated web sites.

The Evans' Trust - the link to Canty Bay [2]
William Edgar Evans (1882-1963) was a botanist, naturalist and photographer, and from 1920 he was the scoutmaster for the group associated with Charlotte Baptist Chapel, Edinburgh.

The link with Canty Bay, North Berwick began in 1921, when the scout group sought a venue for a summer camp. In 1923, Sir Hew Hamilton Dalrymple, 9th Baronet, began to sell off parts of his estate – including Lower Canty Bay and the New Hotel and stables; an offer of £850 was made and accepted. The properties were bought 'for the use of the scouts'. In September 1936 W. Edgar Evans set up the Evans Trust - that took over the Canty Bay properties and administered a capital sum to provide funds for the upkeep of the site. In wartime, naval personnel occupied Canty Bay. In November 1945, the property was de-requisitioned and returned to Mr Evans. Damage was considerable and the compensation given rather small. In April 1946, the first post-war camp was held there, and the same year, W. Edgar Evans' retiral from the botanic garden meant he was there for much of the time (otherwise living in Edinburgh). Scouts recall that camps at Canty Bay in the 1950s included unauthorised exploits after lights-out like trips into North Berwick, and up the Law. In 1956 ill health meant that W. Edgar Evans withdrew somewhat from the Canty Bay activities, while maintaining his support. He died in March 1963. In 1967, the gates made in his memory were unveiled at the entrance to lower Canty Bay.

In 1958, use of Canty Bay was extended to a few groups with links to Charlotte Chapel. By 1971, regular Christmas camps began at Canty Bay, and these - together with the regular summer and easter camps - continue to date. The continuing success of the Charlotte Baptist Chapel Scout Group during the extreme social changes of (particularly) the past 20 years is attributable in no small way to the role of Canty Bay.

Evans Trust Chairman (1991-date) David R. Whitlie gives a personal reflection:
'I attended Charlotte Baptist Chapel as our family church…. There was a thriving scout group at the church and at the age of eight, I joined the cub scouts, then moved onto scouts and then assistant scout leader.

A major part of the scout activity involved travelling to Canty Bay outside North Berwick, which had been purchased by Mr William Edgar Evans for scout use. The influence of camps at Canty Bay, of other leaders and of Mr Edgar Evans himself was profound.

Mr Evans had an incredible knowledge of plants, birds, bees, wasps, butterflies etc, and his knowledge and accounts were fascinating to a young lad. As a scout patrol leader and scout leader, I spent many

Miscellany (cont)

days at Canty Bay, often with only one or two others, with Mr Evans in residence in the big house, and ourselves in the scout cottages. His influence was immense and stemmed from his strong Christian faith and convictions, and played a huge part in my own Christian commitment.

With the passage of time, those who knew Mr Evans personally, affectionately known as 'Pa Evans' are a dying breed. … The Evans Trust is still very active, carrying out the remit laid down by the 1936 trust deed and still responsible for the upkeep of Canty Bay and its use'.

People

Sir Hew Hamilton Dalrymple Bt. GCVO became vice-lieutenant of the county in 1973 (having served as a deputy lieutenant from 1964). Sir Hew was appointed Lord-Lieutenant in 1987. He remains a member of the Royal Company of Archers, the Queen's bodyguard in Scotland in which he holds the ancient court appointment of Gold Stick.

Catriona Lambert, a member of the North Berwick Ladies' Golf Club won the British Ladies' Amateur Championship in 1993. She also played in three Curtis Cup teams before turning professional in 1994.

Catriona Matthew now competes on the US LPGA (Ladies' Professional Golf Association) tour and in 1998 made her debut in the European Solheim Cup team.

Dr James Smith Richardson LL D, HRSA, FRIA (Scot.), FSA Scot. was born in Edinburgh in 1883. The family moved to North Berwick, and lived in Tantallon Terrace. He trained to be an architect and became a part-time inspector of ancient monuments in Scotland, a position he held until 1948 with a break when he served in the great war. On his return he became a full time inspector and was responsible for extensive surveying work throughout Scotland; he led many archaeological excavations both on the Scottish mainland and in the Orkney Islands. He wrote many guide books and, on his return to North Berwick, led many local 'digs'. He became involved in local affairs and was described by Sir Hew Hamilton Dalrymple as 'a thorn in the side of the council and on many occasions, a thorn in the side of many distinguished local people'.

In 1967, at the age of 84, for his public-spirited local work the council conferred on him the Freedom of the Burgh, making him North Berwick's youngest burgess! He fought long and hard for retention of the old burghs, ancient and time-honoured institutions dating from early mediaeval times. In 1957 the burgh museum was opened, largely due to his efforts and he became its first honorary curator. He wanted people to be aware of both natural and local history. He donated many of the items in the collection.

Affectionately known as 'The Doctor', he died on 12 September 1970 and, in May 1971, a plaque was unveiled in the museum by Sir Hew Hamilton Dalrymple in appreciation of 'the love and care he lavished on this museum which was his idea and inspiration'. He loved North Berwick and was much loved by North Berwick.

Lord Stodart of Leaston (1916-) farmed the family farm at Kingston (1934-58), and later at Leaston, Humbie. The Conservative MP for Edinburgh West (1959-74), and author of Land of Abundance: Scottish Agriculture in the 20th Century (1962); president East Lothian Boy Scouts Association 1960-63, Lord Stodart chaired the Committee of Inquiry into Local Government in Scotland (the Stodart Report) Cmnd. 8115, 1981.

Donald J. Withrington, historian (1931-2003), was evacuated to the care of his North Berwick grandmother during the war. He was educated in the town, and thereafter identified with

People (cont)

Scotland. With Ian R. Grant, he was the general editor of the Statistical Account of Scotland, reprinted by county in 1975. He died on 1st June 2003.

This account of North Berwick Parish was initiated and collected by Norman Hall. Additional information, research and essays were provided by the following:

Father John Barry	Belief - the Church of Our Lady Star of the Sea
Desmond Bathgate	Police
Norma Buckingham	Townscapes, Buildings, & Landscapes of Distinction; Homes; Leisure Services; Revisiting the Past - North Berwick Museum; Miscellany - Dr Richardson
Stephen Bunyan	Townscapes, Building, and Landscapes of Distinction – Balgone, Fenton Tower
Margaret Costa	Education
Robert Cowan	HM Coastguard
Anne Cowie	Shops & Services; Transport; Leisure
Lyle Crawford	Economy - Tourism
Bill Gardner	Economy - Tourism, the Scottish Seabird Centre
Rev Dr David J. Graham	Belief - Abbey Church
Norman Hall	Local Government
John Hunt	Environment - Lamb & Craigleith, Wildlife at Bonnington & Castleton Farms; Lifeboat; Leisure - boats, harbour and yacht club; Economy - Agriculture, interviews with Bill McNicol (Castleton) and Andrew Miller (Bonnington) - Fishing, boats & the harbour, from interviews with Leonard Groom, Jim Pearson, Fred Marr, Chris Marr, Ian Hutchinson and Ken MacLean
Rev Canon John Lindsay	Belief - St Adrian's & St Baldred's Church
Robert MacAdam	Belief - Blackadder (to 1989) and St Andrew Blackadder (from 1989) Churches
Rev Dan McCaskill	Belief - Baptist Church
Hugh McMinn	Fire Service
Bill McNair	Economy -Tourism the growth of Gilsland
David Moody	General information
Dr Bryan Nelson	Environment - The Bass Rock
William Nisbet	Belief - North Berwick Christian Fellowship
Douglas C. Seaton	General information; Land Ownership - North Berwick Trust; Homes - Local Structure Plan; Utilities; Leisure - sports centre, town fete; Economy - Tourism interview with Mrs Skwara (landlady); Industry - Golf
James Simpson	Belief - St Andrews Church
Dr Jean M. Walinck	Healthcare
David R. Whitlie	Miscellany - The Evans Trust

References (cont)

And the recollections of: Robert D. Burgon (primary school 1960-67); Margaret Costa (primary and secondary school 1945-58); Anne Cowan (primary school 1950s; growing up in the 1950s); Jacqueline Dillon (primary and secondary school 1955-68); Bernice Graham (primary and secondary school 1953-64); Robert Gray (pavilion concerts); Gillian Lindsay (secondary school 1988-94); Alastair McKay (growing up in the 1970s); Barbara Montgomery (primary and secondary school 1943-55); P.E. Rooney (primary school, 1940s);

Muriel N. Shiel (secondary school 1939-45, primary teacher 1955-90,); Lynne Turnbull (homes & standards of living); James Walker (secondary school 1952-58); Jean Walinck (healthcare), and Anon (primary and high school, 1946-56).

Thanks are also due to the RSPB, and to the Ministry of Defence, Rosyth.

FURTHER READING & REFERENCES

Dunnett, Robert (1968) *East Lothian Farm Buildings* East Lothian County Planning Committee

Ferrier, W.M. (1980) *The North Berwick Story* Royal Burgh of North Berwick Community Council

Hajducki, A. (1992) *The North Berwick and Gullane Branch Lines* Oakwood Press

Jamieson, B. (2000) *Old North Berwick,* Stenlake Publishing

Land Use Consultants for the Countryside Commission for Scotland, CCS (later Scottish Natural Heritage, SNH) and Historic Buildings and Monuments Directorate, Scottish Development Department (first published c 1987, 1997 reprint) *The Inventory of Gardens & Designed Landscapes in Scotland: Volume 5: Lothian & Borders*

McAlister, D.J.B. (1960) *History of Blackadder Church – Dear Stones*

MacLeod, Angus H. (1995) *75 Years of Scouting; the story of the 6th Edinburgh (Charlotte Chapel) Scout Group* John Donald Publishers Ltd. Edinburgh
(re the link to Canty Bay and the Evans Trust)

Scottish Natural Heritage (1994) *An Inventory of Gardens & Designed Landscapes: Supplementary Volume 1: Lothians*

Andrews, Ian J. (1986) *The Birds of the Lothians,* Edinburgh branch of the Scottish Ornithologists' Club

Snodgrass, C.P. (1953) *The Third Statistical Account: The County of East Lothian* Oliver & Boyd

Tindall, F.P. (1998) *Memoirs and Confessions of a County Planning Officer,* Pantile Press

Tully-Jackson, Jack & Brown Ian (1996) *East Lothian at War* East Lothian District Library

Notes

[1] The assessment at age 12 was variously (and erroneously) referred to as the 'eleven-plus', or as the dreaded 'Quallie' ('qualifying' examination). The nationally standardised version of the Qualifying Examination (introduced in 1903) ended in 1922/3 and had been superseded by the Promotion Test, also known as the Promotion Exam. (See also Education, Allen & Bonnar, County Volume, p117).

[2] Summary extracted from MacLeod, Angus H. (1995)

WHITEKIRK & TYNINGHAME
PARISH REPRESENTATIVES: *Peter & Hermine de Iongh*

Introduction

Whitekirk and Tyninghame is a coastal parish with an abundance of rich farmland and woodland, and many attractive buildings. Here the Tyne reaches the sea, and in 2000 the landscape seemed much as it always had been. In the north and east of the parish lie Auldhame, Seacliff, Scoughall and Lochhouses, the fields and farm buildings reflecting major changes in farming methods but the houses little changed. Whitekirk now enjoys a golf course on Whitekirk Hill and is no longer a farm; in 2000, the demolition of the steading in the village (of post-war construction following two major fires) was about to begin, to make way for housing. Only Stonelaws remains as a farm of any size. The fields and policies of Newbyth estate had long since been sold to various owners. In appearance, Tyninghame estate was perhaps least changed but appearances can be deceptive (*see* Land Ownership).

In 1945, this rural parish of some 2950ha (7289 acres) would have been still easily recognisable in visible feature and social reality by a visitor from 1900, with the two great estates of Newbyth and Tyninghame still whole, and Tyninghame village still an estate village. There had been changes of course: where the lovely Binning Wood had stood, a million tree stumps froze the affectionate eye; the shoreline was festooned with concrete blocks, glider poles and barbed wire, and the beaches and dunes heavily mined. But otherwise the second world war had had little impact. Some men had of course gone to war - but farming had been a reserved occupation and many had stayed. Six names only are mentioned on the war memorial in Whitekirk churchyard. A bomb had dropped in Whitekirk at 1.30am on 4 August 1940, and another had demolished one of the Seacliff greenhouses, and Polish army officers had been billeted at Seacliff, but they had left. Some Italian prisoners of war from the camp at Gilmerton were still employed on farms and estates. A sort of prosperous stagnation had reigned, with government regulation covering every aspect of life; there was a sort of bemused anticipation of what the future might hold. Few realised that the next 55 years would see fundamental changes.

Environment

By the end of 2000, the ecclesiastical parish boundaries remained as they had been for generations, though that year, Presbytery had threatened to amend them. The civil parish boundaries too remained unchanged, but the two however, did not exactly coincide.

The floods of 1948 did cause severe damage on that part of the parish bordering the river Tyne, which - until the construction of Buist's embankment and the sea wall on the south bank of the river in 1820 - was largely salt marsh.

At Kirklandhill, the sea breached the sea wall and flooded a large acreage; the wall was repaired by the Department of Agriculture but the land could not be used for two and a half years. Knowes Mill was three feet underwater and Tyninghame sawmill was completely flooded. By comparison the 1992 floods did only moderate damage.

The once majestic Binning Wood, which had boasted the tallest tree in Scotland, a Scots fir over 100 feet tall, had been clear-felled during the war, the beech to make the frames of Mosquito aircraft, the rest for pit props and other uses. Over the 15 years of its replanting, roe deer, badgers, foxes, grey squirrels and numerous birds returned; an effort to control the greys and encourage the red squirrel was begun, with the importation of some darker reds from the

Environment (cont)

Black Forest in Germany. Careful management over the years has made the woods a profitable source of timber and an increasingly beautiful amenity open to the public. On the old Newbyth estate can be found the largest oak plantation in Scotland.

Intensive cultivation of the fields has reduced the partridge population but on the golf course skylarks flourish and the lochans and ponds host mallard and tufted duck. The rabbit and hare population had been the scourge of the land; after the war a determined co-operative effort had vastly reduced their numbers, which still fluctuate with seasons, disease and the attention of stoats.

Many greenfinch nest on the unspoilt whins above Whitekirk village, numerous goldfinch are still summer visitors but there are fewer swallows and swifts. A barn owl has relocated from the tithe barn to an old quarry. Many greylag and pinkfoot geese visit in the winter, as do whooper swans. Crows, rooks and jackdaws have increased as the regular shoots were abandoned. Kestrels, sparrow hawks and several buzzards have taken up residence. A green parrot was seen around Whitekirk for several years.

By an access agreement signed on 18 December 1974 (Tindall, F.P. 1998 p236) the Earl of Haddington agreed to make available to the John Muir Trust the lovely stretch of Ravensheugh Sands, St Baldred's Cradle and the Tynemouth for public use, and at about the same time the Dale family opened Seacliff beach and the Gegan. Large numbers of wading birds, gulls, gannets, cormorants, shelduck and eider, curlews, terns, occupy these outer reaches of the Forth Estuary. There are two designated Sites of Special Scientific Interest (S.S.S.I.s), which in effect stretch along the entire coastline of the parish. The continuation of the North Berwick

Seacliff Harbour with Gegan rock in background.

Environment (cont)

coastal strip is nationally important for turnstone, purple sandpiper and eider, and for its colonies of fulmar and housemartins. The saltmarshes of the Tyne estuary support breeding terns, again of national importance.

The coastal stretches and large swathes of inland country had been restricted areas during the war. A lively fear of possible invasion had led to the deployment of concrete blocks, barbed wire, pillboxes like that at Whitberry Point, and wooden posts set in concrete to deter glider landings on Ravensheugh Sands. Many landmines were laid. These were all slowly cleared in the 1950s, though attempts by the Home Guard to blow up the concrete blocks only served to fill nearby trees with fragments of stone, making them dangerous to fell. At the end of the period some decaying relics of these defences remained.

Land Ownership

In 2000, as in 1945, the parish could be divided into three distinct areas: the land and farms owned by the Dale family; Tyninghame estate; and Newbyth estate. While the ownership of the first two of these had remained relatively unchanged for 55 years, in contrast, Newbyth estate was no more. Broken up in 1946, it was no longer a single cohesive unit.

Auldhame, Seacliff, Scoughall and Lochhouses all remained in the hands of branches of the Dale family, though Auldhame House had been sold to a private buyer and William Dale had bought Lochhouses from Lord Haddington, his landlord, in 1984. The Dales also farmed New Mains in a shared farming agreement with Charles Lambert through their manager, Neil Knox.

The Tyninghame estate is owned by the Earl of Haddington (the 12th earl to 1986, and then the 13th). In 2000, it was either managed by his factor, Alastair Milligan (Tyninghame Links, Lawhead, Binning Wood), or farmed by tenants (Peter Cochrane at Knowes, Robert Carswell at Kirklandhill); the mansion and some lands outside the parish boundaries had been sold. Nevertheless, to all appearances the estate was much as it had been in 1945.

The dowager Lady Haddington had remained at Tyninghame when the rest of the family took up residence at Mellerstain, and then the mansion was sold in 1987 for £250,000 to Kit Martin. He divided it up into nine apartments, preserving the outward appearance of the house, and sold these on to private owners. The owners are obliged to maintain garden and grounds and have their own garden committee on which Lord Haddington or his representative sit as one member.

Tyninghame village had been established in 1761 as a model planned estate village and remained so in 1950. There were about 100 people employed on the estate but 50 years later, as machinery took over, the number had dwindled to five. Many houses in the village had been sold or let privately and ten plots sold for sympathetically designed housing.

From 1946 on, the significant and more visible change of ownership in the parish was the breakup of the beautiful Newbyth estate - mansion, and farms. This had been in the Baird family since the seventeenth century and had included Lennoxlove. The estate was split when the late Sir David Baird inherited Newbyth from an uncle in 1941; Lennoxlove passed to his brother Robert, who lived in the Bahamas, and he then sold his portion to the Duke of Hamilton in 1946. At the same time Sir David, whose roots were in Perthshire, sold the two farms of Newbyth and Whitekirk to the sitting tenants, James Gardner and William Main and, two years later, the remaining land and policies to Irvine Chalmers-Watson from Fenton Barns.

Land Ownership (cont)

*Newbyth mansion, 1972
(Stephen Bunyan)*

*Queen Elizabeth,
the Queen Mother,
visits Tyninghame in 1993,
after attending celebrations
at 'The Lamp of Lothian'
in Haddington.
Here, she is seen with
Sir Alastair and Lady Grant.
(Irene Johnstone)*

Land Ownership (cont)

The stately Newbyth mansion, dating from 1817, had been used during the war as a convalescent home and remained in the hands of the South East Regional Hospital Board. It was briefly considered for use as a Borstal. It passed through various hands ending with Robin Jell, a developer. In June 1972, as work was about to begin on its conversion into nine apartments, it was severely damaged in a huge fire; however, the delayed work was completed a year later. Another developer, Christopher Weekes, turned the fine stable block into four apartments and another, David Gallacher, bought and developed the steading as a settlement of 17 houses.

Irvine Chalmers-Watson had consolidated his holding of Newbyth with Kamehill in an exchange arrangement with James Gardner (who now held Stonelaws with a further parcel of land at Bankhead to make a farm of 650 acres). In 1949, Chalmers-Watson built a new Newbyth House and used the land and the orchard as part of the family's new turkey farming business; in the process he felled a lot of timber for sale and used obsolete trams and double decker buses from Glasgow as improvised turkey sheds. In 1958 he sold all that was left.

The 437 acre Mains of Newbyth, with Newbyth House, was sold to Anthony Hobrow and then by him in 1961 to Bill Elliott. He worked the farm for about 20 years, and planted thousands of trees both to replace the woodlands felled earlier and to add to them: for example Angus's Wood on the East Fortune Road was planted to commemorate the birth of his son. He sold the farm to James Main (who had inherited Whitekirk Mains from his father) and retained Newbyth House with 35 acres of policies; Bill Elliott died in 1986. James Main was forced to sell up in 1988: Robert Dale from Lochhouses bought the Newbyth portion, and George Tuer from Yorkshire bought Whitekirk. George Tuer sold half of Whitekirk in 1999 to Robert Dale and Sir James Grant-Suttie of Balgone, retaining the rest for his golf course, some agriculture and some leasing.

Stonelaws was passed by James Gardner to his son Douglas who, on his retirement in 1985, sold it to David Miller from Cumbria. He in his turn sold the farmhouse and 500 acres to Colin Hunter, retaining 150 acres for intensive pig farming.

Kamehill was split from Newbyth in 1958 and sold to William Bruce from Seton Mains, who set up a pig isolation unit. He sold it in 1967 to William Cunningham from Dunbar who farmed pigs, initially very profitably, and built Ashfield House in 1972; but when the market collapsed he was forced to sell the land to Henry Wason from Fife, and Ashfield House to a private purchaser.

Townscapes, Buildings & Landscapes of Distinction

The parish is rich in beautiful buildings, not all of which are grand in scale. Both villages were designated conservation areas in 1969, and are subject to additional planning constraints; the areas thus designated include the whole of both villages and Tyninghame estate. Historic Scotland has listed the more important of the buildings.

At Whitekirk, the parish church (see Belief) and the nearby tithe barn are both A listed buildings; the former manse (Lady's Field) and Whitekirk Mains farmhouse are B listed. The tithe barn (c1540) had been long abandoned, with several centuries of use as tithe barn and cattle shed, decaying gently with time. In 1999 it was restored as a private house.

Fires at Whitekirk Mains steading in the 1970s led to the erection of modern steel frame sheds, which were demolished to make way for a residential development in 2000.

Townscapes, Buildings & Landscapes of Distinction (cont)

Newbyth old mansion is also A listed, with the stables and east lodge B listed.

Much of Tyninghame village is B listed; properties of note include the post office; smithy and smithy cottage; Teviot, Pear Tree and St Baldred's cottages; the village hall, and the old school.

Tyninghame House too is A listed; on the estate, several of the ancillary properties are B (walled garden with gardener's cottage, south lodge, the dairy, the factor's house, the grieve's house) and C listed.

The designed landscape at Tyninghame dates from the 18th century, with 19th and 20th century additions and amendments. The policies, the woodlands and the gardens continue to have a major impact on the appearance of the parish. In 1946, the Tyninghame foresters began the massive task of clearing, draining and replanting Binning Wood (400 acres), with the help of Italian prisoners of war, and the work lasted until 1961. Lord Haddington insisted on following the exact plan of 1707, with the same rides and clearings, but had to compromise on his wish to replace hardwood with hardwood because of the national shortage of stock, so that 75% of the planting was softwood.

Knowes Mill, once a meal mill, remained derelict throughout the period, apart from the house. The increasingly unsteady footbridge across the Tyne at Knowes Ford was replaced with a new one in 2000. The ford itself was closed to public traffic after a car with a baby on board was swept away and the baby drowned in 1992.

The imposing remains of the pseudo-Jacobean Seacliff, (ruinous since it was destroyed by fire in 1907), have stayed much the same over the period.

Tyninghame Sawmill was a watermill fed from a lade taken off the main river Tyne; it was subject to flooding. Waterpower was replaced by electric motors but the flooding problem remained. It was closed and became a private house.

Population
By parish, from the General Registrar's office

1931	732	357M	375F		
1951	642	313M	329F		
1961	621	315M	306F		
1971	464	230M	234F		
1981	360	180M	180F		
1991	447	225M	222F		
2001	522	251M	271F		
By parish, from ELDC				*By settlement, from ELDC*	
1991	379			---	
1997 (est.)	465 (sic)	225M	239F	77 (*Tyninghame only*)	

Population figures are difficult to compare, as no two sources extract data in the same way.

The steady decline in population (which had already fallen from 1113 in 1861 to 732 in 1931) reflected the trend to smaller families, increased mobility, the decline in agricultural employment and the increasing accessibility of jobs elsewhere. The recovery in the last two decades of the century (which will be sustained) was due to the motor vehicle, the realisation

Population (cont)

among young affluent commuters and retired people of the attractions of country life (of a sort), and the enterprise of local builders.

Here (and elsewhere throughout the text) Hermine de Iongh paraphrases the recollections of a number of Whitekirk residents [1], who willingly shared their memories for this account of the parish.

In 1945 most of the population in the parish were in one way or another connected with farming and estate work. This profile has drastically changed. By 2000 no one living in Whitekirk was involved in farming, the only animals being domestic cats, dogs, a cockerel and three hens. With this change and the mechanisation of the work on the other farms in the parish, the type of people living here has changed too. Farm workers have been replaced by retired, still active persons or commuters, their cottages lovingly done up. In 1945 there were many families with children, on average three to five, living in sometimes cramped circumstances, although the new council houses from just before the war and the Orlits from around 1950 provided more room and more comfort; an altogether healthier environment.

The number of children in Whitekirk itself dwindled to just four by the end of the century, though in 2000 there were ten again. Of the 29 properties, five were still council owned, one privately rented and one a holiday home in 2000.

Most of the inhabitants are native Scots, although there are several from England, two Canadians, one German born, one Dutch born and two New Zealanders. I am not aware of a specific local dialect.

The lady from Germany, an elderly widow, left her native Berlin during the famous airlift after the iron curtain had come down. She answered an advertisement, circulated by the British government asking for people to come and work in Britain. She spoke no English. She was sent with others to East Fortune hospital as a ward orderly. In nearby Gilmerton were still German ex-prisoners of war, who could not return. One of these came from the long disputed lands east of the Oder. They heard about German girls working so close by who went roller-skating on the airport's landing strips. The Polish German married one of them and settled in Whitekirk. This is an illustration of the lack of labour in those early years.

Belief

The historic and humbly beautiful parish church of St Mary, Whitekirk is the only church in the parish. Its red sandstone continued to crumble and flake for most of the period - though a major repair project ten years in the planning was nearing completion in 2000, bringing the church back to its former glory.

In 1945 Whitekirk and Tyninghame was still an independent parish with a roll of about 400. A distinguished incumbent, the Reverend Doctor William D. Maxwell (1950-56) left to become Professor of Divinity at Grahamstown University, South Africa. Then in 1969, as a result of bad management, declining congregations and income, and mounting debts, the living became vacant and the manse had to be sold. After an interval of two years an association was set up with Dunbar Old Church, with the Reverend John Blair as associate minister living in a manse in Tyninghame leased by the estate. This lasted until Presbytery decided to break the association with Dunbar and link Whitekirk instead with Athelstaneford. The new arrangement was finally realised in June 1974 with John Blair as minister in charge and a manse to be built in Athelstaneford. John Blair retired in 1976; the Reverend Kenneth Walker was then appointed to the linked charge.

Belief (cont)

*St Mary's
Parish Church
and graveyard,
Whitekirk.
(above)*

*Fund raising for church repairs, Tyninghame House, 14 July1956.
Left to right on platform: Dr Lamb (New College); Mrs Helen Shepherd; 12th Earl of Haddington;
Rosemary Hume; Miss Mary Malcolm; Chief Constable Merrilees; Lady Haddington;
Mrs Jack Dale; Mrs Lamb; Mr Robert Carfrae.*

Belief (cont)

Ministers

1917-50	J.T. Soutter
1950-56	W.D. Maxwell
1957-69	T.A. Tulloch
1971-76	J.L. Blair

1971-74 Whitekirk & Tyninghame associated with Dunbar Old
1974 Linked with Athelstaneford

1976-date	K. Walker

In 2000 the roll was 180, having held steady for 15 years, the church was solvent and in good heart, offering a weekly service of morning prayer, quarterly communion and a candlelit service of carols and nine lessons on Christmas Eve. There was a small choir and junior church. An annual pilgrimage to St Mary's Haddington and Lennoxlove, begun in 1971 at the instigation of the Earl of Lauderdale, attracted large numbers and international interest in its heyday in the 1980s. The search for the site of the Holy Well, which had attracted thousands of pilgrims in the Middle Ages before it was ploughed over in the 16th century, continued without success.

There were five royal visits: Princess Margaret in 1953 (the first royal to visit since James IV, who had loved the place and come often); Princess Alexandra in 1957 and 1961; Queen Elizabeth the Queen Mother in 1963; and Princess Marina in 1965.

Recollections on church and belief

In 1945 and for some time after, most inhabitants were members of the Church of Scotland, into which they were baptised.and buried. Most marriages were conducted by the minister of the kirk; it was not exceptional to get married in the front room of the manse. During the second half of this period the monopoly of interment was broken and cremation became acceptable.

In our informants' views, not much has changed in the local church services. The Sunday school, twice resurrected since 1992 is a shadow of what it used to be. In past years, the Sunday school enjoyed a picnic in the summer on the beach, for which Mr Dale provided the transport - a wagon, first drawn by horses, then by tractor.

There were two services per Sunday (one in the morning in 2000) so mothers with smaller children and those involved in Sunday farm work could attend at the later time.

One person, long since living in Dunbar, vowed never to set foot in this church again as his farm worker father had been threatened by his boss with the sack if he and his family did not regularly attend church. He declined to give his name or that of the farmer! Harvest Thanksgiving is a fondly remembered service.

The church organised a flower festival lasting a week in 1986, during which concerts were given by organists, a local choir, post-graduate students from St. Andrew's University and St. Mary's Music School, Edinburgh. In later years the building was again a few times used for concerts mainly by musicians from East Lothian.

On rites of passage

Boys and girls mostly married locals. If not from families of the same or neighbouring farm they had probably met at school and Sunday school; after that at the dances in the church hall, which stood opposite the Orlit houses in the glebe. On pleasant evenings the girls would walk up the Leuchie road, arm in arm, giggling, meeting the boys who had been up the hill playing football.

In spite of so many adults around constantly to keep a watchful eye, shotgun marriages were not that uncommon.

Each couple applied to the man's employer for the use of a farm cottage.

For some years after the war the 'creeling' of the groom was still practised; a basket was tied around the groom's neck and the bride had to cut the strings. This was done amid great hilarity from the friends of the couple.

On funerals

Only men attended funerals, in their one and only dark suit and a hat or cap. For close relatives a black armband was worn, for six months if it was for your husband or wife.

On behaviour

The general impression is of quite a close family life, strict discipline exercised by parents on their children, physical punishment not shunned (by the parents), free time (such as there was) spent in the family circle, or with neighbours and others in the village. As one lady said 'There was no pub and it was not everybody's idea of fun to cycle to East Linton on a dark night and back again just to have a few beers. And that over quite hilly roads'. Hogmanay, of course, being the exception.

Homes

The main centres of population in the parish throughout the period were Tyninghame and Whitekirk; the nature of these two places though had changed. In 1945, Tyninghame, two miles from East Linton and six from Dunbar, was still largely home to the families of those who worked on Tyninghame estate. Likewise at Whitekirk, four miles south of North Berwick on the old Edinburgh road, lived farm workers, a minister, a schoolmaster, a teacher and a sub-postmistress (Snodgrass, C.P. 1953 p372). Each farm had some cottages for its workers and perhaps a bothy or two for the itinerant Irish. The great house at Tyninghame was home to Lord Haddington, Newbyth Mansion lay empty and the substantial Mains houses were occupied by owner or tenant farmers.

Tyninghame Village from the east.

Homes (cont)

Whitekirk village from the hill, c1950s. (Ingram Gordon & Co.)

By 2000, there had been extraordinary change. The two great houses and most of their outbuildings passed from the hereditary ownership of distinguished families to multiple occupancy. Though most of the farmhouses were still occupied by farmers, the many farm cottages were now largely in the hands of careful owner-occupiers. New houses, perhaps 50 in all, had sprung up in various well-chosen sites. Buildings where cattle had lowed now echoed to the hum of central heating and the early morning snarl of departing cars.

The district council had built four houses in Whitekirk in 1940, and added eight Orlit houses on the main road in 1948. These were the only council houses in the parish and by 2000 most of them had been bought by the sitting tenants.

Recollections of homes

As far as interiors is concerned there was of course a huge difference between farmhouse and farm workers' cottages or indeed between the former and Tyninghame House. Newbyth mansion was mostly unoccupied during the period until its conversion. One lady I spoke to worked at the 'big house' and one whole long working day a week she had to devote to the polishing of the brass and silver.

The farmhouses were spacious dwellings, with generously-sized rooms, big 'living' kitchens with Aga, utility rooms with boilers and outhouses. They have not changed much over the years, apart from central heating having been put in, some double or secondary glazed and modern appliances in the kitchen.

The council houses and Orlits were built with a range in the main room, which also heated the water and a coal boiler in the kitchen for laundry. The floors were covered with linoleum with mats through the house. (There were of course no stairs). A kettle was singing on the range and the dinner was cooked

Homes (cont)

there. The mothers who worked on a farm or in a farmhouse had to put the pot on the stove before they left. Most cottages had two bedrooms, one for the parents, one for the bairns and beds in the attic. One family lived for several years in a sort of bothy with one bedroom and the attic to be shared by all six children, boys and girls. They were very grateful to move into one of the new council houses.

When the Whitekirk farm was sold six of the cottages were turned into three and they made very comfortable homes for two families, and one a holiday home for an Edinburgh lawyer. The post office cottage was enlarged because the shop became part of the house and the cottage next to it was also enlarged because its 'single-end' was incorporated in it.

Some owners have built a garage or conservatory, but the look of the village in 2000 was very much the same as in 1945.

Recollections of standards of living

Before these changes came, fuel for heating and cooking was coal, the coal lorry coming once a week. At some farms the workers were given sacks of coal as a Christmas gift. Until electricity came in 1953, lighting was provided by Tilley lamps and candles. The paraffin for the lamps was bought from the post office shop, which kept it in a special shed to the right of the house.

Breakfasts were substantial, including porridge, eggs (from 'Granny Main' from Whitekirk Mains) while the midday meal was the main meal, many times 'one-pot meals', a roast on Sundays. After work was done there was 'tea', always with some hot snack, bread, butter and jam. The children got their main meal at school.

A small number of new houses had been built varying in scale from the substantial - Newbyth House, Ashfield House, Old Stonelaws, Howdens, the Pillars at Seacliff - to the modest, mostly in the second half of the period; sensitive small scale developments for sale were planned or in train at Tyninghame and Whitekirk. A proposal in 1990 for 50 houses at Whitekirk received a hostile reception from villagers and was withdrawn. Tyninghame House, Newbyth mansion, stables and steading all housed affluent families from the 1980s. Few of these developments violated agricultural land.

Utilities

Public water supply and sewage schemes were in place throughout the period. Electricity came to Tyninghame in 1948 and to Whitekirk in 1956. Coal was the normal source of heat (though since the 1800s 'the poor find their interest in picking up the broken and decayed branches in Lord Haddington's woods, to which they have at all times free access' – Wallace, J. 1835 p41). The houses had a range for cooking and a hot water boiler. Lighting was by paraffin lamp. During the period, oil and LPG began increasingly, though not completely, to replace coal; a gas main was laid along the road from North Berwick in 1995 but only reached as far as Leuchie.

The only street lighting, which was in Whitekirk, had been in place since the 1960s – also a 30mph speed limit. Tyninghame, as the period closed, coveted the speed limit but could not agree to accept the street lighting, which would justify it. In 2000 the public telephones at Whitekirk and Tyninghame, and the telephone exchange at Whitekirk, were still in use. Also in 2000 a mobile phone mast was erected near Lawhead.

Shops & Services

The villages had changed from their role in servicing a busy estate in 1945, to very different places by 2000:

There were of course still the farmers and farming families themselves with a few workers on their land, a smithy at Merrylaws, a sawmill in Tyninghame, some tradesmen, landscape gardeners, a garage, a farm shop, a coffee/gift shop and an agricultural machinery repair shop. Horses were only kept for riding and there was hardly a house without a car (or two)

The general aura of the parish had changed from rural and all that that implies to comfortable middle class.

The village post office and shop held out in Whitekirk until it closed in 1983 after the retirement of the last postmistress. It did good business in paraffin until the electricity came, and in sweeties for the schoolchildren from next door until the school closed. The property lay empty for two years and then became a private house.

Tyninghame had both joiner's shop and smiddy in the 1950s. The latter became the post office and general store. A coffee and gift shop replaced the general store in the mid 1990s, and retained the post office as well until 1999.

The sawmill at Tyninghame ceased to operate in the 1960s and became a private house, as did the joiners' shops at Tyninghame and Bankhead. Alec Anderson at Merrylaws was the only blacksmith still going strong in 2000.

Gerry Fitzell started in 1990 with a small motor engineering workshop at Whitekirk Mains and moved later to a more modern facility on the Whitekirk golf course, with Alex Sibbald, agricultural engineer as his neighbour.

Grocers, butchers, greengrocers, ironmongers and coal merchants from North Berwick, East Linton and Dunbar had van deliveries for orders, and still in 2000 a fishmonger from Cockenzie called every Wednesday evening. Milk was also delivered throughout the period.

Food was bought from the vans: the butcher, the baker, the ironmonger (who took orders for the following week, also for sewing needs) and the grocer. When the milk was all done in bulk and sent straight to the big dairies the milkman started calling. He had as well to provide the school with its $^1/3$ pint bottles. At Lochhouses they called the grocer 'The midnight man' as he came there at the end of his round - 11pm on a Saturday. Once every six months or so someone from McLeod's Tea called, selling only tea.

A fish man arrived in later years and was in 2000 still there on a Wednesday; the only other one by then being the milkman.

In the early 1950s, Andrew Logan would take a pony and trap from Tyninghame into East Linton on Tuesdays and Thursdays for messages, tethering the pony at the fountain and popping over to the Crown for a pint or two before making his way back. When he retired the estate bought a van, which probably knew the road less well than the pony had done. The Cochrans at the Knowes established a very successful farm shop in 1984, specialising in local produce, eggs and a wide range of homemade fare.

The days of the drapery van were over. For clothing the farm workers and their families went to the Co-op in Dunbar, diligently saving the 'divis'. There they bought as well any of the basic furniture they needed - bedding, floor covering, curtains, kitchenware. Most spent the days in wellies, the evenings in

Shops and Services (cont)

slippers. Nearly all the ladies remember their first nylons, but before that stockings and a corset. The tailor in Dunbar measured the men on the Saturday afternoon and they could collect their suit the following week. Most only had one suit, for Sundays, weddings and funerals. The ladies all possessed a hat.

And on hair care

The men had their hair cut by one of their own, not always too expertly. The ladies and girls too helped each other and put curlers in. The older ladies normally sported some kind of bun. But when money and transport became more readily available, they visited the hairdresser in East Linton and came home with permed curls!

Healthcare

Most people were with the East Linton practice, although some went to North Berwick and one or two to Dunbar, mainly because of having moved from that area. This was still the case in 2000.

Health in the parish seemed to be of a good standard. Before the war there had been problems with diphtheria and tuberculosis. Arthritis was mentioned as the most common affliction. One lady, who worked on the farms said that the doctor expected this as a normal result of her labours. No one could remember local instances of polio.

Before the health service was introduced one had to be very ill before a doctor was called. The high costs were alarming. One lady remembers her nephew's operation for the removal of a mastoid to have cost £10.10s.11d! Great gratitude for the health service was expressed.

The children were examined by the school nurse and the school dentist visited as well.

There were no children with obvious mental problems. During the first half of the period the county ran a school for children with learning difficulties in Tyninghame.

On birth

Up to quite a few years after the war babies were born at home. The father-to-be had to cycle to the midwife, who then came out with him on her bike. Later babies were born in Vert hospital in Haddington, and eventually in Edinburgh. There was no memory of any single mother.

On the elderly

Elderly parents no longer able to look after themselves generally lived with one of the family; there was still a horror of the 'poorhouse'. This attitude changed gradually and in later years old people no longer lived automatically with one of the children. Now most stay as long as possible in their own home with the help of a visiting nurse and/or home help and visits to the day centre in Dunbar. By 2000 the terms 'old peoples' home' or 'nursing' home did not evoke the same instinctive terror.

Traditionally, in Tyninghame, social welfare and care of the elderly had all been handled by families or the estate itself - the five houses in Widows' Row were originally ten, with living room, kitchenette and box bed. If an employee on the estate died, his widow had the house for life. The 12th earl was a caring and unassuming landlord, walking about the village in corduroys and sweater, knocking on people's doors and asking after their welfare.

Education

By 2000, educational provision in the parish had disappeared. Tyninghame school already took infants only in 1946; later it became a school for children with learning difficulties who were bussed in from all over the county until it was closed in 1961 and converted to a private house.

The primary school at Whitekirk (where there were 50 pupils during the war) was full of life for some decades but lost pupils as the population declined. The writing was already on the wall in 1960 when a school inspector's report deemed the building and site unsuitable for modern requirements and envisaged its closure for 1965. It lasted eventually until 1989; in March that year, there were just seven pupils, and the school closed on 30 June 1989. The regional authority then decreed that the building should only be sold as a house if the small school dining room should be used as an employment-creating business venture of some kind. It remained empty for some years until the inevitable happened and the school also became a private house.

There were two teachers, the headmaster for the higher, another teacher for the lower classes. In the first years after the war those who did not pass the entrance exam into North Berwick High School had to stay on at Whitekirk until they reached 14. So there was a huge age range.

There were no school uniforms; the children often had to wear wellingtons to school, especially those who walked from the neighbouring farms. This daily walk could be several miles to and several miles back from school, a long and tiring day for a just-starting five year old! Some of the older ones were the proud possessors of a bike, often recycled from some non-functioning ones. The school lunches were well spoken of.

There were physical exercises on the asphalt in the school playground, but taking into account the distances walked or cycled they were not considered essential by the parents. Marbles was a game for the boys, while the girls played hopscotch or with their skipping ropes.

Bullying was hardly heard of. As one informant said: 'If my Dad had heard I had bullied a little one.... and in such a small community he would always have heard!' And of course there were very likely older brothers or sisters and neighbouring children around.

It was different for the teachers: the tawse was much in evidence. The very few old pupils left in the village were of the opinion that the education they received was adequate.

Tyninghame schoolhouse and village green, 1940s.

Whitekirk Primary School

The children of Whitekirk Primary School with their teachers, Mrs Margaret Martin and Ronnie Grieve c1980s.

Transport

Shank's pony and the bicycle were the main means of transport in 1946 but this soon began to change. The rise of the internal combustion engine was not however an unalloyed blessing, even to the motorist. The A1 bordered the parish, and apart from the A198 the roads were very secondary. They were in a good state of maintenance at the beginning of the period (possibly like small parishes all over the county, because there was a resident roadman) and very little used; then, with a perverse logic as use increased sharply, the standard of maintenance fell equally sharply. By the end of the period half the signposts had disappeared, many road surfaces were breaking up and pothole-dodging had become a necessary sport. The situation was aggravated by irresponsible use. Farmers and others were using ever larger and more powerful machines; haulage contractors' 40-ton articulated lorries broke up the edges as well as the surface of the minor roads, and the smaller roads - first laid down for horse-drawn vehicles - suffered as a consequence. Many farmers forgot their obligation to clean up after themselves, nor did the police enforce the law on this.

Bus services to Dunbar, East Linton and North Berwick were sporadic for much of the period but by 2000 there was a regular hourly service in each direction. Several footpaths and rights of way remained in the parish though walking and cycling both declined after 1945. An occasional pony and trap was to be seen until well into the period – and here and there someone on horseback.

The nearest railway stations were at East Linton, East Fortune and North Berwick - not much more than a four-mile walk for most, so access to Edinburgh was rather easy. After the Beeching cuts (1964) only North Berwick remained.

Leisure

There was never a shortage of things to do, though the nature of what was available did change somewhat over time.

Until there was a bit more money around the only entertainment was that provided by the people themselves: men and boys bowling, darts and dominoes; women and girls from 16 upwards attended the lively local SWRI, which was active in organizing pantos, etc. - another chance for boy to meet girl. Whist drives were organized in the village hall until Bingo arrived in Dunbar. With greater frequency of buses and the car becoming more and more a possibility for the ordinary villager and farm worker this too changed. The cinema in North Berwick became the main attraction. The school began to organize outings, even to the zoo in Edinburgh.

For many years there was a church hall at Whitekirk, which stood opposite the Orlit houses in the Glebe: it was demolished in 1980. There was also a hall owned and used by the Whitekirk SWRI, which remains in the village. It was handed over by the WRI to the local parish church.

Men's and boys' clubs, the British Legion, the Woman's Guild, came and went through the period. The SWRI was very strong in Whitekirk; established in 1923, it finally closed in 1991 when the membership fell to five. During the war they had organised the collection, drying and packing of many herbs in the WRI hall. These were sent by rail to a firm in London and the proceeds (up to £12 in a good year) went to the Red Cross. They ran many entertainments in the hall, particularly whist drives, and entered the SWRI drama festivals, as well as producing a yearly panto in the WRI hall for many years – the cast enlarged by men and children. In 1966 they won the SWRI village history competition, compiling a fine description and history of the parish - a useful source of information.

Tyninghame school was a popular venue in the early days for whist drives and Burns suppers. When the old bakery, long empty except as an ARP post during the war, was restored and brought into use as a village hall in the 1950s the estate opened it for hire and it saw increasing use – for weddings, shooting lunches, harvest lunches, antiques road shows, bring and buy sales, the Lammas fair, and country dances.

There is fair fishing on the Tyne for trout and sea trout, and this continued through the period; there were tales too of running battles between poachers and the Tyninghame gamekeepers. Before it became polluted, the occasional fish was said to lurk in the Peffer Burn, at whose mouth fishermen set lines for eels and flounders - some whoppers, it is reported. The seashore, though dangerous for bathing, also attracts many walkers, birdwatchers, paddlers and picnickers, and wildfowlers on the Tynemouth saltings.

For several years Gladys Dale ran wonderful 4-in-hand events at Seacliff, with a cross-country course through the Tyninghame policies and woods.

From 1977, Tyninghame House, with its ruined Norman church associated with St Cuthbert and St Baldred, opened its lovely grounds and secret garden to the public twice a year.

In the 1950s Tommy Dale offered a stretch of beach at Scoughall to the Scripture Union for a summer camp. This became so popular that a permanent site was built there and remained in yearly use at the end of the period.

A cricket club was founded in 1993 and remained active for several years, the inaugural match on Whitekirk Hill between 15 men of Whitekirk and 15 men of Newbyth.

Economy

Even by 2000, there was little economic activity outside agriculture. A few tourists could enjoy B&B at Whitekirk Mains and Stonelaws in the closing years of the period.

Economy – Industry

The tile and brickworks on the heavy clay by the burn at Newbyth had long since disappeared, though examples of its work could still be seen on roofs and walls in the area.

In 1969, Bernard Mullen obtained permission to extract sand at Lochhouses Links for glassmaking. The sand was taken to a factory in the west of the county and returning lorries brought ash and clinker, which were used to improve roads and paths around Tyninghame estate – particularly in Binning Wood: this lasted till about 1975.

The Dale family set up an engineering workshop for all their farms at Scoughall.

In 1976, Jack Dale and Jim McConnell established Seacliff Haulage but after financial problems hit the firm it split and Jack Dale then specialised in the refrigerated transport of shellfish to Europe.

The modern softwood sawmill set up at Tyninghame Links in the 1960s was purchased by James Brown in 1984 and, combined with a forestry business, was in full swing in 2000, despite competition from cheap imported timber from Eastern Europe. James Brown & Son employ eleven staff.

Economy – Industry (cont)

On Tyninghame estate, the nature of employment had changed radically. In 1950 the pyramid structure went from laird through factor through farm manager and head forester, head gamekeeper, head gardener and so on, each with his own people. Fifty years later that structure had vanished: for example, for work in the woods the factor used a forestry consultant and contractors were called in.

Economy – Agriculture (see also Land Ownership)

Agriculture itself changed beyond recognition, and with it the support services: in 1950 there were five or six pairs of horses on each farm and the village smiddy was busy all day shoeing horses or fitting rims to wheels for carts being made in the joiner's shop - where eight men were employed.

Most men worked on the farms, many with the horses – two horses to a man. But most started off as general labourers. The practice of the hiring market in Dunbar, still remembered by the oldest amongst them - men and women - had stopped by the beginning of our period. The women were employed mainly for the cattle and milking and for helping in the farmhouses. Of course Tyninghame House and Newbyth mansion also employed household staff, as did the minister and the schoolteacher. In addition the two great houses employed several foresters and gardeners. There were also smithies on the big estates.

For the harvest, extra labour was hired, mainly Irishmen, who were housed in Seacliff and bothies around the area. There are no regrets that the old days are gone. Tractors made life so much easier and less worrying for the workers than working with horses had done, although the men loved their animals. The dairy too was hard on the women, especially on their hands and backs.

'… there is no doubt that the agricultural worker has worked harder and for less money than his compatriots; many of these workers have been highly skilled…' Thomas Dale, writing in the WRI book (1966).

This publication told us about the wages in 1966; for the men this was £11, for the women £8.15 shillings per week as a basic wage. There were some perks; oats, barley, potatoes, milk, eggs. And after the Agricultural Board was set up, two weeks holidays + six odd days, shorter working hours and therefore overtime.

As the numbers of farm workers dwindled the population changed. Mechanisation and tractors did not need the same manpower, milking was no longer done by hand and the country people began to leave for employment elsewhere. The steadings lay empty, awaiting conversion into comfortable dwellings with neat gardens and occupied by either retirees, many from elsewhere lured by their dream of country living, or commuters.

Auldhame, Seacliff and Scoughall, owned by J.R. Dale & Sons
With perhaps 700 acres between them, these were mixed farms with land of varying nature and quality. For example, at one point about 210 milking cows and young stock were kept, cereals and 300 acres of vegetables were farmed at Auldhame, but activities changed with the market; a busy market garden at Seacliff supplied North Berwick for some time.

The same would be true of New Mains, about 400 acres farmed in association with Charles Lambert.

Lochhouses, owned by W.P. Dale & Son
Lochhouses extends to about 500 acres. For several years, this branch of the Dale family grew

potatoes, carrots, wheat and barley, and leased ground for a piggery; then carrots were stopped. Winter barley and rape were tried depending on the market and conditions. A fair parcel of land was leased to Stewarts for growing 'The Best Turf on Earth', the firm employing five men on average, taking a crop every two years and adding a cultured elegance to the fields.

Tyninghame Links and Lawhead, Tyninghame Estates Ltd.
Previously under factor John Hume, latterly Alastair Milligan, this covers 950 acres, with 900 acres forestry and 200 acres of grassland. Growing mainly wheat, spring barley and spring rape, with cattle grazing the grassland; 60-70 acres let to Stewart's for turf, and the same to the Knowes for potatoes.

Kirklandhill, Tyninghame Estates Ltd.
Under tenant Robert Carswell, this 520 acres concentrated on wheat, spring barley and potatoes.

The Knowes, Tyninghame Estates Ltd.
Tenanted by Peter Cochran; 380 acres of wheat, potatoes, some spring barley, vegetables and poultry.

Stonelaws, owned by Colin Turner, has 500 acres, grain and potatoes.

The once prosperous, traditional mixed farms of Whitekirk, Newbyth, Kamehill were largely inoperative as units at the end of the period, the fields being leased or sold to owners outwith the farms themselves and laid down to grain, vegetables or potatoes.

Economy – Golf
Latterly the golf course on Whitekirk Hill (designed for George Tuer by Cameron Sinclair) both attracted visitors and offered considerable employment. It opened in 1995, with a club membership growing to over 400 and a very popular bar and restaurant open to all. It became a challenging venue for the PGA Junior Tour. Whitekirk covert, planted with Scots fir and pine in the 1960s, became an integral part of the golf course, which blended happily into the landscape, made exciting use of contours and incorporated two ponds and two small lochans. Work on the leisure and health centre (and creche), and swimming pool began with an opening date set for May 2001.

Miscellany
Apart from the election of the Attlee government in 1945, which profoundly affected the social and economic structure of the countryside, there was little direct impact from outside events during the period. There was the prisoner-of-war camp at Gilmerton, which provided some Italian labour on the farms and estates in the 1940s, but few seemed to have settled after repatriation.

This account of Whitekirk & Tyninghame Parish was written by Peter and Hermine de Iongh. Additional information and research were provided by the following:

Archie Mathieson   Environment - Squirrels
Brian McGuire   General information

And the recollections of Miss J. Anderson; Gladys Dale; Robert Dale; Mrs E. Fitzell; Douglas Gardner; John Hume; Mrs Jacholke; Mr R. Jack; Jean Jackson; Mrs P. Jarvis; Alastair Milligan; Mr & Mrs G. Moffat and family; and Mrs H. Watt.

FURTHER READING & REFERENCES

Land Use Consultants for the Countryside Commission for Scotland, CCS (later Scottish Natural Heritage, SNH) and Historic Buildings and Monuments Directorate, Scottish Development Department (first published c 1987, 1997 reprint) *The Inventory of Gardens & Designed Landscapes in Scotland: Volume 5: Lothian & Borders*

Maxwell, W.D. (nd LHC ref Ae92) *The Story of St Mary's Whitekirk & Tyninghame* (minister 1950-56)

Rankin, E.B. (1914) *Saint Mary's, Whitekirk,* Foulis Edinburgh & London LHC

Ritchie, A.I. (1880) *The Churches of St Baldred: Auldhame, Whitekirk, Tyninghame, Prestonkirk,* Edinburgh

Robinson, Beryl (1999) *A Living from the Land: the reminiscences of Tom Porteous, an East Lothian Ploughboy, forester and 'handyman'* Gullane and Dirleton History Society [2]

Snodgrass, C.P. (1953) *The Third Statistical Account: The County of East Lothian* Oliver & Boyd

SWRI (1966) *The Story of Whitekirk & Tyninghame*

Tindall, F.P. (1998) *Memoirs and Confessions of a County Planning Officer,* Pantile Press

Waddell, P.H. (MDCCCXCIII) *An Old Kirk Chronicle, being a history of Auldhame, Tyninghame, and Whitekirk in East Lothian; from session records 1615-1850,* Blackwood & Sons

Wallace, James (1845) 'The Parish of Whitekirk & Tyninghame' *The New Statistical Account of Scotland*

Notes

[1] For this section, the village of Whitekirk was chosen as a microcosm of the whole parish; it contained the church, a farm, the school, the post office and the village hall. The farm has changed and with it the whole of village life, much as the smaller communities around.
Some of the information had to be built on the memories of just one person. Exact dating was difficult to obtain.

[2] Tom Porteous worked at Newbyth from 1942-58

ABOUT THE EAST LOTHIAN FOURTH STATISTICAL ACCOUNT

It appears that East Lothian is one of the first of the Scottish counties to bring the run of Statistical Accounts (1789-93; 1845; 1953) up to 2000; in this it follows the third East Lothian account, as this too was one of the earliest of that series to be completed.

The driving force behind this work was the East Lothian Antiquarian & Field Naturalists' Society. At the AGM in 1997, the idea of a Fourth Statistical Account of East Lothian was considered; it was agreed to hold a meeting with representatives of the other (around 14) local history and amenity societies. The meeting was held on 18 March 1998, and was supportive; as a result, the East Lothian Fourth Statistical Account Society was set up at a second meeting on 21 May, and formalised on 5 August 1998 with an Executive Committee of Stephen Bunyan as chairman, David Moody as treasurer and Michael Cox as honorary secretary. Lottery funding was sought and £30,000 was granted in 1999 – to be matched by volunteer hours and input.

The editor, Sonia Baker, was appointed in November 2000, parish representatives sought and found by Christmas, and the structure document – a 94 page prompt sheet (or questionnaire) – was sent out to the parish representatives in February 2001. For the parishes with no organised history group, local history enthusiasts were approached for their assistance and input; occasionally, personal circumstances intervened and further support had to be found to complete the work.

A draft list of possible countywide topics was prepared, and authors located, with the last being approached in summer, 2002. The web site (www.el4.org.uk) was up and running by October 2002. Thus far Volume One, the county volume, was published in July 2003 and Volume Two, the first of the parish volumes, in August 2004. Volume Three followed in July 2005. The remaining parish volumes will be published in due course. When the final volume, (Volume Seven) *Growing up in East Lothian,* featuring a series of reminiscences from across the county is published it will be followed by a CD-Rom of the entire work. The CD-Rom will include everything that has been collected in full, and will be available for future researchers. The books and the CD-Rom should not be regarded as the definitive work on the county's economic and social history, 1945-2000, but just the beginning.

For both the parish contributions and the county essays, the response was overwhelming. Material in all formats was welcomed and encouraged. Wherever possible, editorial intervention has been kept to a minimum, and the result is a lively mix of oral and written memories, together with researched material, graphics and photographs, around a specified structure. Local knowledge and access to personal networks were provided largely by the society's executive committee, as well as by other members of the society. In several parishes, the work was done by older members of the community, proving that age is no bar to enthusiasm and the wish to find out more. Without exception, the contributors have done an excellent job.

Once the society has completed its work, it will be wound up. The promised new Cultural Centre for the county in Haddington (due c2007) will hold the account's archive, and future researchers will benefit not only from an electronic version of the account, but room to research in comfort as well.

VOLUME FOUR
BIOGRAPHIES OF PARISH REPRESENTATIVES

Peter & Hermine de Iongh: after national service in the Royal Navy and a degree in modern history at Oxford, Peter taught at schools in England and West Africa. He and Hermine met at a conference at Ibadan University, Nigeria in 1965. She, having studied history at the Free University, Amsterdam, was teaching in Freetown, Sierra Leone. They settled in the UK, and came to Scotland to run Lathallan school, Kincardineshire in 1975. They retired to Whitekirk in 1992, and were invited to join the Kirk Session of St Mary's. The task of producing the account of Whitekirk & Tyninghame was handed over by a fellow member of the Kirk Session.

Malcolm Duncan: has been resident at Needless, North Berwick from 1973, with two children educated through the village school. He is currently treasurer of the Scottish Flag Trust, and chairman of the Athelstaneford Community Association. Author of the county essay on *Local Government.*

Norman Hall: born in Glasgow and educated at Glasgow Academy and Glasgow University, Norman graduated in mechanical engineering. He moved to North Berwick in 1961. He has long been active in local affairs: town treasurer on North Berwick Town Council; member of East Lothian County Council; represented Traprain on Lothian Regional Council. He was also involved in urban regeneration in Wester Hailes and is a past chairman of the Edinburgh Small Business Development Fund and of North Berwick Community Council. He is currently chairman of the North Berwick Trust. Norman has long had an interest in local history, and when no one else would shoulder the responsibility for the North Berwick contribution, he agreed to be the town's representative for the account.

Iain Macaskill MBE: MA, Dip. Ed. is an honours graduate in classics (Edinburgh University). After teaching in Stirlingshire and Glasgow, he was appointed principal teacher of classics at Knox Academy (1965). He was made MBE for services to teaching, and is a co-author of the *Ecce Romani* series of Latin textbooks. A longstanding member of East Lothian Antiquarian & Field Naturalists' Society, and of the Old Edinburgh Club, he considers himself fortunate to have lived in Aberlady for over 30 years, and was glad to acknowledge this good fortune by acting as its representative.

Anne McCarthy: while librarian at Gullane, was involved in the initial stages of Gullane Local History Society. Currently archivist and publications officer of Gullane and Dirleton History Society, editing its millennium booklet Snapshot 2000 which provided the basis for the Dirleton parish entry.

VOLUME FOUR
CONTENTS OF CD-ROM VERSION

The CD-ROM version of Volume Four also contains:

Index

Please note that page numbers in italics refer to photographs.

INDEX (CONT)

169

INDEX (CONT)

INDEX (CONT)